Europe's New Fiscal Union

Pierre Schlosser

Europe's New Fiscal Union

palgrave
macmillan

Pierre Schlosser
European University Institute
Florence, Italy

ISBN 978-3-319-98635-7   ISBN 978-3-319-98636-4   (eBook)
https://doi.org/10.1007/978-3-319-98636-4

Library of Congress Control Number: 2018953998

Cover illustration: Dejan Kolar / Getty Images
Cover Design: Fatima Jamadar

This Palgrave Macmillan imprint is published by the registered company Springer Nature
Switzerland AG
The registered company address is: Gewerbestrasse 11, 6330 Cham, Switzerland

To my daughter Elena and my wife Maria.

CONTENTS

LIST OF FIGURES

LIST OF TABLES

Introduction

If money rules the world, who rules money?
(Margrit Kennedy)

Money rules the world and yet, the real cause of its emergence remains disputed. In their quest to identify the driver behind currencies, economists, historians and anthropologists still disagree over the importance of the transaction needs of market actors as opposed to the financing needs of sovereigns (Goodhart 1998). Yet, it is hard to deny that money and sovereigns are deeply tied together. For instance, it is no coincidence that virtually all modern currencies currently in circulation emanate from a sovereign. All of them? No! In 1999, a 'currency without a state' (Padoa-Schioppa 1999) – the euro – has been launched in Europe and is now the official currency of close to 340 million Europeans who live in the nineteen participating members of Europe's Economic and Monetary Union (EMU). The stateless feature of the European currency was embraced at the euphoric times of its creation as a monetary and political innovation. Back then, the euro was indeed considered – mostly by central-bankers – as a genuine post-modern currency, truly disconnected from the traditional anchors of a currency: gold and the political power (Padoa-Schioppa 2000). More than anything, the euro thus constituted the first large-scale experiment of a sovereign-less currency.

In this introduction I explain why the euro crisis has dramatically impacted EMU's institutional setting and why this has propelled Europe

© The Author(s) 2019
P. Schlosser, *Europe's New Fiscal Union*,
https://doi.org/10.1007/978-3-319-98636-4_1

towards a distinctive fiscal integration trajectory. I then present the actors which embody Europe's fiscal authority, review the existing literature and conclude with a few remarks on the data collected, on the expected contributions of this book and on the roadmap of this book.

A Sovereign-Less and Fragile Currency

Absent a central state, EMU's architecture has been characterised from its inception by an asymmetrical institutional design marked by the co-existence of a centralized, supranational monetary policy capacity on the one hand and decentralized, intergovernmental fiscal and economic policies constrained by EU rules, on the other. During the run up to the Maastricht Treaty adoption, expert observers (Feldstein 1992; Frankel 1992) had however expressed strong doubts that this unbalanced institutional order would be sustainable over time and stressed that EMU would not be resilient enough to satisfy the heterogeneous needs of all euro area economies. No currency, it was argued, could be viable over the long run without some form of central fiscal authority (Eichengreen 1990; Friedman 1997). The crisis which unravelled in the European Union (EU) from spring 2010 until autumn 2012 proved to be the first 'robustness test' for the euro's unbalanced design. It laid bare EMU's shaky fiscal foundations.

Admittedly, crises always played a crucial role in European integration and often acted as catalysts to precipitate agreements on key mutualisation steps. The euro crisis was no exception to that rule. It proved however to be distinctive in both its magnitude and its nature. Often portrayed as the deepest economic recession experienced in Europe since the Second World War, the euro crisis had several dimensions. Economically, it was characterised by a severe slowdown that resulted both in higher debt levels and in a rise in unemployment levels almost everywhere in Europe and in particular in its southern periphery. Socially, the crisis led to deteriorating living conditions as real wages decreased in a number of European countries and social expenditures were cut as a consequence of austerity measures. Politically, the euro crisis proved to be a watershed in the consolidation of populism in Europe, and saw the growth of anti-establishment movements across the continent. During the most heated phase of the crisis, mass public protests proliferated on the streets of Europe's cities.

Without downplaying those three dimensions, I claim in this book that the aspect that really made the euro crisis singular was a fourth feature: its institutional dimension. The crisis put EMU's institutional setting under severe stress: it 'exposed brutally the fiscal void of the monetary union' (Schelkle 2013: 105) and revealed that the absence of a central fiscal backing can bring severe consequences to the EMU's economies, thereby reviving earlier discussions on the inescapability of a fiscal union for the long term sustainability of the euro (Eichengreen and Wyplosz 1993; Goodhart 1998). During the most severe moments of the euro crisis, the constitution of a genuine fiscal union thus seemed unavoidable. This is particularly evident when one considers that the insolvency risks of several euro area countries were posing a systemic and existential threat to the euro. Against this backdrop, one would have expected that the euro crisis, because of its mere magnitude, would have been seized as an opportunity for EU leaders to formally create a genuine fiscal union and to clarify who is EMU's lender of last resort and how it is fiscally supported.

And yet, intriguingly, this did not happen. Calls for a genuine and formalised fiscal union have been resisted and by the end of the euro crisis, no grand fiscal back-up or fiscal capacity had been agreed upon. Instead, a distinctive form of fiscal authority institutionalized through varying informal, *ad hoc* and covert channels. Those newly-centralized powers were not captured by the European Commission, probably for the first time in the history of European integration. Instead, those fiscal powers have been spread across both existing and new executive EMU bodies, a phenomenon that is particularly puzzling and challenging to study for institutionalists.

Against this background, the objective of this book is to analyse the institutionalization dynamics of a European fiscal authority, understood as the centralization of fiscal powers at the European level and taken as the corollary of the EU's policy response to the euro crisis. The book's purpose is hence to both describe and explain the distinctive way through which this European fiscal authority, a new and recent empirical phenomenon in Europe, has institutionalized. The analysis will be guided by the following questions:

• Why did the euro crisis management result in the institutionalization of a central yet fragmented fiscal authority, whose constitutive elements are spread across all EMU executive actors but where no single actor can claim to exert supreme control?

- More specifically, with what type of new fiscal instruments was the euro crisis managed? Did the patchwork of adopted instruments and mechanisms generate a viable fiscal decision-making?
- How does the pattern of fiscal institutionalization integrate within traditional and predominant interpretative models of European integration, if it does at all?
- Looking ahead, how should EMU be reformed to make the euro sustainable?

THE INSTITUTIONALIZATION OF A FISCAL AUTHORITY

I argue that the numerous and diverse institutional changes that occurred during the crisis have prevented scholars and observers from distinguishing an underlying unifying feature. The central claim of this book is thus that the euro crisis response has resulted in the emergence of a fiscal authority, understood as the institutionalization of central fiscal powers at Europe's centre. The analysis hence relies on a distinctive understanding of the concept of 'fiscal authority', in line with the nature of the EU which occupies a middle ground between a confederation and a fully-fledged federation; between a regime and a state. This idiosyncrasy is all the more valid in the fiscal field: while the EU now disposes of a stronger fiscal control over national budgets and has even acquired some borrowing powers, it has no classic, state-like fiscal powers to directly raise taxes and is unlikely to acquire this competence in a foreseeable future. Similarly, it is unlikely that the EU will embark on any grand fiscal redistribution schemes any time soon.

This inquiry therefore deliberately departs from the historical and classic meaning of 'fiscal authority', taken as the legitimate ability of a nation-state to directly raise taxes in order to fund public expenditures. In my assertion, the 'fiscal authority' that has emerged with the euro crisis can better be grasped as the *de facto* and unintended institutionalization of fiscal powers through varied channels. 'Fiscal' is therefore equated with 'budgetary' throughout the book. Table 1.1 below delineates the institutionalization of a fiscal authority into four dimensions: an enhanced fiscal surveillance, a fiscal capacity, a lending of last resort capacity and a banking resolution regime.

The constitution of this fiscal authority, a 'fiscal federalism *sui generis*' (Enderlein et al. 2012), is therefore considered as a hybrid sum of functions whose fragmented centre-formation runs across types of institutions

Table 1.1 Elaboration of the outcome, its dimensions and their operationalization

The outcome	Key dimensions	Key features
Institutionalization of a fiscal authority	Enhanced fiscal surveillance	Tighter surveillance, higher enforcement discretion and stronger sanctioning power
	A fiscal capacity	Commitment and mobilization of public money (as financial assistance)
	A lending of last resort capacity	Discretionary provision of substantial liquidity and acquisition of a *de facto* task of EMU lender of last resort
	A banking resolution regime	Mobilization of private funds and enhanced market discipline

(supranational/intergovernmental) and across nature of institutions (agencies, bodies/mechanisms, EU institutions) while its integration patterns run across types of institutional change (informal/formal; temporary/permanent; covert/overt). This is the political outcome which I will be both describing and explaining in this book. The euro crisis triggered indeed a vast 'institutional tinkering' (Jabko 2013: 132) which partly corrected the initial design flaws of Europe's thin fiscal regime. New rules and procedures have thus been written (e.g. Fiscal Compact, the Bank Recovery and Resolution Directive) or expanded (e.g. the Six Pack and Two Pack which revisited and extended the Stability and Growth Pact) whereas new instruments have flourished (e.g. the Single Supervisory Mechanism and Single Resolution Mechanism). Moreover, a new *ad hoc* body, the European Stability Mechanism (ESM), has established itself in the EMU landscape.

Another chief pattern of change that ran in parallel to the creation of new instruments and mechanisms was the complex institutional transformation of EMU. It was a compound process because the crisis has resulted 'in new actors and new relationships and does not only involve the reshuffling of old actors and relationships. There is more at stake than the redistribution of power among a fixed constellation of players' (Caporaso and Rhodes 2016). Fora for discussions such as the European Council and the Eurogroup have gradually acquired decision-making functions; so has the Euro Working Group (EWG), initially an informal, preparatory body of the Eurogroup. In a different degree, the European Central Bank (ECB) followed similar transformation paths, up to the adoption of a *de facto*

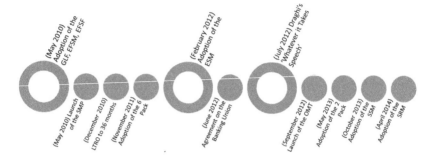

Fig. 1.1   Key euro crisis management measures (2010–2014)

lender of last resort status. The ECB informally expanded its toolkit (with the extension of the Long-Term Refinancing Operations (LTRO), the Securities Markets Programme (SMP) and the Outright Monetary Transactions (OMT) programmes). The European Commission, lastly, often portrayed as a marginal actor during the crisis (Fabbrini 2013; Puetter 2012), also increased its discretion (Bauer and Becker 2014). The below timeline (Fig. 1.1) summarizes the key measures adopted by the EU as part of the euro crisis management.

THE ACTORS OF THE PLAY

As the euro crisis unfolded, a regularity came to the fore: as the arsenal of fiscal instruments expanded, fiscal powers became fragmented among three key EU actors. Those key actors, the ECB, the Eurogroup and the Commission, are mapped below as the key players involved in the exercise of this newly centralized fiscal authority (Fig. 1.2).

The Eurogroup is a body that has been at the core of crisis management during the crisis. Assisted by the Euro Working Group, its preparatory body, and flanked by a new financial assistance mechanism boasting a capacity of € 500 bn, the ESM (an *ad hoc* agency falling under its authority), the Eurogroup is now a central fiscal actor of EMU. Since its creation in 1997, the body has experienced a continuous institutionalization which has been marked by critical junctures, the euro crisis being the latest and most significant one.

The European Commission, an originally marginal actor in EMU and thus in the euro crisis management, has seen its fiscal functions increased with the crisis. This happened on the one hand with the establishment of

Fig. 1.2 Mapping of
the European fiscal
authority's actors

new central capacities such as the new banking resolution regime or indeed such as the European Financial Stabilization Mechanism (EFSM) whose purpose is to assist fiscally vulnerable EU Members; and on the other with the agreement on the 6 Pack and 2 Pack which empowered the institution with a stronger mandate to enforce fiscal surveillance over Member States (notably through a higher discretion) and institutionalised a Commission pre-screening of national budgets.

The ECB, for its part, has evolved from a role of inflation night-watchman towards becoming a leader in crisis management: 'from its initial mandate of providing price stability, the ECB has taken on functions of crisis management that intrude into fiscal policy' (Caporaso and Rhodes 2016: 5; Genschel and Jachtenfuchs 2011). Through strategic interventions, the ECB took over the role of 'de facto lender of last resort' (Winkler 2016) and thereby, arguably saved the euro. Examples of the ECB's interventions include the extension of the Long-Term Refinancing Operation (LTRO) programmes, the Securities Market Programme (SMP), the Outright Monetary Transaction (OMT) instrument and finally the ECB President's declaration on 26 July 2012 to do 'whatever it takes to save the euro'.

To place the European fiscal authority in the wider European institutional context, Fig. 1.3 below presents the formal actor constellation of Europe's fiscal governance which covers a handful of actors and is characterised by a dual form with two distinct memberships: the European Union (EU28) and the EMU (EU 19).

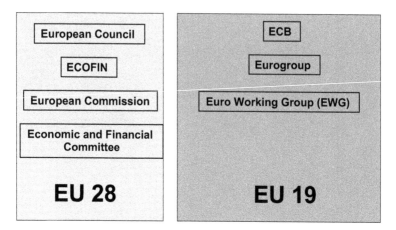

Fig. 1.3   Mapping of all executive actors formally active in EU fiscal governance

In line with its strict focus on the institutional building dynamics of the European fiscal authority, this book leaves out of the scope of its analysis non-fiscal elements pertaining to the wider institutionalization of both the economic pillar of EMU (e.g. Macroeconomic Imbalance Procedure, Euro Plus Pact, Europe 2020) and of the banking union (e.g., European System of Financial Supervision). The EU budget, lastly, whose level and procedure has remained broadly untouched with the euro crisis also falls outside of the scope of this analysis.

LITERATURE REVIEW

The literature on European integration is rich and multifaceted and proves helpful to offer an understanding of the institutional effects of the euro crisis management insofar as 'the processes triggered by the EU responses to the crisis may be considered as constitutionally relevant developments' (Chiti and Teixeira 2013: 685). As far as *intergovernmentalism* and *supranationalism* are concerned, the usual European integration theoretical templates, I contend that not only are they are hard to apply to the EMU due to the complexity of its evolution (Bauer and Becker 2014: 2), they also appear to artificially dichotomize the EU polity. This is particularly problematic in the instance at hand as EMU is becoming increasingly hybrid, combining supranational and intergovernmental features. This book is therefore not structurally framed by the distinction between inter-

governmentalism (Hoffmann 1966; Moravcsik 1998) and supranationalism (Haas 1958; Lindberg 1963; Sandholtz and Stone-Sweet 1998).
Alongside institutionalist approaches, the analysis of EMU's economic
governance has been conducted from various angles, including from a
new governance (Hodson and Maher 2001), eclectic (Verdun 2002) and
constructivist perspectives (McNamara 1999; Dyson 2002).

While it is beyond the scope of this exercise to comprehensively review
all major contributions of the field which are of relevance for this analysis,
a brief assessment of the most recent formulations of the European integration theories is in order. At the heart of this book lies a puzzle that was
well portrayed by an emerging European integration scholarship. The
promoters of so-called *new intergovernmentalism* formulate this contemporary 'integration paradox' in those terms: 'an unprecedented expansion
in the activity of the EU coincides with a definitive shift away from the
further empowerment of traditional supranational institutions' (Bickerton
et al. 2015: 238). They seek to explain the 'post-Maastricht practice of
expanding the scope of EU policy action through new mechanisms of
governance that diverge from the traditional Community method'
(Bickerton et al. 2015: 316).

In this model, EU leaders remain 'committed to closer integration but
very wary of transferring in a last way decision making powers to supranational institutions' (Bickerton et al. 2015: 319). Bickerton et al. (2015)
thus argue that the post-Maastricht pattern of European integration
largely relies on the creation of '*de novo* bodies' (Bickerton et al. 2015:
316), in a broad movement of 'resistance to further supranationalization'
(Bickerton et al. 2015: 7). A regularity of these *de novo* bodies, the authors
further claim, is that 'as a rule, they fulfil functions that could have been
delegated to the Commission and tend to contain mechanisms for member state representation as a part of their governance structure' (Bickerton
et al. 2015: 3).

These observed patterns echo a similar reflection made by Genschel
and Jachtenfuchs, namely that 'Maastricht has unleashed new dynamics of
fundamental change that are unlikely to abate soon' (Genschel and
Jachtenfuchs 2016: 42). Genschel and Jachtenfuchs further claim that the
changing focus of European integration from the creation of an internal
market to the generation of state-like capacities runs in parallel to a shift in
the key actors driving integration (2016: 50–52). While sectoral business
actors were in the driving seat of market integration, state élites, they
argue, are the chief players when it comes to the generation of central

state-like capacities. As regards the consequence that these sweeping changes imply, Genschel and Jachtenfuchs concur with Bickerton et al. (2014) that 'to the extent the integration of core state powers involves the creation of new supranational capacity, the Member States often prefer vesting it into task-specific de novo EU bodies and not the Commission' (Genschel and Jachtenfuchs 2016: 47). As emphasized by Dehousse (2016: 618) this stark view overlooks however the fact that both the ECB and the Commission have seen their tasks strengthened recently.

Applying this frame to the fiscal realm, Genschel and Jachtenfuchs (2013) find that while the EU enjoys a fiscal power, it is limited by its institutional fragmentation and by the absence of a centralized fiscal control (Genschel and Jachtenfuchs 2013: 253). In a dialogue with their contribution, this book will in particular draw on their distinction between 'regulatory integration' on the one hand and integration through 'capacity-building' (Genschel and Jachtenfuchs 2013, 2016) on the other, which I retain to be helpful when assessing the integration pattern of core state powers. Lastly, another strand of the institutional change literature will be at times relied on to deal with the informal and covert integration dynamics at play to characterise a form of European 'integration by stealth' (Majone 2005), as well as veto players' conflict minimizing strategies as a way out of the 'joint decision trap' (Scharpf 1988) and of the 'constraining dissensus' (Hooghe and Marks 2008). A useful distinction between overt and covert integration has been provided in this regard in Héritier (2013: 230).

As far as existing empirical contributions are concerned, several aspects of this book's case study have been addressed by the economic, legal and political science literatures. With a few exceptions (e.g. Heipertz and Verdun 2010; Chang 2013), EMU's fiscal governance has been treated by economists, who have focussed on EMU's rules-based economic coordination (i.e. the Stability and Growth Pact) and its enforcement credibility (Buti and Franco 2005; Brunila et al. 2001; Beetsma and Uhlig 1999). Most political science analyses conducted on the fiscal side of EMU had a micro-scope and seldom attempted to embrace all the elements of the EMU's fiscal governance thereby failing to explain the institutional continuities across actors and EMU's inherent fragmentation. In the remainder of this section, actor-centric contributions are reviewed.

Puetter's account (2006) remains the most extensive analysis that has been carried out on the *gouvernement économique*'s 'first embodiment" (Jabko 2013: 131): the Eurogroup. His contribution treats the Eurogroup as an informal deliberative body and traces its evolving role from its creation until 2005. Crucial elements that have shaped the body after this date such as the establishment of a fixed presidency and the euro crisis management are thus left out. Hodson (2011) covers part of this timeframe but his 'new governance' investigation of the Eurogroup's formalization focusses mostly on the confrontation with the ECB, at the expense of its inner institutionalization dynamics. This analytical choice notably implies that the Euro Working Group – the main preparatory and advisory body of the Eurogroup – characterised by a practitioner as the 'board of directors of the euro area' during the euro crisis (Kasel 2012), has not been addressed. A post-crisis, systematic analysis of the Eurogroup's institutionalization was thus so far missing.

Assessing the evolving role of the European Central Bank during the euro crisis, Salines et al. (2012) have attributed its gradual change to the inherent stickiness of institutions in the EMU. Following similar lines, Schelkle (2013) analysed the ambiguous extension of the ECB's *action repertoire* to unconventional instruments during the crisis. Framing it as a case of 'fiscal integration by default' (Schelkle 2013: 105), she insists on the unintended nature of the fiscal integration process and explains changes 'by stealth' by the absence of a 'federal fiscal authority complementing the centralization of the lender-of-last-resort function' (Schelkle 2013: 117). She also hypothesizes that 'governments ended up with fiscal integration by default for the very reason that they intended to keep the creation of fiscal capacity at a minimum' (Schelkle 2013: 120). In an analogous fashion, Yiangou et al. (2013) explain the same instances of 'unintended consequences' as a product of the EMU's initial monetary financing prohibition. While the causal mechanisms at play remain blurred, these interpretation lines offer however interesting stepping stones for this study.

Using a public policy lens, Bauer and Becker (2014) have re-evaluated the institutional powers acquired by the European Commission in the wider EMU reform and have found it to be 'the unexpected winner of the crisis' (Bauer and Becker 2014: 1). To best account for the Commission's acquisition of new tasks, they invite EMU scholars to decompose the policy process in its various phases and distinguish between the Commission's agenda-setting, implementation, management and interpretation powers. Lastly, in his examination of the Commission's supranational entrepreneurship during the crisis, Hodson (2013) presented several instances where it proved to be influential (6 Pack, 2 Pack). Bringing up a resource argument, Hodson claimed that the Commission's low profile on institutional reform during the crisis could be explained by its limited resources and attributes its focus on 'relatively uncontroversial issues' (Hodson 2013) to an underlying interest in safeguarding its political credibility.

In summary, the existing scholarship has tended to follow the piecemeal pattern of the EMU's economic governance. The emphasis has therefore been placed on the empowerment of particular institutions at the expense of more systematic analyses. So far, no comprehensive account has been carried out on the interaction between the euro crisis, a new empirical development, and the construction of a fiscal authority seen as a sum of functions running across different types of institutions (supranational, intergovernmental, independent) and across different types of institutional change (informal, formal). The aim of this book is to fill this gap.

A FEW REMARKS ON DATA COLLECTION

In line with the inductive nature of the research enterprise, the data collection strategy I relied on has been bottom up and consisted of two main steps in which multiple forms of data were gathered and analysed.

1. During the first period, a deep foray into the case study was performed. Systematic fact-finding and data gathering were firstly conducted based on publicly available information, mainly official documentation, as well as secondary literature dealing with the reform of the EMU's fiscal governance in the context of the euro crisis. More specifically, this process implied the review and analysis of key legal texts (primary and secondary law), official documentation (EU communications and Roadmaps) and secondary literature.

   I then spent a three month field period in Brussels as a visiting fellow within the Centre for European Policy Studies (CEPS). The proximity to EU institutions allowed me to meet EU policy-makers involved in the case on a regular basis. I therefore conducted numerous exploratory interviews and background chats. Those informal meetings allowed me to retrace the dense sequence of the euro crisis events and, more specifically, to gain an insider understanding of the procedures foreseen by the complex and opaque 6 Pack and 2 Pack which form the backbone of EMU's new fiscal surveillance regime.

Also, background discussions with selected policy-makers allowed me to acquire more micro information about the key actors involved in the institutional change process and the critical junctures which had a key impact on the design of a European fiscal authority.

2. After a deep immersion in the intricacies of EMU's fiscal pillar, I conducted 62 semi-structured interviews and 'background chats' over the period October 2014 to July 2016 in the following cities: Brussels (October to December 2014), Rome (June 2015), Helsinki (March 2016), Frankfurt (April 2016), and Brussels (April 2016). I interviewed senior policy-makers of EU institutions (ECB, European Commission, EU Council, Euro Working Group), senior policy-makers of national finance ministries of the EMU countries, senior officials from the European Parliament and a few independent analysts. They provided me with tangible data on the relevant factors that played out in the institutionalization of a fiscal authority.

EXPECTED CONTRIBUTIONS

I expect the book to contribute to the study and the process of European integration in two ways.

- From an academic perspective, the analysis of the European Union's leading sub-system (EMU) could lay the ground for further generalization on the dynamics of polity 'differentiation' within the European Union, generating operational insights for other fields where core state powers are exercised and which are likely to be characterised by similar changes (e.g. the Common Foreign and Security Policy; Justice and Home Affairs). The treatment of the institutionalization dynamics of a fiscal authority, a core state power, within the EMU is indeed particularly important for understanding the wider transformation of the European Union as a polity.
- From a policy and practical perspective, this book will help to provide a better understanding of the institutional pre-requisites of increased fiscal centralization within the EMU. One form that this enhanced centralization could take over the medium term is the performance of what economists term 'fiscal stabilization', i.e. the smoothing of business cycles through automatic or discretionary fiscal measures since this could help accelerate the macroeconomic adjustment process of EMU members during future crises, thus

reducing its currently high social cost. Such an EMU fiscal capacity is viewed as central for the completion of a genuine economic and monetary union (European Commission 2012).

BOOK OUTLINE

Building on the scene-setting provided by this chapter, Chap. 2 looks at EMU's inherently asymmetrical design. It recalls that while early EMU blueprints recommended the simultaneous creation of a monetary union and of a fiscal union, this institutional symmetry vanished with the advent of the Maastricht Treaty. The chapter thus retraces the build-up of EMU with a view to canvassing the regime's asymmetrical institutional design and the key steps of its evolution. For that, its distinctive fiscal nature as well as its key actors and instruments are described. The chapter lastly sets out the institutional balance that EMU had reached before the euro crisis hit the continent. Such a contextualization allows to situate the institutional change in the broader context of EMU institution-building.

Chapter 3 explains that the euro crisis has resulted in a substantial revamp of Europe's fiscal surveillance regime. The central control over national fiscal policies has expanded along the lines of the two earlier critical junctures in fiscal surveillance: the Maastricht Treaty and the Stability and Growth Pact. As a result, the European Commission has gained new implementing powers. The chapter thus retraces the process leading to the adoption of this new fiscal surveillance regime and explains the chief policy changes that led to a shift in the vertical power balance between the centre and Member States. By analysing in depth the negotiations of the 6 Pack, the Fiscal Compact and the 2 Pack, the chapter uncovers the preferences and strategies of key actors involved across these cases, with a view to identifying the most influential actors in this reform process and the pattern of fiscal governance expansion.

Chapter 4 retraces the road towards European leaders' agreement on the creation of a € 500 bn mechanism in early May 2010 meant to provide assistance to euro area countries facing financial stability risks. The establishment of the European Financial Stability Facility (EFSF), later turned into the European Stability Mechanism (ESM), was a critical juncture in the constitution of a European fiscal centre. Its financial capacity is unprecedented, as the fund's lending power amounts to more than three times the size of the annual EU budget. The chapter hence retraces the negotiation that led to the creation of these mechanisms and of the smaller sized facilities that preceded their existence (the Greek Loan Facility and the

European Financial Stabilization Mechanism). Lastly, the chapter argues that the creation of these financial mechanisms has converted the Eurogroup and the Euro Working Group (EWG) into executive bodies.

Chapter 5 describes how the European Central Bank saved the euro. The chapter documents how, through strategic yet conditioned interventions, the ECB took temporarily over the controversial role of EMU's lender of last resort. In other words, the Frankfurt institution autonomously expanded its mandate from securing price stability to safeguarding financial stability. Driven by a twin concern to safeguard the euro without giving up on its monetary dominance, the institution shaped its institutional environment to ensure that its new responsibility for financial stability would be sufficiently 're-insured' so as to not jeopardize its independence to conduct its monetary policy. As the ECB does not formally possess the lending of last resort function, it had to revert to selected, strategic and timely interventions to exert this new quasi-fiscal authority. The chapter recalls that such power could however not be exerted in an institutional vacuum.

Chapter 6 reviews the creation of the Single Resolution Mechanism (SRM) – composed both of a Single Resolution Board (SRB) and of a Single Resolution Fund (SRF) of € 55 bn – during the crisis. The chapter shows how EMU's executive institutions converged on the need for a centralized regime but also documents how Northern Member States' concerns over any further agency drift by the Commission, produced a fragmented decision-making. The chapter's emphasis lies on the institutional design contests that surfaced when the detailed features of this additional fiscal capacity began to be discussed. Lastly, the chapter describes how the Commission's powers were tamed down while additional prerogatives were given to a new agency and veto powers mushroomed.

Chapter 7 summarizes the findings of this book and provides an interpretation of the convoluted trajectory that fiscal power centralization took during the euro crisis. It explains that the height of the crisis management coincided with the institutionalization of a fiscal centre, understood as an incipient and composite fiscal authority that runs across all EMU executive institutions without being embodied by any *primus inter pares*. The emergence of such a fiscal centre was strongly conditioned and constrained by the path-dependence of the EU's past institutional modus operandi: an over-reliance on rules on the one hand and the empowerment of technocratic agencies on the other. The chapter shows that in the absence of an EMU crisis management mechanism, the crisis not only generated its own pressure to define an adequate EU policy response, it also acted as a catalyst for the development of common central fiscal capacities.

Looking ahead, Chapter 8 documents how and why EMU's post-crisis polity is unstable. To address this major challenge, the chapter therefore assesses the EMU polity's reform prospects. It first sets out the crucial features of the most likely outlook for the years to come: muddling-through in the current institutional framework and discusses the costly implications of the perpetuation of this status quo. Departing from muddling-through, the chapter then describes three competing medium term scenarios for the development of EMU's polity: an *executive technocracy*, an *intergovernmental confederation* and *democratic federalism*. After having clearly spelled out the possible institutional directions that EU leaders could embark on, the chapter suggests three policy reform steps to make EMU sustainable, offers the 'technology' behind institutional settlement and provides the closing remarks of this book.

REFERENCES

Bauer, M., & Becker, S. (2014). The Unexpected Winner of the Crisis: The European Commission's Strengthened Role in Economic Governance. *Journal of European Integration, 36*(3), 213–229.

Beetsma, R., & Uhlig, H. (1999). An Analysis of the Stability and Growth Pact. *The Economic Journal, 109*(458), 546–571.

Bickerton, C. J., Hodson, D., & Puetter, U. (2014). The New Intergovernmentalism: European Integration in the Post-Maastricht Era. *Journal of Common Market Studies, 53*(4), 703–722.

Bickerton, C. J., Hodson, D., & Puetter, U. (2015). *The New Intergovernmentalism: States, Supranational Actors, and European Politics in the Post-Maastricht Era.* Oxford: Oxford University Press.

Brunila, A., Buti, M., & Franco, D. (Eds.). (2001). *The Stability and Growth Pact: The Architecture of Fiscal Policy in EMU.* Basingstoke: Palgrave Publishers.

Buti, M., & Franco, D. (2005). *Fiscal policy in EMU: Theory, Evidence and Institutions.* Cheltenham: Edward Elgar.

Caporaso, J., & Rhodes, M. (Eds.). (2016). *Political and Economic Dynamics of the Eurozone Crisis.* Oxford: Oxford University Press.

Chang, M. (2013). Fiscal Policy Coordination and the Future of the Community Method. *Journal of European Integration, 35*(3), 255–269.

Chiti, E., & Teixeira, P. (2013). The Constitutional Implications of the European Responses To The Financial And Public Debt Crisis. *Common Market Law Review, 50*(3), 683–708.

Dehousse, R. (2016). Why has EU Macroeconomic Governance Become More Supranational? *Journal of European Integration, 38*(5), 617–631.

Dyson, K. (2002). *European States and the Euro: Europeanization, Variation and Convergence.* Oxford: Oxford University Press.

Eichengreen, B. (1990, April). One Money for Europe? Lessons from the US Currency Union. *Economic Policy, 5*(10), 117–187.

Eichengreen, B., & Wyplosz, C. (1993). The Unstable EMS. *Brookings Papers on Economic Activity, 1993*(1), 51–143.

Enderlein, E. et al. (2012). *Completing the Euro: A Roadmap Towards Fiscal Union in Europe*, Report of the Tommaso Padoa-Schioppa Group. Notre Europe.

European Commission. (2012, November 30). *Blueprint for a Deep and Genuine Economic and Monetary Union*, Commission Communication, COM(2012) 777 final/2.

Fabbrini, S. (2013). Intergovernmentalism and Its Limits: Assessing the European Union's Answer to the Euro Crisis. *Comparative Political Studies, 46*(9), 5–18.

Feldstein, M. (1992, June 13). Europe's Monetary Union: The Case Against EMU. *The Economist.*

Frankel, J. (1992). On the Dollar. In P. Newman, M. Milgate, & J. Eatwell (Eds.), *The New Palgrave Dictionary of Money and Finance.* London: Macmillan Press Reference Books.

Friedman, M. (1997, August 28). The Euro: Monetary Unity to Political Disunity? *Project Syndicate.*

Genschel, P., & Jachtenfuchs, M. (2011). How the European Union Constrains the State. Multilevel Governance of Taxation. *European Journal of Political Research, 50*(3), 293–314.

Genschel, P., & Jachtenfuchs, M. (2013). Conclusion: The European Integration of Core State Powers. Patterns and Causes. In P. Genschel & M. Jachtenfuchs (Eds.), *Beyond the Regulatory Polity? The European Integration of Core State Powers.* Oxford: Oxford University Press.

Genschel, P., & Jachtenfuchs, M. (2016). More Integration, Less Federation: The European Integration of Core State Powers. *Journal of European Public Policy, 23*(1), 42–59.

Goodhart, C. (1998). The Two Concepts of Money: Implications for the Analysis of Optimal Currency Areas. *European Journal of Political Economy, 14*(3), 407–432.

Haas, E. (1958). *The Uniting of Europe: Political, Social, and Economic Forces (1950–1957).* Stanford: Stanford University Press.

Heipertz, M., & Verdun, A. (2010). *Ruling Europe: The Politics of the Stability and Growth Pact.* Cambridge: Cambridge University Press.

Héritier, A. (2013). Covert integration of Core State Powers: Renegotiating Incomplete Contracts. In P. Genschel & M. Jachtenfuchs (Eds.), *Beyond the Regulatory Polity? The European integration of core state powers.* Oxford: Oxford University Press.

Hodson, D. (2011). *Governing the Euro Area in Good Times and Bad*. New York: Oxford University Press.

Hodson, D. (2013). The Little Engine that Wouldn't: Supranational Entrepreneurship and the Barroso Commission. *Journal of European Integration, 35*(3), 301–314.

Hodson, D., & Maher, I. (2001). The Open Method as a New Mode of Governance: The Case of Soft Economic Policy Co-ordination. *Journal of Common Market Studies, 39*(4), 719–746.

Hoffmann, S. (1966). Obstinate or Obsolete: The Fate of the Nation-State and the Case of Western Europe. *Daedalus, 95*(3), 862–915.

Hooghe, L., & Marks, G. (2008). A Postfunctionalist Theory of European Integration: From Permissive Consensus to Constraining Dissensus. *British Journal of Political Science, 39*(1), 1–23.

Jabko, N. (2013). The Divided Sovereignty of the Eurozone. In P. Genschel & M. Jachtenfuchs (Eds.), *Beyond the Regulatory Polity? The European Integration of Core State Powers*. Oxford: Oxford University Press.

Kasel, A. (2012). La présidence de l'Eurogroupe et la gouvernance économique de la zone euro'. In V. Charlety (Ed.), *Le Système présidentiel de l'Union Européenne après Lisbonne*. Paris: ENA.

Lindberg, L. N. (1963). *The Political Dynamics of European Economic Integration*. Stanford: Stanford University Press.

Majone, G. (2005). *Dilemmas of European Integration: The Ambiguities and Pitfalls of Integration by Stealth*. Oxford: Oxford University Press.

Mcnamara, K. R. (1999). *The Currency of Ideas: Monetary Politics in European Union*. Ithaca: Cornell University Press.

Moravcsik, A. (1998). *The Choice for Europe: Social Purpose and State Power from Messina to Maastricht*. Ithaca: Cornell University Press.

Padoa-Schioppa, T. (1999, December 29). Europas Notenbank ist (Europe's Central Bank Is Lonely), Interview with Die Zeit.

Padoa-Schioppa, T. (2000). *The Road to Monetary Union in Europe: The Emperor, the Kings and the Genies*. Oxford: Oxford University Press.

Puetter, U. (2006). *The Eurogroup: How a Secretive Circle of Finance Ministers shape European Economic Governance*. Manchester: Manchester University Press.

Puetter, U. (2012). Europe's Deliberative Intergovernmentalism: The Role of the Council and European Council in EU Economic Governance. *Journal of European Public Policy, 19*(2), 161–178.

Salines, M., Glöckler, G., & Truchlewski, Z. (2012). Existential Crisis, Incremental Response: The Eurozone's Dual Institutional Evolution 2007–2011. *Journal of European Public Policy, 19*(5), 665–681.

Sandholtz, W., & Stone-Sweet, A. (Eds.). (1998). *European Integration and Supranational Governance*. Oxford: Oxford University Press.

Scharpf, F. (1988). The Joint-Decision Trap. Lessons From German Federalism and European Integration. *Public Administration, 66*(2), 239–278.

Schelkle, W. (2013). Fiscal Integration by Default. In P. Genschel & M. Jachtenfuchs (Eds.), *Beyond the Regulatory Polity? The European Integration of Core State Powers*. Oxford: Oxford University Press.

Verdun, A. (Ed.). (2002). *The Euro: European Integration Theory and Economic and Monetary Union*. Lanham: Rowman and Littlefield Publishers.

Winkler, A. (2016). The ECB as Lender of Last Resort: Banks vs. Governments. *Jahrbücher für Nationalökonomie und Statistik, 235*(3), 329–341.

Yiangou, J., O'Keeffe, M., & Glöckler, G. (2013). 'Tough Love': How the ECB's Monetary Financing Prohibition Pushes Deeper Euro Area Integration. *Journal of European Integration, 35*(3), 223–237.

CHAPTER 2

EMU's Asymmetrical Institutional Design

INTRODUCTION

EMU's institutional design is notoriously asymmetrical (Verdun 1996): it entails a fundamental imbalance between its monetary and its fiscal pillars. While this feature is commonly accepted as a key characteristic of contemporary EMU, it was not self-evident when the first EMU concepts began to be discussed, almost five decades ago. In truth, expectations about the adequate nature of EMU's fiscal regime radically evolved during the ideation phase of EMU. They oscillated between a thick fiscal centre which would have implied institutional capacity-building (e.g. a large central budget and a borrowing capacity) and a thin fiscal centre which would have revolved solely around the establishment of central rules ensuring fiscal discipline. Because they involved varying sovereignty transfers, those competing fiscal centre models also implied drastically opposing institutional and polity choices for EMU. A thin fiscal centre would have been compatible with the pre-Maastricht European integration trajectory based on market integration through regulatory means. A thick fiscal centre, instead, would have required a fundamental constitutional reform to empower or establish the executive actors of this new centre as part of a move towards a political union which would thus have involved institutional capacity-building.

These fundamental institutional questions would underpin the Maastricht negotiations (1990–1991). Yet, the reflection on the needed pre-requisites and institutional form of EMU initiated much earlier. The

© The Author(s) 2019
P. Schlosser, *Europe's New Fiscal Union*,
https://doi.org/10.1007/978-3-319-98636-4_2

preparatory groundwork on EMU mostly occurred as part of the Werner Committee (1970) and of the Marjolin Committee (1975). Those expert groups were launched as a result of the rising monetary imbalances of the 1960s, an instability which departed from the relative monetary stability that marked the 1950s. In those years, European policy-makers started to realize that the stability induced by the Bretton Woods system in the post-war western world was beginning to falter. This, in turn, provided a breeding ground for the first genuine reflections over a stronger monetary unification in Europe. What is particularly striking about the recommendations of the Werner and Marjolin committees is that they unambiguously and explicitly recommended the establishment of fiscal and political centres alongside its monetary core. For instance, the Marjolin Report suggested that EMU's centre should consist of 'a European political power, an important Community budget, and an integrated system of central banks' (Marjolin 1975: 5). Along similar lines, the Werner Report recognized that 'Economic and monetary union thus appears as a leaven for the development of political union, which in the long run it cannot do without' (Werner 1970: 12).

The asymmetrical institutional architecture of modern-day EMU can therefore not be attributed to its early founding fathers, who had a radically different concept in mind. Admittedly, the nature of EMU's ultimately unbalanced fiscal regime was influenced by the evolution of macroeconomic ideas, which contributed to ultimately tame down the importance of fiscal policy. However, it is by and large the product of the intricate and inconclusive Maastricht Treaty negotiations which partly stemmed from the tension between French and German preferences over a fiscal union. Monetary experts were quite successful in Maastricht in bridging divergences over the monetary design of EMU. Politicians however failed to agree on the explicit nature and institutional design of a fiscal and political centre that would underpin EMU. Absent a pressing need to centralize fiscal prerogatives, fiscal policies were therefore kept at the national level. As explained by Verdun (2015: 221), 'member states' governments were unwilling to transfer sovereignty over fiscal policies to the EU level without there being a felt need (e.g. owing to a major shock). Yet it was assumed there would be some kind of crossroads, some kind of upset, that would force the matter back onto the agenda so that member state governments would have to commit there and then, under major pressure, to consider deeper integration' (Verdun 2007: 209). Such critical juncture came with the euro crisis.

Setting out the institutional balance that prevailed in EMU before the euro crisis unfolded fully, this chapter describes the build-up of EMU's asymmetrical institutional design, retraces the convoluted emergence of its thin fiscal centre and introduces the critical junctures of its evolution. As part of this it canvasses the institutionalization of EMU's central actors (the Commission, the Eurogroup and the ECB) and instruments (mainly the Stability and Growth Pact). The pre-crisis institutional set-up has indeed been central to the subsequent evolution of EMU's fiscal arm.

THE RISE AND FALL OF THE IDEA OF A EUROPEAN FISCAL CENTRE

The euro's creation did not happen overnight. It was the result of a long preparation which started in the early 1970s. This preliminary work aimed at setting the right economic and political conditions for the creation of a common currency. A chief element of the reflection over the pre-requisites of a common currency was whether a fiscal centre would be needed to support it. Early EMU blueprints approached the creation of a common currency from a political and federal perspective as opposed to the more economic and functional approach followed in the Delors Committee. Both the Werner Report and the Marjolin Report argue in favour of a symmetric regime: a centralized monetary policy regime should go hand in hand with a centralized fiscal and economic policy regime. This self-evidence disappears however in the Delors Report. In other words, while earlier blueprints (the Werner Report and the Marjolin Report, but also in the 1977 McDougall Report) clearly advocated the creation of a central fiscal regime, the ultimate EMU architecture completely abandoned it. The changing ideational, political and economic context played a role in this shift. The final design of EMU was, by and large, defined as part of another committee: the Delors Committee (1988–1989) which discussed the idea of a fiscal centre – an idea that was later dismissed when the Maastricht Treaty was drafted.

The Werner report's overarching objective was to 'determine the elements that are indispensable to the existence of a complete economic and monetary union' (Werner 1970: 9) to be realised within a decade. The views expressed within the Committee, made up of high level representatives and financial experts stemming from the six countries of the European Community, were split among those who believed that economic convergence was a necessary pre-condition of enhanced monetary coop-eration (the German-led 'economists') and those who were convinced that monetary parity would be needed first to reach enhanced policy con-vergence (the French and Belgian-led 'monetarists'). The Committee made a series of key contributions of which the 'plan by stages' (Werner 1970: 7) which would ultimately influence the implementation of the euro in the late 1990s. Remarkably, the Report put forward a symmetric institutional architecture for EMU's final stage: a common central bank (setting monetary policy) would be matched with an economic policy centre.

A key function of this centre would be to develop a common approach to fiscal policy. Accordingly, the Werner Report highlighted that 'it will be necessary to establish normative and compatible economic budgets each year and to control their realization' (Werner 1970: 10). It stated further, referring to national budgets, that their 'harmonized management' would be 'an essential feature of cohesion in the union' (Werner 1970: 10–11). Also, the report emphasized that 'the margins within which the main bud-get aggregates must be held both for the annual budget and the multi-year projections will be decided at the Community level, taking account of the economic situation and the particular structural features of each country' (Werner 1970: 11). Detailing further this recommendation, the report underscored that 'the essential features of the whole of the public budgets, and in particular variations in their volume, the size of balances and the methods of financing or utilizing them, will be decided at the Community level' (Werner 1970: 12).

In summary, the Werner Report recommended to determine a policy process at Community level to set out an aggregate fiscal stance. The Report lastly acknowledged that these 'transfers of responsibility represent a process of fundamental political significance which implies the progres-sive development of political cooperation. Economic and monetary union thus appears as a leaven for the development of political union, which in the long run it cannot do without' (Werner 1970: 12). As an illustration of this fundamental link between the economic union and the political union, the Report foresaw that 'the centre of decision of economic policy will be politically responsible to a European Parliament' (Werner 1970: 13). In contrast to the advocated centralization of monetary and fiscal policy, the Report remained silent on banking supervision. As is quite often the case in European integration, the policy steps canvassed by the Werner Report were never implemented. This, in turn, triggered the creation of a new expert group which was entrusted with the task of taking stock of the (absence of) progress made on monetary unification and with the mandate of making new recommendations, in what became known as the Marjolin Report.

The diagnosis of the Marjolin Report (1975) was blunt: 'Europe is no nearer to E.M.U than in 1969' (Marjolin 1975: 1). The cause of this stalemate was arguably that 'each national policy is seeking to solve problems and to overcome difficulties which arise in each individual country, without reference to Europe as an entity. The diagnosis is at national level; efforts are made at national level. The coordination of national policies is a pious wish which is hardly ever achieved in practice' (Marjolin 1975: 1). The report also lamented an 'insufficient understanding in the past on the meaning of an EMU and the conditions which must be fulfilled if it is to see the light of day and become operational' (Marjolin 1975: 3). In particular it stated that 'there was an insufficient appreciation of the essential difference between a customs union, as defined by the Treaty of Rome and an Economic and Monetary Union' (Marjolin 1975: 4).

Despite its rather gloomy assessment, the Report also emphasized what a step change EMU would require, politically and institutionally: 'in an Economic and Monetary Union, national governments put at the disposal of the common institutions the use of all the instruments of monetary policy and of economic policy whose action should be exercised for the Community as a whole. The institutions moreover must have a discretionary power similar to that which national governments possess now, in order to be able to meet unexpected events' (Marjolin 1975: 4). The report further outlined that central EMU institutions 'would have to include a European political power, an important Community budget, and an integrated system of central banks. They would be called upon to function in the appropriate fields in a comparable way to those of a federal State' (Marjolin 1975: 5). More specifically, EMU's regime would require the following: 'concerning the distribution of authority: a common monetary policy, a common economic policy, a common social policy; concerning institutions: a central community bank or system of central banks responsible for the management of a monetary policy; a decision making centre responsible for economic and social policies and able to act by means of a budget of significant size; a democratic control by means of an European Parliament elected by universal suffrage and endowed with real legislative powers' (Marjolin 1975: 29).

Looking at the long term outlook of EMU, lastly, the report stressed that 'it is clear that in the final stage of unity, the Community must in its budget fulfil the three traditional functions of every public authority, namely: provision of public goods (allocation function), stabilisation policy; and, distribution policy' (Marjolin 1975: 32). What is lastly remarkable is that the Marjolin Report foresaw that 'in the longer term, this approach must stress the development of the proper stabilisation function of the Community budget' and stressed that 'over a longer span it would be unavoidable to bestow on the Community powers of short and long-term community debt management' (Marjolin 1975: 33–34). In this regard it recommended the set-up of a 'community unemployment benefits scheme' whose design was developed in quite some detail in a dedicated annex.

How such a fiscal centre might look like was the object of yet another expert report, the so-called McDougall report, published in 1977, drawn up on the invitation of the Commission. It outlined the key institutional features of a fiscal centre in Europe with a focus on the size of the federal budget. By contrast to the Werner and Marjolin reports which offered steps towards EMU, the McDougall Report took a clear public finance focus. It suggested a progressive increase in the financial capacity of the EU budget, in a 'pre-federal integration' 2–2.5% of GDP in the short term, on to 5–10% of GDP in 'an earlier stage would be a federation with a much smaller federal expenditure' and even concluded that 'it is possible to conceive, presumably at some distant date, a Federation in Europe in which federal public expenditure is around 20–25% of Gross Domestic Product as in the U.S.A. and the Federal Republic of Germany' (McDougall 1977: 12–13). Yet, within little more than ten years, the idea of forging a thick fiscal core as well as establishing a symmetry between the monetary, fiscal and political dimensions of the Community would suddenly disappear from the agenda of the Delors Committee (1988) and of the Maastricht Treaty negotiations (1990–1991).

A fundamentally changing macroeconomic and ideational context played a role in this. As a result of the 1970s oil-shocks, fiscal deficits rose constantly in OECD countries which in turn fuelled its own vicious cycle as debt services increased and no build up buffers were created during good times, thus limiting the effectiveness of fiscal stabilization and thereby, of government action in hard times. The persistence of stagflation was a fertile ground for the take up of new macroeconomic ideas and corresponding policy beliefs. New economic policy paradigms emerged and slowly became mainstream, in particular among central bankers and finance ministry officials (McNamara 1999). 'Their emergence was to be explained by the discrediting of Keynesian orthodoxy with the economic shocks of the 1970s and the subsequent opportunity for ideas that were more relevant to the problems of inflation and competitiveness' (Dyson and Featherstone 1999: 752).

While the post-war years led to the triumph of Keynesianism with its primary focus on fiscal policy and its relative neglect of monetary policy, the new monetary world order initiated by the Nixon and oil shocks and their resulting fiscal imbalances would lead the way to the advent of monetarism, a new economic policy paradigm that revolved around a more cardinal monetary policy. In short, a decade of stagflation had brought a breeding ground for a convergence of ideas on the evils of inflation and discretionary fiscal policy and on the benefits of price stability enforced through central bank independence. Central bankers, being at the core of the new monetary turbulences, would be the first actors to become impregnated by these new ideas.

EMU's Genesis in the Delors Committee and in Maastricht

EMU's contemporary history started with the Hanover European Council (June 1988). The latter summit tasked Europe's central bankers – under the aegis of Commission President Jacques Delors – to come up with an operational proposal on how an Economic and Monetary Union could be achieved and how it should function. The lion's share of EMU's institutional design bargain thus occurred as part of the so-called "Delors Committee" which provided a key venue for consensus-building on the future EMU. The Committee, which always gathered at Basel's Bank for International Settlements (BIS) – the *central bank of central banks* – did not perceive its task as political in nature: 'as Delors stressed, the committee was asked to supply an answer to the question of 'how' EMU might be established, not 'whether' it should be' (Dyson and Featherstone 1999: 773). Nevertheless, despite its alleged apolitical nature, the Committee happened to lay down the blueprint of the Maastricht Treaty as only a few amendments were ultimately made to transform its final report into the Treaty: 'the basic structure and ingredients of EMU, remained as they had been specified in the Delors Report' (Verdun 1999: 122).

Central bankers thus proved largely influential in the process of the EMU-polity shaping. The committee, whose composition was determined by the European Council, was principally made up of central bankers which were assisted by selected independent experts. Meetings were chaired by Commission President Jacques Delors who was aided by a rapporteur, Tommaso Padoa-Schioppa, vice-governor of the Bank of Italy and by a second rapporteur, German national Gunter Baer, from the BIS. The work process valued from the start the input provided by central bankers. For instance, while the agenda of the first meeting was shaped upfront by written questions formulated by Commission President Delors, its second meeting was structured along the presentation of a few thematic papers by central bankers themselves. In the view of Jacques Delors, ensuring that central bankers managed to acquire ownership of the EMU project was crucial for EMU's final success. He therefore was keen to be perceived as an honest broker. As Verdun (1999) documented, the Delors Committee was characterised by a deep sharing of common beliefs and habits among its participants and thus qualified as an epistemic community (Haas 1992).

Notwithstanding the fact that it operated under the distant control of the European Council and notably of Germany, the Commission had the upper hand on the agenda-setting process. The Commission was very active inside and outside the Delors Committee. It nurtured an ideational investment, developing arguments based on the functional imperative of creating a single currency to exploit the full benefits of a single market (Jabko 2006), and in particular of deeper capital markets. Building on the contribution of Padoa-Schioppa (1988) – former head of the Commission's Directorate General for Economy and Finances – who provided a strong building block towards the theoretical justification of EMU (the so-called 'inconsistent quartet'), the official arguments for EMU were developed by the Commission as part of its famous report *One Market, One Currency* (European Commission 1990). The latter, elaborated by the Commission services but also with the support of academic economists, underlined the transactional benefits of a common currency.

Delors Committee discussions mainly focussed on the steps and conditions to be met to proceed towards monetary unification. Following the spirit of the Werner Report, a three steps approach was outlined to accomplish EMU: (1) complete the internal market and lift restrictions to capital movements, (2) carry out economic convergence and set up the European Monetary Institute, (3) fix exchange rates and set up the European System of Central Banks (ESCB), which would be composed of a central body (the ECB) and of national central banks. The committee defined so-called 'convergence criteria' in order to assess qualification from one EMU step to the next ones. The road to EMU was however also marked by institutional novelties. Crucially, it was agreed that the ESCB's mandate would focus on price stability: 'the System would be committed to the objective of price stability; subject to the foregoing the system should support the general economic policy set at the Community level by the competent bodies' (Delors 1989: 19).

Overall, the flavour of the Delors Report was much less Keynesian than the Werner Report, largely because the 'basic economic policy consensus had changed in eighteen years' (Dyson and Featherstone 1999: 785). While no fiscal centralization steps were strongly advocated, the broad 'recommendation that budgetary authority should be given to a European body' was however made (Thygesen 1989: 639). Also, the Report still stated the need to determine an 'overall policy stance for the Community as a whole, avoid unsustainable differences between individual member countries in public sector borrowing requirements and place binding constraints on the size and the financing of budget deficits' (Pisani-Ferry 2006: 825). The key argument used was that 'some authority over the sum of national budget deficits and national expenditures is required if the Community is to achieve a proper balance between monetary and fiscal policy' (Thygesen 1989: 640). Also, concerns about the likely effects of excessive deficits in a fixed exchange rate mechanism were voiced. A counter-argument to wide-ranging budgetary authority was however also formulated, namely the fact that market discipline can be expected to exert a restraining influence on deficits within the union. The proceedings of the Delors Committee were finalised in April 1989, on time to ensure a sound discussion of its conclusions in the subsequent Madrid European Council (held in June 1989). The latter took the decision to move towards stage 2 of EMU which implied Treaty change. As a result, two parallel Inter-Governmental Conferences (IGCs) were constituted.

The two separate IGCs on EMU and on political union opened as ministers gathered for the first time in Rome in December 1990. The new Treaty negotiations were characterised by a fundamental imbalance between the intensity and depth of the monetary arrangements of EMU on the one hand and its institutional and political underpinning on the other. The discussions within the IGC on EMU proved to be at an advanced stage whereas the political and institutional reflections on the

IGC on the political union were very premature: 'EMU was on track and speeding ahead, and in a much better state of health than the debate about political union. Indeed, almost three years of debate and analysis had preceded the IGC on EMU. It was hence far better prepared than the IGC on political union, where the French and German governments had very contrasting approaches' (Dyson 1994: 146). Therefore, a disconnection between the monetary union and the political union appeared. The 'neglect of the relationship between EMU and political union (was) a major asymmetry in the Maastricht negotiations' (Dyson and Featherstone 1999: 746). Compared to the early blueprints of EMU that foresaw fiscal capacity-building of some form, fiscal federalism approaches were ultimately dismissed as part of the IGC. The deliberations over the political union stalled mainly because of a French-German disagreement over the design of the fiscal policy regime that should underlie EMU.

The negotiations have been indeed characterised by a strong eagerness of delegations to specify the design of the monetary union (in its most intricate details) and a lack of ambition to establish the political institutions that would have been necessary to shape EMU's legitimate and democratic governance. According to Dyson and Featherstone, part of the explanation of this segmentation between the monetary and the fiscal/political unions lies with the fact that the bulk of the Treaty negotiations were conducted by monetary and financial experts and that those 'actors were disposed to promote the interests of the institutional milieu in which they operated' (Dyson and Featherstone 1999: 748). Put differently, 'bureaucratic politics of competition to control the territory of the EMU negotiations played a key role in shaping outcomes. The more EMU negotiators had insisted on the linkage to political union, the more they would have been inviting EC foreign ministers and heads of stage and governments to take up EMU in their own institutional venues' (Dyson and Featherstone 1999: 747).

The disregard for the political union in the negotiation would have long-term consequences as it locked-in a politically and institutionally unsettled EMU framework. Tracing the key institutional design flaws in the Maastricht Treaty negotiations, Dyson and Featherstone (1999) concluded that: 'the biggest gap of all was caused by the lack of attention to the requirements of political union for a sustainable EMU' [...]. What was lacking was a model of transnational democratic polity to underpin a venture that directly affected all Europeans' (Dyson and Featherstone 1999: 800–801). This political void appears particularly puzzling in the light of the failure of EMU to qualify as an Optimal Currency Area (OCA) and of the resulting conclusion to this debate which pointed at the importance of endogenous mechanisms that could turn EMU into an OCA by fostering economic convergence, for example through fiscal transfers.

Maastricht's Heavy Legacy: An Ambiguous French-German Compromise

Discussing the institutional shape of EMU necessarily involved the confrontation of varying models of economic policy. The starting points and preferences of France and Germany – the two initiators of the euro – over EMU's institutional groundwork were notoriously different. Deep down, their views diverged over the respective role that should be attributed to rules and to discretion in economic policy. Germany displayed however a stronger bargaining power. Germany's central bank, the Bundesbank, and its monetary policy benefited from a strong credibility, earned after decades of stable prices in line with the economic philosophy of *ordo-liberalism*. France's situation, instead, was characterised by a high inflation that resulted from a strong reliance on Keynesian demand management. Moreover, Germany had made its agreement to the whole idea of a single currency conditional on an orthodox institutional regime (Dyson and Featherstone 1999). Institutionally, France focussed on strengthening the European Council in line with its previous claim for the constitution of a *gouvernement économique* while Germany envisaged an enhancement of the European Parliament (Dyson 1994: 146).

The first concrete clash came at the time of the French proposal to turn ECOFIN into a *gouvernement économique*. Germany reacted with clear distance and feared that a strong EU executive arm, i.e. ECOFIN, would risk 'undermining the authority of the ESCB and of developing an interventionist approach' (Dyson 1994: 147). What appeared at first sight to be an institutional struggle was however more deeply rooted into two opposing normative approaches on economic policy: 'on the one hand, a school of thought has consistently been arguing that once a core set of fiscal discipline principles are enforced, there is no need for further constraints on national economic policy autonomy; on the other hand, another school of thought has been as consistently claiming that a well-functioning union cannot be based on fixed rules alone and that some form of fiscal coordinated decision is also required' (Pisani-Ferry 2006:

824). Ordo-liberalism on the one hand, republicanism on the other (Dyson and Featherstone 1999: 794).

The French-German tensions were so strong that they even made their way into the final provisions of the Maastricht Treaty which, also for this reason, appears as an ambiguous and eclectic treaty. As Pisani-Ferry highlighted (2006: 827) there was a clear difference in the enforcement capacity of the French and the German pillars: 'a crucial difference between the two pillars was however that they were of unequal strength: while Art. 104 includes a specified objective, numerical targets and a detailed procedure (the excessive deficit procedure, or EDP) leading up to pecuniary sanctions, Art. 99 [on economic policy coordination] is a general-purpose provision with no corresponding policy rule or 'teeth' (...) With no legal basis for sanctions, the most Art. 99 can lead to is a non-binding recommendation by the Council' (Pisani Ferry 2006: 827). Furthermore, the strong focus put by the Maastricht Treaty – on German insistence – on fiscal discipline *de facto* neutralized all reflections about the definition of an aggregate fiscal stance, i.e. the institutionalization of some, even loose, kind of fiscal federalism regime. While 'early official thinking on monetary union regarded some form of fiscal union as a natural and necessary complement to the creation of a single currency' (Pisani-Ferry 2006: 824), others contended that the strict definition of rules would be sufficient to avoid negative externalities in a currency union. As a result, EMU remained characterised by a fundamental imbalance – 'an outright structural fault' – (Delors 2012) between its monetary and its fiscal pillars.

These fundamental distortions led many observers to consider that the EMU architecture in the form it was given in the Maastricht Treaty would not be solid enough to sustain the euro area's high economic diversity. Absent a large-scale institutional settlement that would have clarified roles and responsibilities of fiscal actors, the EU muddled through based on its old, functionalist working method which was inherited from economic integration. The functional rationale of the euro would be subsequently used as a key argument to promote the 'necessity of the euro' and was later synthesised in the Commission's motto: 'one market, one money' (European Commission 1990). With the Stability and Growth Pact, Europe created a *de minimis*, rules-based instrument that was deemed to be more compatible with the requirements of sovereignty. The Maastricht Treaty was the second occasion when a constitutional settlement over the European political authority was disregarded. The first was when the federalist Spinelli project was abandoned in the course of the 1980s in favour of a relaunch of the single market project centred around economic integration. With hindsight, the disregard of the Spinelli project was a critical juncture in European integration: it put a provisional halt to deep reflections over the advent of a political union in the EU.

THE ORIGINAL ACTORS AND INSTRUMENTS OF EMU

The Maastricht Treaty established one central monetary actor and empowered a series of executive actors which became entrusted with the coordination of decentralized economic policy powers. Post-Maastricht reforms would attempt to – unsuccessfully – bridge this gap. The institutional spirit of the Maastricht Treaty is largely inspired by decentralization, except when it comes to the supranational and centralized European Central Bank.

The ECB is indeed the central, supranational actor created by EMU. It is tasked with the role of setting the monetary policy of the euro area. For this it is entrusted with the mandate of maintaining price stability, in full independence. To avoid that the ECB becomes trapped in fiscal dominance, the designers of the Maastricht Treaty provided indeed for the bank's independence from government pressures. Article 123 of the Treaty on the Functioning of the European Union (TFEU) therefore prohibits 'monetary financing' while article 125 TFEU in its 'no bail-out' clause, prevents the European Union 'to be liable for or assume the commitments of central governments, regional, local or other public authorities'. The Maastricht Treaty is also revealing in terms of the tasks that it did not attribute to the ECB, in particular banking supervision and lending of last resort, which remained national competences.

The ECOFIN, an institutional incumbent whose creation goes back to the Rome Treaty, is the EU's key formal executive actor and as such a key player on EMU and on fiscal policy coordination. In many ways ECOFIN is the formal lead orchestrator of EMU's economic policy coordination. Being the official EU Council formation in charge of Economic and Financial Affairs, it acts both as a forum for the coordination of economic policies and as the formal legislator on economic and financial affairs for the European Union. Like all EU Council formations, ECOFIN is assisted in its works by the Committee of Permanent Representatives (COREPER). The latter is the formal diplomatic body that prepares the deliberations of the EU Council.

The proceedings of the ECOFIN are also prepared by the Economic and Financial Committee (EFC), 'the EU's expert committee for EMU affairs' (Puetter 2006: 73). The EFC acts in support of ECOFIN but also, in theory more than in practice, of the Commission. It is made up of ministry of finance and central bank representatives. The Maastricht Treaty's article 134 foresaw its set up 'in order to promote coordination of the policies of the Member States to the full extent needed for the functioning of the internal market' (art. 134–1 TFEU). Among its chief tasks lies the function to monitor 'the economic and financial situation of the Member States and of the Union' (art. 134–2), to 'contribute to the preparation of the work of the Council (…) and to carry out other advisory and preparatory tasks assigned to it by the Council' (art. 134–2). These broad tasks should however be executed without prejudice to article 240 which lays down the tasks of the COREPER (the Committee of Permanent Representatives). In other words, the EFC 'shares competences with COREPER' (Puetter 2006: 74). The EFC saw the daylight with the Maastricht Treaty but its predecessor, the Monetary Committee, was created at the time of the Treaty of Rome (art. 105–2). The EFC is therefore one of the oldest monetary and financial body of the European Union.

While being very influential in the run up to and during the Maastricht negotiations, the European Commission did not become as crucial an EMU actor as it would have wanted to be or as its role in the Community method, mostly applicable to single market issues, would have suggested. In truth, it only disposes of limited autonomous powers under the Treaty. Its function consists in the general monitoring of economic developments (art. 103a), the issuance of recommendations, such as in the case of the BEPGs (art. 103 – see below) or the preparation of proposals in view of the opening of a formal procedure of sanctions (such as in the case of the Excessive Deficit Procedure, art. 104b) or of assistance (such as in the case of financial assistance under exceptional circumstances, art. 103a). Overall, it is more expected to act as a secretariat on EMU rather than as its executive. Lastly, while formally outside of the negotiation process – as co-decision did not apply to EMU – the European Parliament nevertheless obtained the right to be informed regularly on the choices made to support Europe's monetary policy.

In terms of policy instruments, the Maastricht Treaty foresees provisions on the fostering of economic policy coordination. In this context, the key instrument designed is the 'Broad Economic Policy Guidelines' (BEPGs). These guidelines are recommended by the Commission, endorsed by the ECOFIN and reported to the European Council who adopts them in the form of conclusions. The BEPGs are an illustrative case of the institutional spirit of EMU's economic governance: the Commission initiates and supports administratively the process, ECOFIN is the expert forum for discussion while the ultimate political authority on policy coordination is retained by the European Council. As Puetter (2006: 42–43) put it: 'the BEPGs are generated through a complex and essentially intergovernmental procedure' while 'the Commission plays the role of a watchdog' (Puetter 2006: 43) that 'cannot enforce non compliance' (Puetter 2006: 43). However, as Pisani-Ferry outlined, the BEPGs have so many imperfections that they are far from being an operational instrument: 'the economic rationale and analytical basis of the BEPGs remain fuzzy [...]. They involve far too many guidelines to deliver a selection of priorities, and the EU is deprived of any meaningful instrument to ensure that they are effectively implemented' (Pisani-Ferry 2006: 836; Pisani-Ferry and Sapir 2006).

THE POST-MAASTRICHT INSTRUMENTS OF EMU

The decades succeeding the Maastricht Treaty (1992) were characterised by a series of institutional reform which were driven by the need to deal with the institutional 'left-overs' (Castiglione et al. 2007) from Maastricht, given the relative failure of the IGC on the political union. The aim was to both deepen and consolidate the European Union before the 'big bang' 2004 EU enlargement. Every new Treaty (the Amsterdam Treaty in 1997; the Nice Treaty in 2001; the Lisbon Treaty in 2009) thus came in with its share of institutional layering. They affected EMU unevenly in terms of the new actors and instruments which they produced.

Despite its early creation as an informal discussion body in the year 1974, the European Council which regroups heads of state and government, saw its role evolve ever since. Admittedly, the European Council was always a strong actor during 'history-making moments' of European integration. In line with this high-level role it met only a few times per year (twice or three times) until well into the 1990s. However, its formalisation as an official institution of the European Union and, as such, as a genuinely constitutive part of the EU polity only started with the Maastricht Treaty and even more significantly with the Lisbon Treaty. The Maastricht Treaty paved the way for the institutionalisation of the European Council as an 'arbiter of the last resort' (Richardson 2006) and as the strategic body which determines the policy agenda. It has 'turned into the key institution in the institutional architecture of the EU polity' (Wessels 2013: 753), putting it at 'the apex of the Union's institutional pyramid' (Wessels 2013: 754) where it exercises 'the prerogatives of ultimate leadership' (Wessels 2013: 754). While the Maastricht Treaty formalised the frequency of three European Council meetings per year, clarified its animating spirit (i.e. 'provide the Union with the necessary impetus for its development and shall define the general political guidelines thereof' (art. 4, TEU)), it did not recognize the European Council as an official EU institution. The genuine institutionalisation of the European Council only occurred after Maastricht. On top of officially recognising the European Council as a Union institution (art. 13), the Lisbon Treaty crucially established a stable, permanent and full-time presidency for the European Council (art. 15), a turning point in the evolution of its decision-making.

Created in December 1997, the Eurogroup, experienced several stages in its gradual institutionalization. Assigned with the rather anonymous name 'Euro X' or later 'Euro XI' group, it was originally meant to be a low profile and informal discussion group of finance ministers. Its mode of functioning clearly 'emanates from the practice of the ECOFIN Council formation. The Eurogroup seems to be a kind of limited version of this formation, a – euro area ECOFIN' (Puetter 2006: 11). The fundamental feature of the Eurogroup is the fact that it is 'deprived of the ability to conclude formal decisions' (Puetter 2006: 11). Like the European Council, its role was however set to evolve over time. During its first ten years of existence, the Eurogroup operated as a low key body, working under the shadow of the ECOFIN. Yet, during this same period, it increasingly took on new responsibilities in terms of economic policy coordination – in particular when it comes to multilateral fiscal surveillance and peer review, imposing itself as the core node of economic policy-making in EMU. The below graph (Fig. 2.1) which evidences the growing number of documents processed by the Eurogroup, the EFC and the Economic Policy Committee illustrates the growing centrality of the Eurogroup.

A major step in its institutionalization was its unilateral decision, in September 2004, to move from a presidency characterised by a rotation every six months, to a permanent presidency. Eurogroup members autonomously decided that the group should have a permanent chairman elected for a period of two and a half years, thereby moving away from the previous model of rotating presidencies which is still characterising

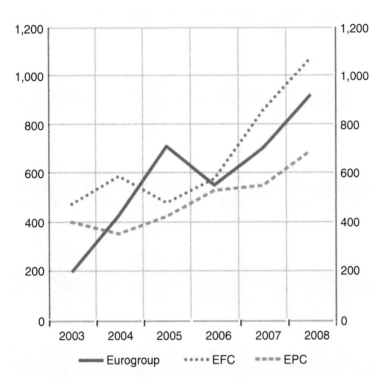

Fig. 2.1 The Eurogroup deals with an increasing amount of documentation. (Source: ECB 2011)

ECOFIN Council formation and indeed more generally EU Council meetings. The so-called Scheveningen agreement also foresaw the following: 'in addition to preparing, chairing, and reporting on Eurogroup sessions, the President was given responsibility for formulating meeting agendas, preparing a long-term work programme, and representing euro area members on the international stage' (Hodson 2011: 42). In 2009, the Lisbon Treaty formalized the creation of the Eurogroup and recognized – in protocol 14 annexed to the Treaty – that 'the ministers of the Member States whose currency is the euro shall meet informally'. It therefore *formally* recognised the existence of this *informal* body.

Often portrayed as a purely intergovernmental instance, the Eurogroup is in reality more complex in nature. The intensity and interactivity of the exchanges among its members, and overall, their socialisation, ('many of them stay in permanent telephone contact and consult each other on numerous issues', Puetter 2006: 83) ensures that its inner dynamic goes beyond the pure bargaining over national interests and entails some supranational attributes. It is characterised by a strong 'esprit de corps' (Puetter 2006) and could thus even qualify as an 'epistemic community' (Haas 1992). The Eurogroup is also a functional institution as its membership base (finance ministers) also extends to the Commission (in the person of its Economic and Financial Affairs Commissioner) and the ECB (its Executive Board Member in charge of the coordination with the European institutions). The body therefore also performs a horizontal function across EMU's institutions.

The Eurogroup is assisted in its work by the Euro Working Group (EWG). Ever since its creation as the Euro Working Party in the 1990s, the EWG is gathering the highest ranked officials of Finance Ministries from the euro area, i.e. usually Treasury directors. The EWG is the informal euro area formation of the advisory Economic and Financial Committee (EFC) which is officially recognised by the Lisbon Treaty in its article 134. At the time, central bank governors formed also part of the EFC and hence of the EWG, a practice which progressively faded away with the advent of the Eurosystem. Over time, the EWG has gradually established itself as EMU's expert body over economic policy coordination. With the creation of the Eurogroup in 1997, the EWG has added the preparation of Eurogroup meetings and more generally of economic policy coordination to its tasks. In the absence of a COREPER for the euro area, the latter, despite being the traditional preparatory instance of all Council formations, is often 'by-passed' by the informal EWG which, as a matter of fact, fulfils its function when it comes to EMU matters.

Besides EMUs fiscal institutions, one fiscal coordination instrument stands out as a central element of EMU's architecture: the Stability and Growth Pact (SGP). The SGP was adopted in 1997 (on German suggestion) at the occasion of the Amsterdam Treaty, which also saw the creation of the Eurogroup (on French suggestion). This institutional outcome is in line with the hybrid use of both discretion and rules in EMU. The SGP's acclaimed aim was to incentivize European governments to bring their public finances in balance also in stage 3 of EMU, which featured a lack of disciplining device compared to the stages 1 and 2 of EMU where pressure to act was exerted by the perspective of joining EMU. In its original version, proposed in September 1995 by German Finance Minister Theo

Waigel, the 'Stability Pact for Europe' foresaw 'automatic fines for coun-tries with excessive deficits' (Beetsma 2001: 23). Its fundamental objective was to protect EMU 'against the unsound fiscal policies of individual member states' (Stark 2001: 86). For this, 'it sought to convert the 3% of GDP reference value from its then perceived status as a 'target' into an 'upper ceiling' which could only be breached in extreme exceptional cases' (Costello 2001: 106) and which would rest on a uniform 1% medium term deficit objective. However, the automaticity of the sanction mecha-nism was met with scepticism, not least for reasons of incompatibility with the existing provisions of the Maastricht Treaty. In the face of Member States' resistance for Treaty change, Germany thus settled for a solution that took the form of secondary legislation (i.e. two Council regulations and one Council resolution). The Commission, keen to remain a key actor on multilateral surveillance, was key in 'framing the SGP within the EU legal framework' (Verdun 2007: 205).

As part of its preventive arm, the SGP provides the obligation for Member States to submit every year a Stability and Convergence Programme in which they clarify their 'medium term budgetary objec-tive' – which should be 'close to balance or in surplus' (Regulation (EC) 1466/97) – and describe the adjustment path towards this aim. Its correc-tive arm, on the other hand, operationalizes in further detail the Excessive Deficit Procedure (EDP) which was designed at the time of the Maastricht Treaty but remained vague and un-enforceable. In case of a persistence of excessive deficits the corrective arm would, going forward, lead to con-crete financial fines through a clear and established procedure. One mea-sure proposed by the Commission was interestingly not adopted. It would have consisted in 'the submission of annual programmes [which] would provide an ideal opportunity for ministers to assess the aggregate fiscal stance for the euro area in light of monetary conditions' (Costello 2001: 116). The proposal was however quickly abandoned in the face of Member State opposition as it 'stocked suspicion that the Commission was intent on centralising budgetary authority in EMU, by attempting to define a target deficit/surplus for the euro area as a whole' (Costello 2001: 117).

In the year 2003, as France and Germany both ran similarly expansive fiscal policies, they became confronted with the opening of an EDP by the Commission. Due to the discretionary powers retained by the Council (the powers for which Germany fought ironically hard at the time of the SGP genesis), France and Germany managed however, on 25 November 2003, to suspend the SGP by constituting a blocking minority when the

Commission came up with the recommendation of fines. The Commission attacked this decision in front of the European Court of Justice whose 13 July 2004 ruling, in turn, precipitated the SGP's reform as all Member States agreed that a credible framework was required. The reformed SGP in its 2005 version puts more emphasis on flexibility, debt sustainability, cyclical effects on fiscal positions and, overall, on country-specific conditions. However, this comes at the cost of simplicity and transparency. An element of its reform was notably the fact that correction factors were included in the assessment of Member States' fiscal policies, thus departing from the previous single focus on the output (the headline figures) to include elements related to the input (the fiscal measures taken). According to several interviewees, part of the complexity of the post-crisis EMU fiscal surveillance can be retraced to this 2005 innovation.

EMU's Pre-crisis Design in a Nutshell

In summary, EMU's intellectual groundwork – first laid down in abstract concepts throughout the 1970s – aimed at setting the adequate economic and political conditions for the creation of a common currency. A chief element of the reflection over the pre-requisites of the euro was whether a fiscal centre underpinned by a political union would be needed to support the currency. While the Werner Report and the Marjolin Report clearly advocated the establishment of a central fiscal regime (which the McDougall Report further specified), fiscal policies remained ultimately decentralized in the institutional design put forward for EMU in the Maastricht Treaty. This choice was 'symptomatic of a desire to reject fiscal federalism and to maintain national responsibility for budgetary management' (Dyson and Featherstone 1999: 789). As a result of the privileged focus put on the monetary constituency of EMU, its institutional design became asymmetrical. This marked a clear departure from the federal logic of early EMU concepts. The final outcome thus consisted in the centralization of monetary policy in the hands of a single federal actor – the ECB – while Member States kept the upper hand on fiscal policy, yet coordinating their economic policies in the ECOFIN and later, also in the Eurogroup. The emphasis was put on the reliance on disciplining rules which in turn made a political union arguably unnecessary.

Pre-crisis, EMU's constitution thus consisted of the following key features: a single, one-size-fits-all monetary policy (to cope with symmetrical shocks); the prohibition of bail-out and the resulting lack of financial assistance mechanisms among EMU members to deal with spill-overs of too harsh asymmetrical shocks; decentralised fiscal policies constrained by softly enforced EU rules; inexistent banking supervision mechanisms, and, most crucially, an absent political union. Despite the attempted corrections made to its original design during the 1990s (i.e. the establishment of the Stability and Growth Pact and the creation of the Eurogroup) and the years 2000 (mostly with the Lisbon Treaty), the pre-crisis euro remained an ambiguous 'currency without a state' (Padoa-Schioppa 2004). However, the absence of a fiscal and political centre standing behind the euro would prove to be destabilizing and made EMU's Maastricht compromise tumble as the euro crisis unfolded.

By establishing such an imbalanced monetary union, Treaty designers restated their preference to consider the EU as a 'regulatory polity', which has been the EU's genuine polity nature since its creation. The EU strives indeed on the adoption of regulations, directives and guidelines, and with the exception of competition policy, rarely adopts far-reaching autonomous executive decisions. Its weak and limited executive power is furthermore characterised by a high division of labour and in particular by a 'growing polycentrism' (Dehousse 2013: 15), a phenomenon which is most notable ever since the institutionalization of the European Council with the Lisbon Treaty. On the one hand, discretionary executive powers are split between the European Council, the EU Council, the Eurogroup and the Commission while on the other hand, implementing executive powers are divided between the European Commission and independent regulatory agencies, which have been proliferating over the past two decades. Lastly, whereas in the past, the Commission used to be *the* uncontested executive actor to become empowered when further centralization steps were undertaken, ever since the Maastricht Treaty European integration has been characterised by a growing 'desire to define a viable intergovernmental alternative to the transfer of powers to the Commission' (Dehousse 2013: 23) with the Eurogroup standing out as a very telling example of this aspiration.

References

Beetsma, R. (2001). Does EMU Need a Stability Pact? In A. Brunila, M. Buti, & D. Franco (Eds.), *The Stability and Growth Pact: The Architecture of Fiscal Policy in EMU*. Basingstoke: Palgrave Publishers.

Castiglione, D., Schönlau, J., Longman, C., Lombardo, E., Perez-solorzano Borragan, N., & Aziz, M. (Eds.). (2007). *Constitutional Politics in the European*

Union: The Convention Moment and its Aftermath. New York: Palgrave Macmillan.

Costello, D. (2001). The SGP: How Did We Get There? In A. Brunila, M. Buti, & D. Franco (Eds.), *The Stability and Growth Pact: The Architecture of Fiscal Policy in EMU*. Basingstoke: Palgrave Publishers.

Dehousse, R. (2013). *The Politics of Delegation in the European Union*. Paris: Centre d'Etudes Européennes de Sciences Po, *Cahiers européens de Sciences Po*.

Delors, J. (1989). *Report on Economic and Monetary Union in the EC*. Brussels: CEC.

Delors, J. (2012). *Speech*. In Notre Europe and EPC Conference: The Maastricht Treaty 20 Years on, 29 February 2012, Brussels.

Dyson, K. (1994). *Elusive Union: The Progress of Economic and Monetary Union in Europe*. London/New York: Longman.

Dyson, K., & Featherstone, K. (1999). *The Road to Maastricht: Negotiating Economic and Monetary Union*. New York: Oxford University Press.

European Central Bank. (2011, September). *Beyond the Economics of the Euro: Analysing the Institutional Evolution of EMU 1999–2010* (ECB Occasional Paper Series No 127).

European Commission. (1990, October). One Market, One Money: An Evaluation of the Potential Benefits and Costs of Forming an Economic and Monetary Union, *European Economy*, Commission of the European Communities, Directorate-General for Economic and Financial Affairs.

Haas, P. M. (1992). Introduction: Epistemic Communities and International Policy Coordination'. *International Organization, 46*(1), 1–35.

Hodson, D. (2011). *Governing the Euro Area in Good Times and Bad*. New York: Oxford University Press.

Jabko, N. (2006). *Playing the Market: A Political Strategy for Uniting Europe, 1985–2005*. Ithaca: Cornell University Press (Cornell Studies in Political Economy).

Marjolin Report. (1975, March). *Report of the Study Group 'Economic AND Monetary Union 1980'*. Brussels: European Communities, Commission, Directorate General Economic and Financial Affairs.

McDougall, D. (1977). *The Role of Public Finances in European Integration*. Mimeo. Brussels: CEC.

Mcnamara, K. R. (1999). *The Currency of Ideas: Monetary Politics in European Union*. Ithaca: Cornell University Press.

Padoa-Schioppa, T. (1988). The European Monetary System: A Long-Term View. In F. Giavazzi, S. Micossi, & M. Miller (Eds.), *The European Monetary System*. Cambridge: Cambridge University Press.

Padoa-Schioppa, T. (2004). *The Euro and Its Central Bank: Getting United After the Union*. Cambridge: MIT Press.

Pisani-Ferry, J. (2006). Only One Bed for Two Dreams: A Critical Retrospective on the Debate Over the Economic Governance of the Euro Area. *Journal of Common Market Studies, 44*(4), 823–844.

Pisani-Ferry, J., & Sapir, A. (2006). Last Exit to Lisbon, Policy Contribution, Bruegel, Brussels.

Puetter, U. (2006). *The Eurogroup: How a Secretive Circle of Finance Ministers Shape European Economic Governance.* Manchester: Manchester University Press.

Richardson, J. (Ed.). (2006). *European Union: Power and Policy-Making.* Routledge: Research on European Public Policy.

Stark, J. (2001). Genesis of a Pact. In A. Brunila, M. Buti, & D. Franco (Eds.), *The Stability and Growth Pact: The Architecture of Fiscal Policy in EMU.* Basingstoke: Palgrave Publishers.

Thygesen, N. (1989). The Delors Report and European Economic and Monetary Union. *International Affairs* (Royal Institute of International Affairs), *65*(4), 637–652.

Verdun, A. (1996). An "Asymmetrical" Economic and Monetary Union in the EU: Perceptions of Monetary Authorities and Social Partners. *Journal of European Integration, 20*(1), 59–81.

Verdun, A. (1999). The Role of the Delors Committee in the Creation of EMU: An Epistemic Community. *Journal of European Public Policy, 6*(2), 308–328.

Verdun, A. (2007). A Historical Institutionalist Analysis of the Road to Economic and Monetary Union: A Journey with Many Crossroads. In S. Meunier & K. McNamara (Eds.), *Making History: European Integration and Institutional Change at Fifty.* New York: Oxford University Press.

Verdun, A. (2015). A Historical Institutionalist Explanation of the EU's Responses to the Euro Area Financial Crisis. *Journal of European Public Policy, 22*(2), 219–237.

Werner, P. (1970). Report to the Council and the Commission on the Realisation by Stages of Economic and Monetary Union in the Community. *Supplement to Bulletin 11-1970 of the European Communities.* Luxembourg.

Wessels, W. (2013). The Maastricht Treaty and the European Council: The History of an Institutional Evolution. In T. Christiansen & S. Duke (Eds.), *The Maastricht Treaty: Second Thoughts after 20 Years.* London/New York: Routledge.

CHAPTER 3

Enhancing EMU's Fiscal Arm: Towards Stronger Regulatory Surveillance

INTRODUCTION

With the adoption of the Six Pack, Fiscal Compact and of the Two Pack, Europe's central fiscal surveillance regime, previously revolving only around the Stability and Growth Pact (SGP) has been significantly enhanced: it has been made stronger, broader and more intrusive. To illustrate the magnitude of this regulatory transformation, Table 3.1 below summarizes the density of fiscal rules prior to the crisis and post-crisis. It exemplifies the legalization process which Europe's fiscal governance underwent during the euro crisis, confirming the claim that 'if challenged in its regulatory endeavour, the EU tends to respond with more regulation' (Mabbett and Schelkle 2009: 1). In truth, strengthening Europe's arsenal of rules has been the first European reaction to the euro crisis.

Enhancing the credibility of EMU's fiscal regime was the common thread of the reform packages which was formerly notorious for its weak enforcement capacity. In other words, EMU's fiscal rules were on paper tough but given that Member States still had the last word to decide on the enforcement of their own commitment, their enforcement was conditional on their circumstantial willingness to sanction one of their peers. The 6 Pack and the 2 Pack aimed at going around this collective action constraint by delegating more enforcement powers to the Commission. As a result, a hardening of decision rules and sanctions occurred, both on the preventive and corrective arms of the Stability and Growth Pact. Overall, the new fiscal agreements allowed for further intrusion into the domestic

© The Author(s) 2019   45
P. Schlosser, *Europe's New Fiscal Union*,
https://doi.org/10.1007/978-3-319-98636-4_3

Table 3.1   Density of fiscal rules in EMU: Pre-euro crisis vs post-euro crisis

Pre-crisis (as of 2007)	Post-crisis (as of 2017)
Maastricht Treaty provisions & Protocol	Maastricht Treaty provisions & Excessive Deficit Procedure (EDP) Protocol
SGP's two Regulations + one resolution	SGP's two reformed Regulations (part of Six Pack)
	Directive on minimum requirements for national fiscal frameworks (part of Six Pack)
	Regulation on the effective enforcement of budgetary surveillance (part of Six Pack)
	Treaty on Stability, Coordination, and Governance (Fiscal Compact)
	Regulation on financial stability (part of Two Pack)
	Regulation on draft budgetary plans (part of Two Pack)

budgetary processes of Member States. The Six Pack and Two Pack have proven to be key legislative steps in the strengthening of Europe's fiscal surveillance regime. By contrast, the Fiscal Compact appeared as a largely *ad-hoc* and symbolic gesture to clear the way for new liquidity provisions by the ECB.

The alignment of interests among supranational actors seems to have led to an empowerment of the European Commission in fiscal surveillance. A crucial factor at play in this task expansion has been the fact that the previous rules-based system which featured the Commission as its watchdog proved path-dependent and cast a strong shadow over the reform of the SGP. Whereas the pre-crisis regime was already geared towards 'ruling Europe' (Heipertz and Verdun 2010), Europe's fiscal framework post-crisis revamp is even more rules-based than before: the density and formalization of Europe's fiscal surveillance regime has been dramatically increased.

Moreover, the Commission's task expansion appears to have been enhanced by the increased ambiguity of the fiscal rules, absent an external dispute settlement authority (so far the European Court of Justice has been quite silent on the interpretation of the SGP enforcement mandate) that could help to clarify the rule interpretation. At times, the activist reform process has also produced institutional results which were unintended, as is well illustrated by the increasing discretion gained by the European Commission on the implementation of the Stability and Growth Pact. All three central supranational actors (European Commission,

European Parliament, European Central Bank) have been instrumental in shaping the policy process and its outcome. The supranational actors' preferences converged when it came to the Commission's empowerment on sanctions, monitoring and compliance in the negotiations on the Six and Two Pack. Whereas the ECB proved particularly consistent in its policy shaping attempts over all three cases, the Commission and EP leveraged more influence on the Community legislations (Six Pack and Two Pack). Germany, the SGP's original initiator, proved to be influential in setting the fiscal surveillance reform agenda but proved less effective in shaping the design features of the new regime.

Against this background, this chapter retraces the negotiations which led the way to the adoption of the major fiscal surveillance reforms and the corresponding redesign of the Stability and Growth Pact's original rules and its extension by the Six Pack (2011), the Fiscal Compact (2012) and the Two Pack (2013). As part of this retracing exercise, the preferences and strategies of key actors involved in the negotiations are examined. The chapter also documents this fiscal governance expansion and stresses the ways in which the adoption of the new rules has affected the Commission's role in fiscal surveillance – a typology of new tasks created is notably provided.

EMU's Key Actors and Their Preferences

Given the high density of the fiscal surveillance reform, this analysis only accounts for a selected number of influential actors in EMU's fiscal governance, namely: the Commission, the European Central Bank, the European Parliament and the SGP's originator and principal advocate, Germany. The Commission has been acting as the monitoring and compliance agent of Member States on fiscal surveillance since the adoption of the SGP. This put the institution in the centre of Europe's fiscal framework. The ECB, instead, did not exist when the SGP was adopted but showed a marked interest since its creation for a sound fiscal framework in Europe. The European Parliament, for its part, was a marginal EMU actor when the SGP was conceived. It proved however to be a crucial player in the adoption of the Six Pack and Two Pack, in particular because of the new legislative role that the Lisbon Treaty granted to the EP on multilateral surveillance.

The European Commission has traditionally considered itself to be the uncontested EMU executive, drawing on its decades-long experience as the central executive actor of the EU's internal market and in particular as its competition policeman. Moreover, the Commission could rely on its function of 'guardian of the treaties' to claim a central EMU role. Yet, this conventional narrative wrongly ignores the fact, as I have illustrated in Chap. 2, that EMU was ever since the Maastricht Treaty a largely inter-governmental construct in which the Commission's role has traditionally been minimal. Denying this reality, the Commission has always sought a strong role for itself in the management of EMU's economic governance, and in particular on the control and coordination of fiscal policies. In some way, the establishment of the SGP in 1997 provided the Commission with an opportunity to claim the function of EMU's fiscal policy coordinator. When the Pact's credibility was attacked in 2003, the Commission – acting as a guardian of the SGP – brought the Council in front of the ECJ. Yet, the Court restated the centrality of Member States discretion in applying sanctions. During the euro crisis, the Commission rhetorically championed the widespread use of the 'Community Method', also to EMU, as its President explained during its 2011 State of the Union speech.

The European Parliament (EP) was not an actor of the original EMU design where its only prerogative was to be regularly informed about the Council's multilateral surveillance (i.e. the non-binding broad economic policy guidelines). The Parliament was also granted a right to be consulted should further provisions on the Excessive Deficit Procedure be adopted. Having a 'foot in the door' of EMU, the EP has usually pushed for more transparency and more information provision (through economic dialogues or hearings). Along those lines, the EP reached a major success when it was empowered by the Lisbon Treaty's Article 121–6 to adopt, in co-decision, 'detailed rules for the multilateral surveillance procedure'. This change in the rules of the game would affect the law-making process (Héritier et al. 2015). During the euro crisis, the European Parliament was particularly vocal on three aspects: (1) the development of a more effective and automatic EU fiscal surveillance, (2) the development of euro-bonds in whatever form, (3) safeguarding the Community method. In this analysis, the EP is treated as a unitary actor, notwithstanding the presence of major cleavages on some issues of Europe's economic governance reform, which however go beyond the three above issues (e.g. the set-up of solidarity instruments such as Eurobonds polarized the EP considerably). O'Keefe et al. (2016) have conducted a thorough and rich analysis of the partisan politics in the EP on both the negotiations on the European System of Financial Supervision and the 6 Pack. They, however, also conclude that 'cross party support' on institutional matters was granted when it came to 'reinforcing supranational institutions and ensuring greater legitimacy and transparency, notably through securing its own involvement' (O'Keefe et al. 2016: 226).

The ECB is the central actor of EMU. Since the Frankfurt institution's mandate focuses on monetary policy, it has no direct control over fiscal policy. However, this does not mean that the ECB is deprived of clear preferences when it comes to fiscal integration; quite on the contrary. The ECB has routinely defended stringent fiscal rules and advocated automatic sanctions in case of non-compliance. In the context of the euro crisis, it co-sponsored the Fiscal Compact and pushed on a number of occasions for a strong enforcement of the SGP in its revised form (Trichet 2018). Setting up constitutional rules to constrain the behaviour of fiscal actors in a monetary union must be understood under the particular light of a strategic fight for monetary dominance over fiscal dominance. Another element which derived from its rather high concern for credibility, a typical trait of a young central bank, is the fact that the ECB has always been very sceptical of a central fiscal authority that would strive to manage the euro area's aggregate fiscal stance. For instance, as the Eurogroup started to voice some of its pretentions in that area, the ECB reacted strongly.[1]

Germany, for its part, has been traditionally the most influential Member State in the reform of EMU's fiscal governance, being the original and principal sponsor of the SGP. Due to its strong economic fundamentals, Germany has arisen from the euro crisis as EMU's key decision centre, fuelling claims that Germany's political capital is ruling Europe. Historically, the German government has often operated in the shadow of a central domestic player, the German Bundesbank, a strong advocate of stringent fiscal rules at the EU level, which was instrumental in convincing Theo Waigel (then Germany's finance minister) to promote a Stability Pact for Europe in 1995. A similar pattern was to be observed during the euro crisis when the Bundesbank made no secret of pressuring the German government to restore a 'stability culture' in EMU through 'harder rules' (Weidmann 2011). More recently, the German Constitutional Court has increasingly acted as a domestic constraint on Germany's fiscal agreements too.

THE SIX PACK: REFORMING AND EXPANDING THE SGP

While the SGP, in its first (1997) and second (2005) versions stayed in the logic of the Maastricht grand bargain, the euro crisis led to a fundamental reshuffle and expansion of EMU's fiscal surveillance architecture.

However, the regime remained in the same Maastrichtian spirit of a rules-based coordination. The reform of EMU's fiscal governance started with the so-called 'Six Pack'. Adopted in November 2011, the Six Pack's aim was to both broaden and strengthen the top down monitoring at EU level over Member's States economic policies. While the 6 Pack included several legal acts geared towards limiting economic imbalances, the better coordination of fiscal policies and in particular the limitation of fiscal externalities lied at the core of the package. Its adoption thus resulted in a change of the vertical power balance between the fiscal centre and its periphery.

Only a few months after the advent of the Greek debt crisis in November 2009, consensus emerged among EU leaders in March 2010 for a substantial reform of the SGP's framework; in particular when it comes to reinstating more positive market expectations on the EU's capacity to take action against fiscal 'sinners'. Put under pressure to act jointly, the revamp of the SGP thus constituted the first crisis response measure undertaken – hastily, as interviewees recalled – by EU leaders. While, it might appear naïve with hindsight to think that changing rules would be sufficient to stabilize market expectations, one must bear in mind that the magnitude of the crisis was unknown at the time. Moreover, EU leaders were all very conscious that the SGP framework had suffered a strong credibility blow in 2003 (when France and Germany had unilaterally decided not to enforce it) and that inaction further to the Greek public finances crisis would lead to the Pact's *de facto* abeyance. Furthermore, reforming Europe's rules was in line with the dominant narrative of the crisis's root cause: fiscal profligacy in Southern Europe. As a result, the political imperative 'was about respecting the rules'.[2]

Convening on 26–27 March 2010, the European Council called on both Commission and European Council presidents in its Conclusions to come up with recommendations to resolutely reform EMU's fiscal governance, and urged them to ensure 'better budgetary discipline, exploring all options to reinforce the legal framework' (European Council 2010). This dual mandate, insistently demanded by France and Germany, can be explained by one of the Lisbon Treaty's institutional novelties: the creation of a permanent European Council President. Consensus-building among EU institutions and Member States on the key provisions of the Six Pack thus occurred within the inter-institutional "Task Force Van Rompuy", a new institutional venue. The Task Force gathered representatives from the Eurogroup, the European Commission and the ECB. Yet it operated under the control of the European Council President. Its creation led to a power game between the European Council and the European Commission, the latter being keen to defend its institutional turf. In an attempt to gain back control over the fiscal governance reform process, the Commission autonomously published a communication on 12 May 2010 outlining its intention to 'resolutely strengthen (the) surveillance mechanism in order to prevent a Member State from slipping into such a situation again' (Commission 2010a: 10).

Its swift move was most likely driven by the ambition to shape the discussions of the first meeting of the Van Rompuy Task Force set to convene only ten days later, on 21 May 2010. Content-wise, among the first concrete mechanisms proposed, one can note the willingness, 'to increase the ex-ante dimension of the [SGP] process and by giving it teeth' (EC 2010a: 4). In the first Task Force meeting, a consensus rapidly emerged on the key principles of the reform with two particular elements standing out: the need on the one hand 'to strengthen the Stability and Growth Pact and make it more effective' (Van Rompuy 2010: 1) and the 'need to find means to reduce the divergences in competitiveness between the Member States, at least when these divergences are too big' (Van Rompuy 2010: 1). The shadow cast by the SGP on the surveillance reform was palpable.

Meanwhile, the Commission was already elaborating another Communication, ultimately published on 30 June 2010, in which it specified the key measures it envisaged to propose in a legislative package after the summer. The Commission's package, issued on 29 September 2010 later coined as the 'Six Pack' came out – rather unsurprisingly, given the institutional competition with the European Council's Task Force – about a month prior to the finalisation and publication of the Van Rompuy report. It was made up of 5 Regulations and one Directive to reform and strengthen rules and procedures of EMU's fiscal surveillance. It also aimed at broadening the scope of economic policy coordination in Europe to avoid the build-up of macroeconomic imbalances. Taken together, these measures would contribute to substantially reinforce the Commission's powers in fiscal surveillance. The key recommendations which were finally made by the Task Force Van Rompuy when its report was released in October 2010, addressed the five following pillars: (1) the reform of the SGP; (2) the inclusion of macroeconomic imbalances in the economic surveillance process; (3) greater coordination; (4) a framework for crisis management and (5) stronger fiscal institutions. Most of the key proposals of the report had previously been fuelled to the Commission's preparation work for the subsequent legislative proposals. In reality, the reform process of the Six Pack was partly conditioned by the Lisbon Treaty reform. The latter had foreseen the creation of a permanent European Council President in its article 15 while it had also enshrined a more active role of the European Parliament in the definition of the multilateral surveillance procedure (the Lisbon Treaty extended a few areas to co-decision in this case increasing the EP's involvement in economic policy coordination).

The overarching objective of the Six Pack was to enhance both enforcement capabilities and compliance of the Stability and Growth thereby 'limit(ing) discretion in the application of sanctions' (European Commission 2010c): an actor involved in the early discussions remembers a diffused agreement that 'the rules were the right ones but the enforcement was the issue'.[3] As the Commission put it in its press release accompanying the new legislative package, 'the SGP will become more "rules based" and sanctions will be the normal consequence to expect for countries in breach of their commitments' (European Commission 2010c). This goal is achieved through a large collection of new legal principles and stringent instruments that cover all steps of the fiscal surveillance procedure. The general thread of the reform was to extend the circumstances under which the Commission would subject Member States to closer scrutiny.

The SGP's preventive arm reform (Regulation (EU) 1175/2011) focussed on the addition of new measures that, together, incentivize further Member States towards their 'Medium Term budgetary Objectives' (MTO). Financial sanctions, which take the form of an interest-bearing deposit of 0.2% of GDP (and even of a non-interest bearing deposit if no action is taken) can now be applied earlier in case of a too significant deviation from the agreed fiscal consolidation path, regardless of the opening of an Excessive Deficit Procedure. Specifically, this would occur 'in the event of a 'major gap' with its medium-term budgetary objective or with the adjustment path designed to achieve it (a reduction in its structural deficit of 0.5% of GDP) and if that gap has not been corrected after a year' (Fernandes 2014: 8). Moreover, an 'expenditure benchmark' was set up that warrants the matching of new expenditures by adequate resources, *de facto* 'placing a cap on the annual growth of public expenditure according to a medium-term rate of growth' (Commission 2011c). Lastly, a fine on the manipulation of statistics (an obvious follow-up to the Greek crisis) was also introduced on a 'Member State that intentionally or by serious negligence misrepresents deficit and debt data' (Regulation (EU) 1173/2011, art. 8).

The reform of the SGP's corrective arm, traditionally centred on its key instrument – the Excessive Deficit Procedure which can lead up to fines – was substantial too. The key novelty was the adoption of a system of Reverse Qualified Majority Voting in Council voting upon the proposal of sanctions falling on Member States, thereby limiting the decision-making power of the Council on sanctions. This shifted part of the decision power over the activation of sanctions to the Commission (who initiates the procedure) and would for example make it difficult for the same, French-German led coalition (that vetoed the Excessive Deficit Procedure's sanctions in 2003) to block the fines proposed by the Commission. Another crucial innovation of the corrective arm reform is the operationalization of the debt criterion (previously, surveillance was solely centred on deficit developments) and the development of a new benchmark of debt reduction of 1/20th for countries in excessive debt.

Overall, the reforms imply that the Commission disposes over both additional means, a greater variety of action levies, more progressive and more automatic sanctions which can be initiated at an earlier stage. Summed up, this leads to an overall surveillance regime which is more stringent, at least in theory. The Six Pack reform featured new requirements which went beyond the original scope of the SGP: (1) the set-up of minimum requirements for national budgetary frameworks, with an insistence on constraining Member States to move towards 'multi annual budgetary planning' (Commission 2010b). The underlying objective is however to increase the 'ownership' of European rules by national fiscal actors, i.e. the internalisation of the spirit of the EU's fiscal rules into the national budgetary process. Last but not least, the Six Pack also included the establishment of new procedure, called the European Semester, a policy tool whose aim is to integrate and centralise all surveillance procedures into a single cycle that precedes the development of national fiscal plan for the year t+1. This inversion of the budgetary calendar ensures that the logic of budget-making in EMU becomes more top-down and vertically institutionalized.

Based on these new provisions, I have regrouped the powers gained by the Commission in fiscal surveillance into three categories (1) sanctions; (2) monitoring and compliance; (3) enhanced control over national fiscal processes. Each of these categories encompasses several channels through which the Commission has seen its powers expanded; they are summarized in the below table (Table 3.2).

Table 3.2 Mapping the Commission's task expansion in the Six Pack

Types of power	Policy outcome	Type of measure/instrument	Impact on commission task expansion
1. Sanctions	Higher automaticity of sanctions	– RQMV	(+)
	Higher variety of sanctions	– Application of financial sanction also under preventive arm – Data misrepresentation	(+)
	Broader eligibility for sanctions	– Operationalization of the debt criterion	(+)
2. Monitoring and compliance	Higher use of quantitative measures Broader mandate Additional reporting requirements	– Expenditure benchmark – Debt reduction benchmark	(+)
3. Enhanced control over national fiscal processes	Higher synchronization of policy cycles	– Multi-annual fiscal planning – European Semester	(+)
	More reliable data	– Surveillance missions – Minimum requirements on systems of budgetary accounting and statistical reporting	(+)
	Partial delegation of compliance to national mechanism(s)		

In reality, the Commission operated under the close watch of the Task Force Van Rompuy, which, acting as a 'police patrol' for the European Council (Chang 2013), constrained the Commission's autonomous agenda-setting power. Given these conditions, the Commission hence did not win all battles. One of its drawbacks has been for example the refusal by co-legislators to support the Commission in its intention to monitor public finances 'based on the new concept of prudent fiscal policy-making' (European Commission 2010c). Instead of the open-ended discretion requested by the Commission, quantitative benchmarks were designed to assess national fiscal policies. Another setback was that the Treaty limited the Commission's ambition to be alone in the driving seat of the EDP implementation as the RQMV only applies to the decision on sanctions, not on the opening of an EDP as such.

The ECB's position on fiscal rules has always been rather consistent over the years and can be derived from its concerns to keep a regime of monetary dominance so as to safeguard its room for action. Historically, the ECB's dominance has been enhanced by the absence of a single European or Eurozone fiscal policy, unlike in normal economic constituencies. The ECB has been a staunch defender of the *status quo* on this, and repeatedly warned against the risks of having a fiscal *pendant* to the ECB, in particular at the time of the creation of the Eurogroup in 1997 (Hodson 2011). In the instance of the Six Pack, the ECB called for quasi-automatic rules, 'based on less discretion over outcomes' (Trichet 2010: 3) and has been a regular supporter of the SGP reform to restore its credibility. ECB President Trichet declared in November 2009 that the 'SGP is more important than ever' (Trichet 2009: 1). Moreover, Trichet was an active participant in the Task Force Van Rompuy, being present in 4 of the 6 working sessions of the Task Force. Speaking in November 2010 about the recommendations put forth in the final version of the Van Rompuy Report, ECB President Trichet regretted however the report's lack of ambition: 'the Governing Council of the ECB considers that they do not represent the quantum leap in the economic governance that is needed to be fully commensurate with the monetary union we have created' (Trichet 2010: 3).

Following the Lisbon's Treaty entry into force, the European Parliament (EP) had the opportunity for the first time to shape the reform of EMU's economic governance. Perhaps keen to set a precedent, it actively contributed to the 6 Pack negotiations. Although not all legislative proposals were to be adopted in co-decision (only five out of six texts), the European Parliament had a clear centralization stance. It notably insisted on the creation of the European Semester which the Commission had initially ideated. The ultimate centralization steps that the 6 Pack entailed can thus to some extent be traced back to the activist role of the EP which – as often mobilized its power through packaged deals. This comes in contrast to the findings of Bressanelli and Chelotti (2016), whose focus on the influence of the European Council on the 6 Pack generally overshadows the respective roles played by the Commission and the EP.

More concretely, the EP lobbied in favour of the introduction of a Reverse Qualified Majority system when assessing the compliance to the SGP (Héritier et al. 2015). The EP also made several attempts at exercising its agenda-setting powers. A noteworthy example is the inserted article 13 in Regulation 1173/2011 which foresees that the Commission presents a report to the EP on the introduction of euro-securities. This was one of the several contributions made by the EP towards the mutualisation of liabilities in EMU. Lastly, and in line with the previous endeavour of the EP to increase its own power, the EP managed to put 'a foot in the door' of economic governance by institutionalizing the 'economic dialogue', a forum for exchange between the ECB, the Eurogroup, the Commission and the EP.

In line with its historic insistence on the relevance of rules to constrain fiscal policies in EMU, Germany was among the leading actors to promote a new set of more stringent rules at the EU level. The German government favoured automatic sanctions and quantitative targets. Although Berlin preferred to take action at the level of constitutional/primary law, it also mobilized resources on the Van Rompuy report. The summary table included in the Van Rompuy Task Force report[4] helps to get an idea of the involvement of Germany in the drafting process of the report. Compared to the other Member States who made only one single contribution over the whole lifetime of the Task Force, Germany made three written contributions. Moreover, its first set of comments were the first to arrive on Herman Van Rompuy's cabinet desk. This involvement pattern, while offering no evidence of Germany's negotiation success/failure, goes however a long way in explaining the intentionality of Germany to influence the final Van Rompuy report.

THE INTERGOVERNMENTAL FISCAL COMPACT

On 2 March 2012, all Member States of the European Union (bar the United Kingdom and the Czech Republic) adopted the inter-governmental 'Treaty on Stability, Coordination and Governance' (the so-called 'Fiscal Compact') with a view to 'develop(ing) ever closer coordination of economic policies within the euro area' (TSCG 2012: 1). The initial (German) concept had foreseen however that the Lisbon Treaty itself would be revised to include a so-called 'debt-brake'. The fact that the Fiscal Compact was formalised as an international treaty was therefore a second best, both for the EU and for Germany. Its peculiar design resulted from the UK's strong reluctance – and ultimate veto – to revise the EU Treaty. The timing of the Fiscal Compact negotiation is noteworthy. It occurred in a period when market pressure was significantly increasing on Spanish and Italian bond markets. In functional terms, given that it did not have a direct bearing on the existing EU fiscal governance procedures, the Fiscal

Compact did not lead to enhanced supervision powers given to the European Commission. The Compact should rather be seen as the product of a diplomatic game between Germany and the rest of Europe: the German government was very keen to be perceived by its electorate as standing firm on its principles and by claiming success for an after all symbolic "debt brake" rule. In truth, both observers and policy actors have at times been puzzled by the very limited added-value of the Fiscal Compact (Laffan and Schlosser 2016).

The Fiscal Compact centred on the 'introduction of specific rules', including a 'balanced budget rule' and an 'automatic mechanism to make corrective action' (TSCG 2012: 1). It contributed to reinforce the fiscal centre in Europe by exporting European norms to the domestic level, thereby ensuring the internalisation of EU commitments within national fiscal governances. As such it was an instance of Europeanization as the balanced budget logic of EU's fiscal surveillance regime has been imported to the national level. Compared to the Six Pack and the Two Pack, adopted by and large by ordinary legislative procedure, the Commission's task expansion was however very limited in the Fiscal Compact, an intergovernmental treaty. The Commission was equipped with new monitoring tools to enhance its grip on Member States (e.g. creation of a debt reduction benchmark and obligation for Member States to submit Economic Partnership Programmes in case it enters an Excessive Deficit Procedure).

The key objective of the Fiscal Compact was to root the notion of 'balanced budgets' in EMU's domestic constituencies. The TSCG's article 2 foresees that 'budgetary position of the general government of a contracting party shall be balanced or in surplus' (TSCG 2012: 2). Moreover, the Compact introduces two new measures of fiscal monitoring: the structural deficit is set at '0.5% of the gross domestic product at market prices' (TSCG 2012: 2) while a 'correction mechanism shall be triggered automatically' when deficits display significant deviations from the Medium Term Objective of a Member State (TSCG 2012: 2). The Compact also requires that the rules are transposed into national law 'through provisions of binding force and permanent character, preferably constitutional, or otherwise guaranteed to be fully respected and adhered to throughout the national budgetary processes' (TSCG 2012: 3). A last provision is worth mentioning: art. 16 specifies that within five years following the entry into force of the Treaty, efforts should be made to absorb the Compact's substance into EU law (TSCG 2012: 12).

Of particular relevance is the fact that signatories of the Fiscal Compact have committed themselves to adopt a Reversed Qualified Majority Rule in the *opening* phase of an Excessive Deficit Procedure (compared to the RQMV which applies to the decision on sanctions in the *closing* phase of EDP), thereby reinforcing the automaticity of the SGP's corrective arm. Compared to the task expansion granted to the Commission by the Six Pack (and the Two Pack, as I will illustrate), the Fiscal Compact did not lead to significant new implementing powers gained by the Commission. Also, the Fiscal Compact has not been enforced (Alcidi and Gros 2014) and there remains legal uncertainty on the 'effectiveness of the control mechanisms' (Dehousse 2012: 1).

Based on the press coverage and the available secondary literature, two key actors appear to have played a distinctive role in shaping the Fiscal Compact and pushing for its adoption: Germany, its initiator, and the ECB, its activist public defender. They could both rely on a unique resource: the availability of money/liquidity which they could exchange as a *quid pro quo* for the adoption of additional fiscal rules. Their strength can also be explained by the absence of formal participation of the EP and the Commission in the negotiation process. Indeed, unlike in the cases of the Six and Two Pack, there was no supranational alignment between the ECB, the Commission and the EP on the Fiscal Compact, mostly because the text was negotiated outside the Community method framework.

Concerned by the risks of sustained fiscal profligacy which had been heightened by the moral hazard implications of the new financial firewalls (e.g. EFSF/EFSM), set up in May 2010, Germany elaborated a new proposal in the hopes of restoring financial responsibility at the national level. Probably inspired by its own experience as a federal state, the German government started pushing for the widespread adoption, by all EU Member States, of a constitutional or quasi-constitutional debt brake to ensure fiscal discipline in the EU. Indeed, the legal nature of the Compact – an international treaty whose key provisions should be transposed into national law through either constitutional or organic law – has to be ranked higher in the hierarchy of norms than the Six Pack. This is a chief reason why the Fiscal Compact has been staunchly advocated by Germany which managed to rally the 26 other foot-dragging Member States. As an interviewee involved in the negotiations recalls: 'apart from the Germans, the others were not convinced'.[5]

This legalistic approach is fully aligned with Germany's historic preferences on the matter. Germany has always been a strong defender of 'fiscal discipline' through rules-based governance as the SGP instance illustrates.

A brief foray into the genesis of the Stability and Growth Pact allows to understand that, in the end, the Fiscal Compact's design and content is nothing but "old wine in new bottles". In his original proposal for a 'stability pact' – made in November 1995 – to ensure that fiscal discipline is also safeguarded in stage 3 of EMU, German Finance Minister Theo Waigel made four key demands: (1) his key objective was to ensure fiscal discipline also in stage 3 of EMU, fearing a 'Maastricht fatigue' (Fatas and Milow 2003); (2) to meet this objective he asked for automatic fines in case of deviation from their trajectory; (3) he requested to set up a European 'Fiscal Council' which would be in charge of enforcing the agreement on Member States and, lastly, (4) as uncovered by Heipertz and Verdun (2010), in the first meetings in which the proposal was presented, Theo Waigel made it a point to enshrine these fiscal provisions in a separate treaty. Under this historic light, the Fiscal Compact suddenly loses its novelty, be it either in its form or in its content.

The ECB, for its part, pushed unambiguously for the adoption of the Fiscal Compact, acting most clearly as a 'supranational agent'. In his first Brussels speech in his new capacity and first appearance in front of the European Parliament on 1 December 2011, the newly appointed ECB President Mario Draghi declared: 'what I believe our economic and monetary union needs is a new fiscal compact – a fundamental restatement of the fiscal rules together with the mutual fiscal commitments that euro area governments have made [...]. A fiscal compact would enshrine the essence of fiscal rules and the government commitments taken so far, and ensure that the latter become fully credible, individually and collectively [...] it is definitely the most important element to start restoring credibility' (Draghi 2011: 2). What the ECB President did not say in his speech, however, is that the adoption and implementation of a Fiscal Compact would be the pre-condition for the further provision of liquidity. Here again it is worth contextualising and specifying that the timing of his speech was one of very high market pressure with Spanish and Italian bond yields hovering around 6%.

Moreover, at this time, no new credible financial assistance scheme was in sight due to the disagreement of several veto players in the European Council over new financial commitments. The ECB was therefore in a strong bargaining position when it offered governments to increase liquidity for banks through an extension of its Long Term Refinancing Obligations (LTRO) programme from 1 to 3 years as a *quid pro quo* for the adoption of a Fiscal Compact (Wyplosz 2012). This could hardly be resisted by Member States (Wyplosz 2012). As a matter of fact, the first extended LTRO programme was offered on the 21 December 2011, only a few days after the European Council met to align on the key principles of the Fiscal Compact. This political commitment was then captured in a separate statement made by the euro area heads of state or government (European Council 2011). This LTRO-Fiscal Compact *quid pro quo* would only be the first of a series of linkages between financial assistance and the adoption/support of more stringent rules. Schimmelfennig recalls that both 'ESM and ECB assistance is dependent on implementation of the Fiscal Compact' and argues that this linkage 'is now institutionalized' (Schimmelfennig 2014: 330).

Due to the reluctance of two veto-players (UK and Czech Republic) to agree on the Fiscal Compact and enshrine new fiscal provisions into EU law, EU institutions such as the European Parliament and the European Commission were by and large left out of the negotiation on the Fiscal Compact. To keep a foot in the door of the discussions they could only refer to the argument of consistency with existing EU-EMU rules and procedures, i.e. the unity of EU law or to legitimacy concerns. Despite the Parliament's ambitious demand to be treated as an 'equal partner' in the drafting of the Fiscal Compact (European Voice 2011), the Parliament only managed to secure three observer seats to attend the (technical) discussions where the design features of the Compact were elaborated. A key EP request made was the incorporation of the Fiscal Compact provisions into EU law after 5 years of adoption.

The Commission, formally not involved in the negotiation of this intergovernmental agreement, managed nevertheless to secure a few provisions in its favour. It has thus been attributed some implementation powers (in the monitoring, compliance and enforcement the agreement). But the Commission also tamed down its own ambitions, being reluctant to become empowered on the grounds of an intergovernmental treaty. As Commission President José Manuel Barroso declared, referring to instances in which some Member States were calling for a stronger role of the Commission in implementing the Fiscal Compact: 'some of the tasks we do not want to perform them, precisely because we want to keep our role deriving from the treaties, from the EU treaties and not from an intergovernmental treaty' (Barroso 2012: 6). This is why, like the EP, the European Commission has always supported an integration of the Fiscal Compact provisions into EU law as its official website confirms it: 'the Commission clearly supports the objective to incorporate key provisions of the TSCG in EU law as soon as possible' (Commission 2014).

The Two Pack: Getting Closer to the Core of Fiscal Sovereignty

The so-called Two Pack was agreed in May 2013. Following the achievements of the Six Pack, the Two-Pack aimed at further reinforcing Europe fiscal 'regulatory state'. A new Lisbon Treaty legal basis made it possible for euro area Member States to 'strengthen the coordination and surveillance of their budgetary discipline' (art. 136–1) and thus go beyond what the 6 Pack was already providing. Focused on enhancing the resilience of the euro area, the two elements of the Two Pack were bundled together by the necessity of dealing with left-overs from the 6 Pack negotiation. The 2 Pack entailed several additional delegations to the Commission. Running in parallel to the Fiscal Compact, the negotiation of the 2 Pack (proposed in November 2011, agreed in May 2013) was therefore set in the similar background of rising bond spreads in Southern Europe. Interviewees suggested that the Commission was the genuine policy entrepreneur which drove the 2 Pack forward. It was the Commission which ideated and pushed for the adoption of the 2 Pack.

Apart from this high level objective of preventing contagion in EMU, the two regulations had quite different objectives. Regulation 472/2013 essentially codifies the regime of 'enhanced surveillance' which euro area Member State enter when they are either in a situation where their financial stability is threatened or in a situation where they receive financial assistance. This financial assistance regime is differentiated into two: (1) 'regular enhanced surveillance' which applies when a Member State is in a severe situation but where no financial support is granted; (2) 'enhanced surveillance with precautionary financial assistance' which applies when a Member State receives financial assistance from the ESM/EFSF. Moreover, it sets the legal frame of 'macroeconomic adjustment programmes' in case of the request of financial assistance and compliance with the programmes conditions the granting of financial support. The regulation also determines a regime of 'post-programme surveillance' that clarifies the type of obligations that Member States under financial assistance are subject to until they reach 75% of repayment. The post-programme may be extended on the proposal of the Commission to be approved by Reverse Qualified Majority Voting by the Council. Several new tasks are delegated to the Commission. Provided it is able to offer evidence (against a set of predefined indicators) of a serious risk to financial stability, the Commission is allowed to make specific requests to Member States to obtain additional information (e.g. disaggregate data on banking system, fiscal data, stress tests). The Commission has also the privilege to prolong, in full autonomy, the enhanced surveillance of a Member State, every six months. The Commission is also tasked with the monitoring – along with the ECB and the ESAs and where relevant the IMF, of the implementation of adjustment measures by Member States. As part of this, it shall, where appropriate, conduct regular review missions. Regulation 472/2013 builds on previous rules agreed as part of operational guidelines of the EFSF and of the ESM (European Commission 2013) and therefore also attempts to bring in some coherence between the international and EU legal regimes.

Regulation 473/2013, on the other hand, sets a clear timeline in terms of the evaluation of euro area Member States' draft budgets. It also foresees some corrective measures should euro area Member States run into excessive deficits. Driven by the need to reinforce further the central control over fiscal policies, Regulation 473/2013's main purpose is to specify further the workings of the European Semester. It therefore sets out a common budgetary timeline with three milestones (April, October, December) with a view to synchronizing the preparation of budgetary plans among EMU members. It requests euro area Member States to submit medium-term fiscal plans in the Spring and blueprints of national budgets expected to be submitted to Brussels for examination in the Autumn. Should the Commission note a 'serious non-compliance' from the planned deficits submitted as part of the SGP procedure, the European Commission is entitled to request a new draft budgetary plan. Moreover, Regulation 473/2013 creates the obligation to Member States under an EDP to present economic partnership programmes which includes the 'policy measures and structural reforms that are needed to ensure an effective and lasting correction of the excessive deficit' (art 9).

It also features higher reporting requirements on budget and financial risks for Member States under EDP. On this, the Commission can adopt delegated acts and can request a 'comprehensive independent audit of public accounts of all subsectors of the general government' (art. 10). Lastly, it provides for the creation, at national level, of independent bodies monitoring compliance with fiscal rules. Overall, Regulation 473/2013 ensures a higher intrusion of the Commission in domestic economic policies. Interviewees confirmed that in their reading the Two Pack's 473 Regulation pushed the existing Lisbon Treaty provisions to its maximum. The below table maps the task expansion of the Commission based on the provisions of the Two Pack (Table 3.3).

Table 3.3 Mapping the Commission's task expansion in the Two Pack

Types of power	Policy outcome	Type of measure/instrument	Impact on EC task expansion
1. Sanctions	Higher automaticity of sanctions Higher variety of sanctions		
	Broader eligibility for sanctions/corrective measures	– Commission subjects Member States to 'enhanced surveillance in case of risks to financial stability'	(+)
2. Monitoring and compliance	Higher use of quantitative measures		
	Broader mandate	– Monitoring of implementation of Macroeconomic adjustment programmes – Discretion to extend the post-programme	(+)
	Additional reporting requirements	– Economic Partnership Programmes (countries under EDP) – Debt issue plans reporting (*ex ante*) – Financial risks (countries under EDP)	(+)
3. Enhanced control over national fiscal processes	Higher synchronisation of policy cycles	– Common budgetary timeline	(+)
	More reliable data	– 'Comprehensive independent audit of public accounts of all subsectors of the general government' – Independent forecasts	(+)
	Partial delegation of compliance to national mechanism(s)	– 'Independent bodies monitoring compliance with fiscal rules' are set up	(+)

When proposing the package in November 2011, the Commission had decided to unveil the two regulation proposals together with a green paper on stability bonds, maximizing its autonomous agenda-setting power even at the cost of 'upsetting' Germany. Overall, the Commission's interests largely overlap with the objectives of the Two-Pack, i.e. 'to enhance both the coordination and the surveillance of budgetary processes for all euro area Member States and especially those with excessive deficits, experiencing or at serious risk of financial instability, or under a financial assistance

programme' (European Commission 2011b). The Commission's ambition was indeed to have a 'common and graduated framework' for the
surveillance of fiscal policies (European Commission 2011b).

A comparative analysis between the versions finally adopted compared
to the initial proposals has been conducted. It reveals that as far as the
regulation on budgetary plans is concerned, the following crucial differences in terms of Commission preferences came to the fore, although the
bulk of the texts remains broadly identical: (1) the initial text foresaw a
provision (art. 4–1) that imposed the adoption by Member States of
'numerical fiscal rules on the budget balance that implement in the
national budgetary processes their medium-term budgetary objective'
(European Commission 2011a). The proposed provision also foresaw that
such rules 'be of binding, preferably constitutional nature' (European
Commission 2011a); (2) the initial text did not include the economic
partnership programmes which is a document summarizing the policy
reforms that a Member State under EDP commits to conduct to correct
its excessive deficit. Arguably, this provision of the Fiscal Compact has
been imported into the Two-Pack at the request of the Parliament and the
ECB, who both asked for it. As far as the financial stability regulation is
concerned, fewer changes were introduced. One aspect where the
Commission did initially not foresee many provisions was transparency,
publicity and regular reporting procedures to Council and European
Parliament, in hearings or economic dialogues (De La Parra 2013).
Another aspect, due to the insistence of the European Parliament on this
issue, was the social rights provisions and the involvement of social partners. Lastly, the initial Commission proposal foresaw that the extension of
the post-programme surveillance would occur on a qualified majority vote
by the Council. The final version foresees a Reversed Qualified Majority
Vote which further increases the Commission's authority.

Despite being a rule-maker on EMU's fiscal governance since the
Lisbon Treaty, the European Parliament's involvement in the day to day
surveillance procedure is limited compared to the Commission and the
Council. For example, the European Parliament does not exert a political
control over ECOFIN and Commission in matters of economic governance. This ensures a constraint on the scope and level of involvement of
the EP in the enhanced surveillance process. Against this background, it is
interesting to note that it is the Parliament which managed to prolong the
discussion on the package for a year and set the tone for the Two-Pack's
amendment in a power struggle with both the Council and the Commission.

The EU Council had indeed found a political compromise on the text on 21 February 2012, i.e. only a few months further to the Commission's proposal suggesting its broad alignment (and that of Germany) with the Commission.

The Parliament's preferences were clearly spelled out in a resolution on economic governance adopted on 20 November 2012.[6] Ultimately, it managed to secure the following: (1) the integration of some Fiscal Compact provisions in EU secondary law (De La Parra 2013), (2) regular information on the surveillance measures taken and (3) the ability to organize a hearing to be informed on the assessment of budgetary plans as part of an economic dialogue as well as on the outcome of both the enhanced and post-programme surveillance processes. (4) Last but not least, in a side-deal with the Commission, the EP secured a high level report on a redemption fund and euro-bills in exchange for its support of the Two Pack. Previously, it had managed to include a light provision on the reporting of debt issuance (present in the Fiscal Compact), a first step in the synchronization of debt issuance. It failed however to rally the Council on its proposal to ask Member States 'experiencing or threatened with serious difficulties with respect to their financial stability in the euro area' to submit 'a draft sovereign debt issuance schedule'.

The provisions of the Two-Pack are broadly in line with the traditional preferences of the ECB for a strong top-down fiscal surveillance, and derives from its interest in securing a regime of monetary dominance in EMU. Since the ECB was formally invited by the Council in December 2011 to provide detailed comments on the Two Pack proposal, a thorough account of the ECB's preferences on the Two-Pack is publicly available, in an ECB opinion that includes general observations and even concrete amendments to the Two-Pack's two regulations.[7] The ECB made the following key proposals in the document: (1) extend the scope of revised budgetary plans from the cases of 'particularly serious non-compliance' with the obligations of the SGP to simple cases of 'non-compliance', the consequence of which would be to give more occasions to the Commission to ask for revised budgetary plans; (2) promote tougher sanctions including 'a greater use of (reputational) sanctions'; (3) encourage the Commission to get more discretion by not restricting *ex ante* the cases of serious or severe financial difficulties that justify the placement of a Member State under enhanced surveillance by the Commission; (4) advising that the 'reversed qualified majority voting rule should be used where appropriate' which would *de facto* reinforce the Commission's discretionary power.

In line with the previous expectations of Germany over the design of a fiscal union, Wolfgang Schäuble, Germany's finance minister, was keen to attribute a veto-right to the European Commission over national budget adopted (Spiegel 2012). But Germany failed to obtain this. Apart from this, interviewees reported a fast convergence of views on the 2 Pack in the Council.

The Commission texts, proposed on 23 November 2011, did not raise key controversies and as a matter of fact, a political agreement was found by the EU Council on 21 February 2012, i.e. roughly three months after the proposal of the Commission was made.

CONCLUSION

EMU's fiscal centre has undoubtedly expanded during the euro crisis. Pre-crisis it had a thin structure and a narrow scope. The Commission's role in fiscal surveillance has been increased. It now marshals a higher intrusion capability which it mainly gained with the adoption of the "Six Pack" and "Two Pack". With the advent of the European Semester, the Commission is now entitled to ask Member States for a revised draft budgetary plan in case the draft plan submitted seriously deviates from the SGP rules. The below table summarizes the extent and variation in the Commission's task expansion stemming from the newly adopted legal instruments. Overall, the Commission has gained a series of new powers to enforce fiscal discipline. However, whereas formally the Commission will be entitled to use those powers, it is questionable – as before – whether the Brussels institution has a sufficient thick political legitimacy to enforce those measures on non-complying Member States, in particular large Member States (Table 3.4).

Retracing the negotiations revealed that no single actor displayed a strong and uniform influence over the three analysed instances of fiscal surveillance expansion. While the ECB showed a more marked interest in the exporting of norms to the domestic level, as a condition for financial provision, the EP and the Commission converged on the promotion of the use of the Community method in EMU. The Commission was pivotal in advocating and acquiring new monitoring and compliance tasks. The ECB proved central in EMU's fiscal surveillance reform process as it mobilized resources to shape the design of the new rules. It could also play in this instance the 'conditionality card' being able to inject liquidity under conditions. The European Parliament, instead, has managed to maximize

Table 3.4 A summary of new powers gained by the Commission in fiscal surveillance

	Sanctions			Monitoring and Compliance			Leverage over national fiscal processes		
	Higher automaticity	Higher variety	Broader eligibility	More quantitative assessment	Broader mandate	More reporting to EC	Higher synchronisation	More reliable data	Delegation of compliance
Six Pack	+	+	+	+			+	+	
Fiscal Compact	+					+			+
Two Pack			+		+	+	+	+	+

its new legislative powers on the redesign of fiscal rules and procedures as enabled by the Lisbon Treaty. Together, these three supranational institutions reinforced the fiscal centre and expanded the Commission's intrusiveness into domestic fiscal processes. As far as Germany is concerned – EMU's fiscal framework's principal among Member States – it proved central in setting the agenda during the early years of the crisis. Germany was however less successful in pushing through its preferences when it came to the specific design of the new fiscal surveillance regime. For example, the automaticity of sanctions as well as the constitution of a central veto power over national budgets, ideas defended by Germany, did not stick on the agenda.

This chapter also singled out a stickiness in EMU's fiscal governance as existing features of EMU's fiscal regime have been reinforced (Laffan and Schlosser 2016). Crucially, the reliance on integration by regulation has been confirmed. With the advent of the Six and Two Packs, the EU is now increasingly looking at how to 'regulate governments' (Schelkle 2009: 831), providing apparent support for the claim of an emerging regulatory state in fiscal surveillance (Schelkle 2009: 829; Majone 1994). Past institutional choices such as the fiscal designs decided upon and enshrined in the Maastricht Treaty and in the Stability and Growth Pact – acted as self-reinforcing critical junctures. They pre-determined and constrained to a large extent the trajectory of fiscal governance reforms, discounting institutional alternatives (e.g. utter decentralization of fiscal responsibility; centralizing of fiscal control by a European finance minister). This path-dependence, confirmed during the interviewees conducted for this book, is usually explained by the short term horizon of political actors who tend to heavily discount the long-term effects of their decisions (Pierson 2000: 261) and thus dismiss more efficient alternatives as too costly when they deviate too much from the existing equilibrium. This concern for the preservation of an institutional balance was confirmed by the agenda-setting contest between the Commission and the European Council.

The density of European fiscal rules has been increased, in a laborious attempt, as an interviewee indicated, to elaborate 'complete contracts'.[8] Another interviewee further underlined that 'Member States pushed the Commission towards clarifying the SGP and render it so complex that today no one understands it'.[9] The unintended consequence of the fiscal surveillance reform is therefore that it results to be much more complex: the Pact is now 'a very complicated box'.[10] As the density of rules grows and their complexity increases, room for their interpretation becomes larger. Yet in the absence of a neutral third party (the ECJ has so far been rather passive in the fiscal field) which would clarify the rules and provide an unbiased and formal interpretation of their meaning, the reform process seems to have unintentionally resulted in the creation of more discretion and interpretation room by the Commission itself. As an interviewee testified: 'actually I must congratulate the Commission for having found more loopholes in the new SGP than in the past'.[11] In the same spirit, a Finnish-German memo leaked by the Financial Times[12] denounced a 'somewhat arbitrary approach' in the definition of the methods through which the Commission assesses Member States' consolidation efforts and compliance with the SGP. The methodology is formulated as a 'black box'.

Lastly, a new development came forth with the reform of EMU's fiscal surveillance regime: the control over fiscal policies has vertically spilled-out from the EMU level to the domestic level. European norms have been exported back to national constituencies, thereby ensuring the internalisation of EU commitments and potentially mobilizing the use of domestic enforcers (i.e. national courts). Since its establishment, EMU's fiscal framework could be analysed through the simple lens of international cooperation between Member States who agree on common international rules (the Maastricht Treaty and the SGP) and have to rely on a third-party enforcer for the compliance and enforcement of those rules and to ensure the credibility of their agreement. The adoption of the Six Pack, Fiscal Compact and Two Pack, with the notable adoption of the European Semester, the minimum requirements on national budgets and the delegation of compliance to national independent agencies, has been a breakthrough in this respect. Overall, the analysis thus concurs with Hinarejos (2014) that post-euro-crisis EMU occupies a middle ground between 'two ideal models': on the one hand a fully-fledged fiscal federation with its own resources and a true, autonomous fiscal authority and on the other a reductionist 'surveillance model' where all fiscal powers have remained at the decentralized level.

Notes

1. On this see for example Hodson (2011).
2. Interviewee 22 – Italian Ministry of Finance official.
3. Interviewee 22 – Italian Ministry of Finance official.
4. https://www.consilium.europa.eu/uedocs/cms_data/docs/pressdata/en/ec/117236.pdf

5. Interviewee 20 – Independent analyst.
6. http://www.europarl.europa.eu/sides/getDoc.do?pubRef=-//EP//NONSGML+TA+P7-TA-2012-0430+0+DOC+PDF+V0//EN
7. https://www.ecb.europa.eu/ecb/legal/pdf/c_14120120517en00070024.pdf
8. Interviewee 23 – Bank of Italy official.
9. Interviewee 44 – European Commission official.
10. Interviewee 18 – Italian Ministry of Finance official.
11. Interviewee 32 – European Central Bank official.
12. *Financial Times*, 'Berlin attacks EU's easing of austerity demands', February 28 2014.

REFERENCES

Alcidi, C., & Gros, D. (2014, November 5). The Case of the Disappearing Fiscal Compact. *CEPS Commentary*.

Barroso, J. M. D. (2012). European Governance and the Community Method, *Speech*, In Conference on the Community Method, 28 February 2012, Brussels.

Bressanelli, E., & Chelotti, N. (2016). The Shadow of the European Council. Understanding Legislation on Economic Governance. *Journal of European Integration, 38*(5), 511–525.

Chang, M. (2013). Fiscal Policy Coordination and the Future of the Community Method. *Journal of European Integration, 35*(3), 255–269.

De La Parra, S. (2013). *The Two-Pack on Economic Governance: An Analysis* (Background Analysis). European Trade Union Institute.

Dehousse, R. (2012, February). The Fiscal Compact: Legal Uncertainty and Political Ambiguity. *Notre Europe Policy Brief*, N#33.

Draghi, M. (2011, December 1). Introductory Statement by Mario Draghi, President of the ECB at Hearing before the Plenary of the European Parliament on the Occasion of the Adoption of the Resolution on the ECB's 2010 Annual Report.

European Commission. (2010a, May 12). Reinforcing Economic Policy Coordination. *Commission Communication*, COM(2010) 250 Final.

European Commission. (2010b, June 30). *Enhancing Economic Policy Coordination for Stability, Growth and Jobs and Tools for Stronger EU Economic Governance.* Commission Communication, COM(2010) 367/2 final.

European Commission. (2010c, September 29). EU Economic Governance: The Commission Delivers a Comprehensive Package of Legislative Measures. *Commission Press Release*.

European Commission. (2011a, November 23). *Proposal for a Regulation of The European Parliament and of the Council on Common Provisions for Monitoring and Assessing Draft Budgetary Plans and Ensuring the Correction of Excessive Deficit of the Member States in the Euro Area.*

European Commission. (2011b, November 23). New Action for Growth, Governance and Stability. *Commission Press Release.*

European Commission. (2011c, December 12). EU Economic Governance "Six Pack" Enters into Force. *Commission Press Release.*

European Commission. (2013, May). The Two-Pack on Economic Governance: Establishing an EU Framework for Dealing with Threats to Financial Stability in Euro Area Member States. *Occasional Papers,* DG ECFIN.

European Commission. (2014). DG ECFIN Website: http://ec.europa.eu/economy_finance/articles/governance/2012-03-14_six_pack_en.htm (visited on 28 September 2014).

European Council. (2010, March 26–27). European Council Conclusions.

European Council. (2011, December 9). Statement by the Euro Area Heads State or Government.

European Voice. (2011, December 14). MEPs Demand Role in Drafting Fiscal Compact.

Fatas, A., & Mihov, I. (2003). The Case for Restricting Fiscal Policy Discretion. *Quarterly Journal of Economics, 118*(4), 1419–1447.

Fernandes, S. (2014, October 13). National Budgets and European Surveillance: Shedding Light on the Debate, *Notre Europe Policy Paper n°118.*

Heipertz, M., & Verdun, A. (2010). *Ruling Europe: The Politics of the Stability and Growth Pact.* Cambridge: Cambridge University Press.

Heritier, A., Moury, C., Schoeller, M. G., Meissner, K. L., & Mota, I. (2015, October). *The European Parliament as a Driving Force of Constitutionalisation.* Brussels: European Parliament.

Hinarejos, A. (2014). *Fiscal Federalism in the European Union: Evolution and Future Choices for EMU* (Legal Studies Research Paper Series). University of Cambridge.

Hodson, D. (2011). *Governing the Euro Area in Good Times and Bad.* New York: Oxford University Press.

Laffan, B., & Schlosser, P. (2016). Public Finances in Europe: Fortifying EU Economic Governance in the Shadow of the Crisis. *Journal of European Integration, 38*(3), Special Issue EU Policies in Times of Crisis, 237–249.

Mabbett, D., & Schelkle, W. (2009). The Politics of Conflict Management in EU Regulation. *West European Politics, 32*(4), 699–718.

Majone, G. (1994). The Rise of the Regulatory State in Europe. *West European Politics, 17*(3), 77–101.

O'Keefe, M., Salines, M., & Wieczorek, M. (2016). The European Parliament's Strategy in EU Economic and Financial Reform. *Journal of European Public Policy, 23*(2), 217–235.

Pierson, P. (2000). Increasing Returns, Path Dependence, and the Study of Politics. *American Political Science Review, 94*(02), 251–267.

Schelkle, W. (2009). The Contentious Creation of the Regulatory State in Fiscal Surveillance. *West European Politics, 32*(4), 829–846.

Schimmelfennig, F. (2014). European Integration in the Euro Crisis: The Limits of Postfunctionalism. *Journal of European Integration, 36*(3), 321–337.

Spiegel, Der. (2012, October 17). http://www.spiegel.de/international/europe/schaeuble-presents-euro-reforms-and-broad-new-powers-for-eu-a-861529.html

Trichet, J-C. (2009). Interview by Jean-Claude Trichet, President of the European Central Bank, with *Het Financieele Dagblad*, The Netherlands, Conducted by Mssrs Cor de Horde and Klaas Broekhuizen on 16 November 2009 and Published on 25 November 2009.

Trichet, J-C. (2010, September 27). *Hearing at the European Parliament's ECON Committee.*

Trichet, J-C. (2018, February 16). *Lecture*, "Leaders Beyond the State", European University Institute.

TSCG. (2012). *Treaty on Stability, Coordination and Governance in the Economic and Monetary Union (March 1–2, 2012).* http://www.consilium.europa.eu/european-council/pdf/Treaty-on-Stability-Coordination-and-Governance-TSCG/

Van Rompuy. (2010, October 21). Van Rompuy Task Force Report. *Strengthening Economic Governance in the EU: Report of the Task Force to the European Council.*

Weidmann, J. (2011, November 22). Zur Verantwortung Deutschlands als Stabilitätsanker in der Europäischen Währungsunion. *Speech in Berlin.*

Wyplosz, C. (2012, July). The Role of the ECB in Fiscal Adjustment Programmes. In *The Role of the ECB in Financial Assistance Programmes.* Study for the ECON Committee, Monetary Dialogue.

CHAPTER 4

Building Central Financial Assistance Capacities

Introduction

When the euro crisis gathered pace in early 2010, EMU's crisis management 'toolbox was empty' (Van Rompuy 2012: 3). EMU suffered an institutional 'lack of last resort mechanisms of assistance capable of securing the stability of the euro area in the face of a sovereign debt crisis' (De Gregorio 2012: 1644). An interviewee confirmed this: 'we were unprepared to the crisis institutionally, Europe did not have the right instruments'. As market tremors and financial stability increased in late-Winter/early Spring 2010, the blind enforcement of the Maastricht-designed 'no-bail out clause' looked increasingly unlikely. Acting in a context marked by astounding uncertainty, EU leaders refrained however from creating a Hamiltonian fiscal union and preferred to go down the route of incremental change: 'the EU responded with haphazard decisions that were often announced and then followed soon by other announcements to deal with the immediate aftermath' (Verdun 2015: 223; Buti and Carnot 2012). An interviewee confirmed that 'there was no appetite at the start to revise the architecture'.[1]

However, EU leaders also understood in May 2010 that the sovereign debt crisis would not be solved solely through the layering of new rules. Money had to be put on the table. After months of procrastination which fuelled the contagion of the sovereign crisis further, EU leaders hence agreed to depart from regulatory integration and embarked on the mutualisation of fiscal capacities as a new crisis management tool. However,

© The Author(s) 2019   73
P. Schlosser, *Europe's New Fiscal Union*,
https://Doi.org/10.1007/978-3-319-98636-4_4

'rather than creating right away a financial assistance arrangement, the euro area went through an intermediary stage of additional layering' (Salines et al. 2012: 675). Both the Greek Loan Facility (GLF) and the European Financial Stabilization Mechanism (EFSM) were hence set up and entrusted to the European Commission in early May 2010 to address contagion risks. Yet, market pressure grew further. Only a few days after the adoption of those two facilities, EU leaders therefore settled on the creation of a new *ad hoc* and temporary body, the European Financial Stability Facility (EFSF). The latter would be turned in March 2011 into the permanent European Stability Mechanism (ESM). Established to provide financial assistance to distressed euro area Member States facing prohibitive market conditions for their debt financing, the ESM boasts a financial capacity of € 500 bn which makes it the largest financial firewall in the world. Its main rationale was functional as the ESM was meant to address market pressures which were threatening the existence and integrity of the euro.

Institutionally, the setting-up of the ESM marked the centralization of the financial assistance function to the European level. Because of the Maastricht unsettlement over who disposes of the political authority over the euro, the centralization of the financial assistance function occurred however through a convoluted process and ended up being scattered among several actors. After documenting this complex process, this chapter explains why and how the ESM has, in a feedback loop, converted the Eurogroup from a deliberative informal body into an executive decision-making institution. The central argument brought forward is that the creation of the largest financial firewall and its singular decision-making durably locks-in a chain of command on economic governance that sees the Eurogroup at its executive helm and the Euro Working Group at its bureaucratic core. The chapter further substantiates Gocaj and Meunier's claim (2013) that the EFSF creation 'enshrined an intergovernmental modus operandi' in EMU.

The ESM was formally created outside of and in parallel to the EU legal order. Its legal existence and rules of functioning are indeed laid down in an international treaty which provides for the creation of the ESM as an international body, based in Luxemburg. The fact that the instrument, unlike the EFSM, was deliberately not attributed to the European Commission – usually regarded as the EU's executive arm – constitutes a watershed in European integration. It suggests that EMU governance is further departing from the classic Community method and that intergovernmental practices have been reinforced. The ESM's governance rules indeed formally foresee that strategic decisions are taken by a Board of Governors composed of euro area finance ministers while more operational decisions and day to day oversight of the mechanism are attributed to a Board of Directors composed of EMU's treasury directors. However, those bodies overlap on a one-to one basis with an existing EMU decision-making apparatus: the Eurogroup on the one hand, and the EWG, its preparatory and advisory body, on the other. In other words, while being formally a distinct and autonomous international organization, the ESM is in reality the *informal* agency of the Eurogroup, which, for its part, remains also an *informal* body. Despite being the product of an international treaty, the ESM thus affects the balance of power of existing EMU institutions. Overall, this suggests that in spite of its undeniable centralization, the financial assistance function is subject to fragmentation forces and remains so far incompletely formalized.

DESIGNING THE GLF AND THE EFSM: EMPOWERING THE COMMISSION

From spring 2010 onwards, the Greek debt crisis amplified and, through contagion and increasing market pressure, morphed into a genuinely European systemic crisis. As the promise of new and tougher rules against fiscal 'sinners' proved ineffective in reassuring markets, EU leaders became dragged into the mutualisation of financial resources to address contagion risks. As Chap. 3 highlighted, the first policy response of EU leaders to the Greek sovereign debt crisis in March 2010 focussed on strengthening and expanding rules to restore the credibility of EMU and of the Stability and Growth Pact. Yet, the announcement of those measures proved insufficient to reassure markets: financial actors went on speculating against Greek debt obligations. As market fears and contagion progressively affected other euro area countries (mainly Ireland, Portugal, Spain and Italy), it began to be ever clearer to European policy-makers that 'the public debt crisis was not confined to Greece' (De Gregorio 2012: 1618). The previous crisis response stance was thus not commensurate to the stakes. As an interviewee remembered: 'it became clear in April 2010 that we needed to do something'.[2] The growing systemic nature of the crisis forced EU leaders to change course and to put money on the table for euro area countries, for the first time since the start of the crisis.[3] As another interviewee recalled, 'it became apparent that without explicit fiscal mutualisation we wouldn't solve it'.[4] Yet given that 'no existing instrument allowed us to provide a solution',[5] a new mechanism had to be invented on the fly, the Greek Loan Facility (GLF).

A crucial difficulty of institutional engineering was however that a 'train of mutualisation'[6] would be launched, meaning that beyond the decision on the provision of money 'the problem was creating the precedent'[7] in terms of the type of arrangement under which financial solidarity would be institutionalized. Early May 2010 proved to be a critical juncture in this process. During the first two week-ends of the 1–2 May and of the 7–8 May three new financial assistance mechanisms of previously unimaginable magnitude were established. Recognising that the disbursement of financial assistance was necessary to contain the euro crisis, the first obvious action was however to confront the Greek problem. On 11 April 2010 the EU's finance ministers thus agreed on a € 30 bn financial loan package meant to 'deter speculators'.[8] Its activation was however subject to a Greek formal request for assistance which only arrived on 23 April 2010. By the time however, more money was needed to fill the gap. Euro area finance ministers gathering in the Eurogroup hence agreed on 2 May 2010 to set up a new lending facility to assist Greece in its debt financing.

In line with the design of the first financial assistance mechanism, it took the form of a pool of bilateral loans, guaranteed by euro area Member States and packaged together by the European Commission (EU Council 2010: 1). The arrangement, termed the Greek Loan Facility (GLF), was given an overall financial capacity of € 110 bn made up of € 80 bn commitment by euro area countries and an IMF top-up of € 30 bn. In terms of governance, the facility granted the Commission a quite substantial coordination and operational role under the supervision of the euro area ministers (i.e. the Eurogroup): 'the European Commission acts as coordinator, administrator and disbursement counter on behalf of the member states that provide the loans' (Dutch Court of Auditor 2016: 1). Yet, as the contagion of the sovereign debt crisis progressed, new mutualisation of resources would prove necessary to reassure markets – as I will show in the next sections.

What is important to understand is that the path leading to the creation of these various financial assistance mechanisms was far from linear. It entailed a significant variation in terms of financial capacities and EMU institutions' empowerment. Institutionally, a wedge can in fact be inserted between the very first instruments created and the subsequent ones. In a first phase, the Commission was the lead coordinator on financial assistance provision. However, the standard mode of institutional operation suddenly changed just a few days after. In sum, whereas the Commission was central in the operation of the GLF and the European Financial Stabilization Mechanism (EFSM), agreed on 8 May 2010 and whose functioning is uncovered below, its role became marginal with the advent of the EFSF/ESM. As contagion progressed further, euro area heads of states and governments – convening in an informal setting held on 7 May 2010 – were left with little choice but to take action to contain the damages and avoid further contagion. The Summit ushered in a mandate given to the Commission: 'taking into account the exceptional circumstances, the Commission will propose a European stabilization mechanism to preserve financial stability in Europe' (Euro Area Statement 2010: 2). Earlier, France and Germany had apparently settled bilaterally on a € 500 bn figure in the hopes that this round and high amount would create a positive market shock.

The Summit conclusions put the Commission under tremendous pressure to act. But it also entrusted the latter with a crucial facilitating and coordinating role on financial assistance. An interviewed Commission official remembers that on Saturday 8 May: 'ministers were waiting for a Commission proposal that they would discover for the first time: this was unseen before'.[9] The Commission came up with a workable 'proposal within 24 hours, an incredible speed'[10] and most of the key features of the proposed instrument, called European Financial Stabilization Mechanism (EFSM), were perceived as unproblematic due to its mimicking of the Balance of Payments facility (Olivares-Caminal 2011), this time for euro area countries.[11] Agreed on the 8 May, the EFSM would be formally adopted a few days later on 11 May 2010. While early rumours had actually reported an extension of the Balance of Payments facility to € 110 bn, the mechanism amounted in the end to a more modest € 60 bn facility, a limited size that is explained by the fact that the EFSM is only backed by the EU budget, used as a guarantee, 'no direct Member State financial liability is involved' (Tuori 2012: 13).

Another crucial feature of the EFSM was that the instrument 'is administered by the Council and the Commission' (Tuori 2012: 13). Concretely, this means that while assistance provision is decided by the Council, the Commission is in charge of the daily operation of the mechanism and raises bonds on financial markets. Much like in the GLF case, the EFSM foresees that the Commission acts as a borrower on behalf of the

EU. Moreover, when compared to the other legal forms taken by financial assistance mechanisms, the EFSM 'constitutes an exception to the general policy of reliance on legal and institutional frameworks outside the Treaty architecture' (Tuori 2012: 12). It relies on the EU Treaty's exceptional circumstance provision (art. 122(2) TFEU). Despite this institutional conquest, the Commission failed however to convince European finance ministers on a crucial EFSM design feature that foresaw the possibility for the Commission, in the event that the fund's core resources were depleted, to conduct direct borrowing through the use of Member State guarantees, in a sort of extension of the concept underpinning the GLF. A key reason for this blockade is that the Treaty did not provide the Commission with a sufficient legal basis to borrow money on behalf of Member States. Another factor was the reluctance of non-euro area member states to design EU arrangements to solve euro-specific problems. The following section elaborates further on this.

SETTING UP THE EUROPEAN FINANCIAL STABILITY FACILITY (EFSF): EMPOWERING THE EUROGROUP

The EFSM negotiations revealed Member States' reluctance to grant the Commission with an additional policy tool that would have implied financial commitments which, in turn, would have gone beyond the funds guaranteed by the EU budget. Member States were interested in keeping 'the Commission at arms' length' Hodson (2013: 307). Whereas the EU executive was given responsibility for raising funds for the EFSM, a new and larger fund would be entrusted to a new administrative entity. Initially however, the Commission proposal had included the possibility – in its article 3 – of having a 'stabilization fund under EU authority that would sell bonds backed by guarantees from member states' (Gocaj and Meunier 2013: 243). Concretely, the proposal envisaged that 'loans and credit lines above the ceiling referred to in Article 2 (2) shall benefit from the joint and pro-rata guarantee of the euro-area Member States'. This ambitious proposal intended also to confirm the role of the Commission as the EU's fiscal agent: selling 'bonds and borrow(ing) against guarantees from Member States' (Gocaj and Meunier 2013: 250). Article 3–3 of the Commission proposal even foresaw that 'in the cases covered by this Article, the Commission may rely on the services of the national debt offices of the euro area Member States, which offices shall be at the disposal of the Commission to this end' (Commission 2010).

However, EMU 'outs' were not very keen in creating large EU mechanisms: 'outs did not want to use EU funds'.[12] Moreover, interviewees also pointed to the fact that legal constraints impeded the creation of such an instrument. An interviewee remembers very clearly that the EU Council's legal service blocked the proposal: 'they said: no way'.[13] Legal experts identified at the time that the proposal would go against the letter of the Treaty as the latter does not foresee the possibility for the European Union to have its own resources: 'the Council's legal service told us that the proposed scheme would not work out and that something had to be done through the intergovernmental way'.[14] Voicing its concerns in the ECOFIN meeting, the Council's legal service explained that an 'an act of secondary law cannot engage the budgetary sovereignty of a Member State' recalling that the proposal would engage the fiscal liability of Member States'[15] which is in breach of the Treaty. Yet, an institutional puzzle remains open. While it is acknowledged that 'the Greek Loan Facility (GLF), set up on 2 May 2010, served as a model for the EFSF' (Verdun 2015: 225) it is legitimate to ask why the GLF was legally acceptable while the EFSM's state guarantees provision was not. By the same token, one can wonder why it was accepted that the Commission was granted a coordination role under the intergovernmental GLF while it became dwarfed into *ad hoc* administrative tasks under the EFSF, a model later replicated in the ESM. The mainstream view on the EFSF/ESM creation is that 'the ESM was set up outside the EU framework because a fully-fledged revision of the EU Treaties would have entailed significant political and procedural risks' (Salines et al. 2012: 677). However, as stressed by Bickerton et al. (2015) 'although the Treaty was amended to allow for the creation of this fund, its statutes are set out in an intergovernmental treaty between the participating member states. In this treaty, finance ministers are assigned a key role but the Commission is involved in an observer capacity only' (Bickerton et al. 2015: 11).

The legal conundrum prolonged discussions about the creation of a new firewall and concomitantly gave an intergovernmental design to the mechanism which are clearly set up outside of EU law, but use some of the EU institutions as external resources for their operation. This intergovernmental pattern was repeated at later stages of the euro crisis to circumvent Treaty constraints, veto players or domestic pressures, the Single Resolution Mechanism (SRM) being in case in point. Behind the legal argument, the negotiation centred on the new mechanisms' institutional underpinning: 'dynamics behind the deal included a polarized debate on whether the

Council or the Commission would lead the new mechanism' (Gocaj and Meunier 2013: 245). According to Bickerton et al. (2015), the creation of the ESM as a 'de novo body', proves to be a typical illustration of post-Maastricht delegation patterns. In this reading, the ESM performs 'functions that could have been delegated to the Commission and tend to contain mechanisms for member state representation as a part of their governance structure' (Bickerton et al. 2015: 3).

As the negotiation progressed, it became increasingly clear that the Commission's role in the mechanism would need to be tamed down ('several Member States didn't want the Commission to be the financial backstop for the euro area'[16]), in spite of the Commission's and France's efforts to find solutions that did not disempower the Commission altogether. Those attempts were faced, time and again, by a reluctant Germany which purposefully interpreted the legal service's opinion as an impossibility to delegate substantial tasks, even coordination and non-discretionary tasks, to the European Commission, which it started to distrust: 'Germany set the parameters of the response and the institution' (Gocaj and Meunier 2013: 244). The German government was indeed sceptical about the whole idea of setting up financial assistance mechanisms. It attempted first to limit its size and to avoid any 'institutionalized EU rescue scheme that could fall foul of its constitutional court'.[17]

The negotiation on the European Financial Stability Fund (EFSF) was hence of a rather sterile nature for quite some time, until the moment when, 'in a side discussion with EWG Chairman Thomas Wieser[18] and German minister Thomas De Maizières,[19] Dutch senior official Martin Verwey – who was chairing the alternate EWG meetings – suggested the creation of a Special Purpose Vehicle (SPV)'.[20] In the end, 'it was Germany who made the suggestion. This unblocked the situation, everyone in the room being pleased that Germany finally puts something on the table'.[21] The SPV institutional structure was convenient to Germany in two respects: it 'was the solution to Germany's resistance to Commission control' (Gocaj and Meunier 2013: 245) and it 'also allowed efficiency, as the intergovernmental structure allowed the institution to be set up very quickly' (Gocaj and Meunier 2013: 245). Due to the broad contagion of the crisis and its escalation, German Chancellor Merkel could not resist the need for the creation of such a large scale arrangement. She could only shape its design.

With the agreement on the EFSF's as an SPV, the overall set of measures agreed in the course of the 7–8 May 2010 week-end would amount to € 500 bn, thereby reaching the symbolic amount discussed in the bilat-eral French-German talks. Overall, while France was successful in the agenda-setting of the fund, Germany won on the institutional design front, and kept the Commission[22] in distance from the management of the EFSF. Apparently, this latter aspect did not however prove sufficient to reassure supporters of the old EMU paradigm of 'everyone keeping their house in order', a senior German ambassador, who on the day the agree-ment was done, explained that 'France has won' [...], 'this is what they have wanted for years',[23] later claiming that France 'has finally got its way on the creation of an 'economic government''.[24]

The Euro Working Group (EWG) was tasked with the implementation of the EFSF agreement. Faced with the operational challenge of creating an SPV, a structure usually used by the private sector, the public finance experts from the EWG were thus arguably confused: 'it was a nightmare'.[25] Until the Luxemburg representative suggested to his peers that he could 'create a fund just by going to notary Delvaux in Luxemburg'.[26] Since this rather casual yet operational proposal was the only one on the table, it became implemented and allowed the EWG to keep a hand over the EFSF establishment process. The detailed arrangements were then discussed over the four subsequent weeks as part of a Task Force of the EWG.

THE EFSF: AN OPERATIONAL BUT SHAKY SOLUTION

Finally, 'by notarial deed dated 7 June 2010, the EFSF was formed as a Luxembourg public limited liability company' (Jansen 2011: 418). Decision and operation rules were encapsulated in a so-called 'Framework Agreement between the EFSF and its 17 "high shareholders" setting out the (very intergovernmental) decision-making rules of the Facility and substantive guidance for its operation' (Beukers and De Witte 2013). It has been argued that 'the set-up of the EFSF reflects Germany's effort to control the institution and keep it out of the EU's 'technocratic' manage-ment' (Gocaj and Meunier 2013: 245), for example allowing to have only 'observers from the Commission and ECB' (Gocaj and Meunier 2013: 245). Yet, despite the fact that the EFSF agreement has been made outside of EU law and is considered to be an *ad hoc* vehicle that is not attributed to any established EU actor (and is therefore, on paper, distinct from them), its governance is embedded within the EU institutional landscape, formally and informally. As part of the legal literature on 'institutional bor-rowing', Beukers and De Witte (2013: 814) have emphasized that the

Framework Agreement (FA) on the EFSF foresees 'entrusting supporting roles to three EU institutions, the Commission, the ECB and the Court of Justice', on top of the EIB which provides technical support to the EFSF.

Besides, Beukers and De Witte also pointed at a less documented phenomenon of what they refer as 'a curious hybrid' of the mechanism's governance, i.e. the fact that 'all formal decision-making powers are entrusted to organs composed of representatives of the Members; but those representatives happen to be the same persons who represent their country in the EU's informal Eurogroup and Euro working group' (Beukers and De Witte 2013: 814). Despite its lack of formal institutional affiliation, the EFSF's decision-making is anchored on the existing EMU institutional landscape: it is therefore a Eurogroup instrument. This affiliation occurs mostly informally however: on the one hand through the mentioned Eurogroup since the top decision-making body of the EFSF is indeed the so-called Board of Governors (which gathers euro area finance ministers) and on the other, through the Euro Working Group (EWG) since members of the EWG constitute the more operational Board of Directors of the EFSF. There is however also a direct reference to the Economic and Financial Committee (EFC), for which the Lisbon Treaty formally foresees an advisory and preparatory role while it does not provide for the existence of the EWG at all.

The EFC is formally recognised in the Framework Agreements while its president is a central operational actor of the mechanism. More surprisingly, given its lack of legal existence, the EWG has also been granted decision-making powers within the EFSF. A look at the EFSF's decision-making structure reveals indeed that 'the President of the EFC[27] serves as Chairman of EFSF's Board'[28] and that 'each EFSF shareholder shall propose for nomination to the Board of EFSF its representatives in the EWG' (Jansen 2011: 418). The concrete example of an EFSF disbursement very well illustrates the distinctive centrality of the EWG in the process. The key preliminary step that precedes the decision – by euro area finance ministers, i.e. EMU ministers grouped in the EFSF's Governing Board – to disburse EFSF funds, provides for a central role for the Euro Working Group which approves 'the terms of the Financial Assistance Facility Agreements' (art. 2 of the EFSF Framework Agreement).

The procedure foresees that following the EWG's 'approval of the relevant MoU, the Commission, in liaison with the ECB, shall make a proposal to the Eurogroup Working Group of the main terms of the Financial

Assistance Facility Agreement to be proposed to the Beneficiary Member State based on its assessment of market conditions and provided that the terms of such Financial Assistance Facility Agreement contain financial terms compatible with the MoU and the compatibility of maturities with debt sustainability; (iii) following a decision of the Eurogroup Working Group, EFSF (in conjunction with the Eurogroup Working Group) shall negotiate the detailed, technical terms of the Financial Assistance Facility Agreements' (art. 2 of the EFSF Framework Agreement). This procedure lends support to the view that the EWG, despite being an informal body, has been empowered by the EFSF creation as an operating agent. By contrast, the Commission has been undermined and downgraded to a secretariat of the EWG, which is only 'authorized to sign the MoU on behalf of the euro area Member States, after it has been approved by the Eurogroup Working Group' (Tuori 2012: 14) – and should then ensure the compliance of the agreement. In other words, it is the Euro Working Group that retains the final word and that decides on the main terms of the financial assistance facility. These institutional innovations and the liberty taken with the existing EU Treaty broadly survived the transition from the temporary EFSF towards the permanent ESM, but crucially, also triggered the transition itself.

Despite the unprecedented financial magnitude of the EFSF, it 'soon became apparent that a permanent stability mechanism would be necessary to continue to safeguard the financial stability of the euro area as a whole and of its Member States and to prevent further crises' (Jansen 2011: 421–422). Calls for a permanent instrument began to be voiced[29] already in September 2010. They came on top of an inherent time limit (the EFSF was set up for a duration of 3 years only) that was central in legally justifying the temporary set-up of financial firewalls at the European level. Financial assistance was provided to address exceptional circumstances, and that in legal terms, 'exceptional means temporary' (Louis 2011: 985).

However, as much as 'people like to talk about the temporary/permanent distinction it wasn't this'[30] factor which explained the move from the EFSF to the ESM. The key issue according to the same interviewee was 'exclusively' linked to Member States 'internal cost in terms of public deficit calculation'.[31] In this interpretation, the transition from the EFSF to the ESM was triggered by an usually technical actor, Eurostat, the European statistical office. In its decision issued on 27 January 2011, the statistical body forcefully argued that national contributions to the EFSF would not be exempted from national accounts recording and stressed 'that the funds raised in the framework of the European Financial Stability Facility must be recorded in the gross government debt of the euro area Member States participating in a support operation, in proportion to their share of the guarantee given' (Eurostat 2011). In other words, Member States contributing to the EFSF's financing would see their deficits statistically increasing because of this, thereby fuelling a vicious circle that would not have existed had the EFSF been set up as an international organization (in which case contributions would have been excluded from national debt recording). This decision precipitated the end of the EFSF and accelerated the transition towards a permanent mechanism EU leaders thus 'wanted to make an international organization with a big I and a big O'.[32]

Eurostat's assessment also stressed that, institutionally, the EFSF 'cannot be regarded as an international financial institution' (Eurostat 2011: 2) because the 'EFSF does not possess all the normal characteristics of an institutional unit under ESA 95. It has no capacity for initiative and a limited autonomy of decision in the exercise of its primary function, providing loans to countries in difficulty and their financing' (Eurostat 2011: 1–2). What is particularly noteworthy about Eurostat's decision is the institutional dimension of its analysis. When the statistical organization argues that the EFSF 'cannot also be consolidated with any of the European institutions established by the Treaties (such as the European Commission, Council or Parliament)' it also allows itself to publicly recall the institutional inexistence of the Eurogroup and to define its institutional nature: 'in practice, the EFSF only reports on its activities to the Eurogroup (recognized in the Treaty of Lisbon as just a working group of the Council) and is not under the control of existing European institutions' (Eurostat 2011: 2). This interpretation thus lends support to considering the EFSF as an instrument of the Eurogroup instead of looking at it as an institution in its own right.

Eurostat's decision accelerated the negotiation on a permanent financial assistance mechanism but the switch to a permanent organization was also convenient for other reasons. First, 'the rating agencies did not understand it [the EFSF]'.[33] This is an important dimension as the *raison d'être* of the EFSF was to place bonds on the market and for that 'Europe had to show to the outside world that it had something sustainable'.[34] Secondly, the idea of having a genuine international organization also found support in Berlin as 'the Germans thought that by constituting an international structure, there would not be any problem with the *Grundgesetz* clauses on the German Parliament and Europe'.[35]

THE ESM TAKES OVER AND EXTENDS THE EFSF STRUCTURE

Whilst the EFSF was created over a week-end, EU leaders had plenty of time to design its permanent successor, the European Stability Mechanism (ESM). However, they settled for a replica of the EFSF's structure. This points at the existence of a path-dependence mechanism (Goucaj and Meunier 2013) within EMU: the Eurogroup was kept at its strategic centre, the EWG at its operational centre and the Commission, 'at arm's length' (Hodson 2013). Yet, to comply with the Eurostat decision and in particular the features required to comply with the 'institutional unit' criterion, a *façade* of international financial institution was constructed and the path of institutional parallelism was followed in an even more extreme form.

To turn the EFSF into a permanent mechanism, euro area leaders gathered on several occasions towards the end of 2010. Yet, negotiations followed a stop and go pattern. From the principle agreement on a permanent mechanism creation on 28–29 October 2010 to the final adoption on the 2 February 2012, fifteen months passed, and the ESM was in reality adopted in two different versions. Over this period, 'the discussion on the new ESM has been plagued by misunderstandings and confusion, often amplified by politicians pandering to domestic public concerns' (Micossi et al. 2011: 1). This occurred against the background of a hesitating stance on private sector involvement, which in the end disappeared from the second Treaty version. As market pressure kept on ravaging, euro area Member States had to increase the financial capacity of the EFSF on 24 June 2011 to 780 bn to ensure that the overall financial stability provision (i.e. EFSM + EFSF) would reach the announced figure of 500 bn. In this way, another initial shortcoming of the EFSF could be addressed: the fact that its lending capacity was limited by the necessity to safeguard a triple A rating. This diversification of financial instruments would later be imported into the ESM's second version too, thus contributing to a greater operational toolkit and decision-making power of the ESM's Board of Directors.

Institutionally, the ESM Treaty (ESM Treaty 2012) takes over the decision-making structure of the EFSF with only a few modifications. In particular both the ESM Board of Governors (BoG) and the ESM Board of Directors (BoD) are the replica of the EFSF BoG and the EFSF BoD, thus extending 'the overlap in terms of composition between the EU Council and ESM structures' (Salines et al. 2012: 676). However, in contrast to the EFSF, the

ESM is established as 'an international financial institution' (ESM Treaty, art.1). To comply with ESA 95's 'institutional unit' criterion that requires a certain autonomy of decision, the ESM Treaty no longer foresees a direct link between its decision-making governance and EMU's governance made up of the informal Eurogroup/Euro Working Group or the formal EFC. In practice however, the ESM is informally subordinated to the Eurogroup. This has been confirmed by interviews: 'in real world terms, yes the ESM is a Eurogroup instrument'; 'the ESM body only makes the legal decision as the actual negotiations happen in the Eurogroup and the EWG'[36],[37].

The ESM governance thus relies on a softer principle of 'institutional parallelism' (Tuori 2012: 47) between the ESM and the Eurogroup as they are considered as two different entities. An illustration of this informal institutional parallelism can be found in current working practices. Although euro area finance ministers do not exert officially as Eurogroup formation, real life observations of this 'double-hatting' show that the BoG of the ESM gather in back to back meetings with the Eurogroup while the BoD meets in back to back meetings with the EWG. Since the ESM is headquartered in Luxemburg, those meetings mostly occur in Brussels. Despite the existence of formally distinct agendas for the Eurogroup and the EWG on the one hand and the ESM Board of Governors and Board of Directors on the other,[38] 'what usually happens is that you have Eurogroup and EWG meetings, and then the Chair says, so let us break for 1 or 2 min, people change hats and then Klaus Regling [the CEO of the ESM] is taking over the meeting'.[39] Another interviewee explains that sometimes in the EWG, 'you have 5 additional minutes in the meeting and that's it'.[40] Occasionally, meeting agendas are even merged. This led an interviewee to wonder in a EWG session 'why the ESM Managing Director was sitting next to the EWG Chairman'.[41] While the EWG completely disappears from the ESM Treaty (in contrast to the EFSF Framework Agreement), the only reference made to the Eurogroup relates to the possible nomination of the Eurogroup President at the helm of the ESM's Board of Governors. In contrast to the Treaty's letter, the practice of ESM decision-making thus reveals the ESM's subordination both to the Eurogroup and to the EWG.

Moreover, compared to the EFSF, the ESM Treaty provided a relative extension of both the BoG and the BoD powers. As far as the Board of Governors is concerned, a notable novelty is a departure from a pure reliance on unanimity in the decision-making process. The intergovernmental nature of the EFSF and the fact that no fiscal liabilities could be engaged without the explicit agreement of some national parliaments (e.g. the German Bundestag and the Finish Parliament) had led to the 'sanctifica- tion' of unanimity. Convinced that the multiplicity of vetoes would how- ever be very likely to lead to a joint-decision trap, the Commission – among others – 'always pushed to lift the unanimity requirements'.[42] The final ESM agreement thus foresees a procedure of super majority that allows for a swifter decision-making in case of emergency. Besides, articles 10 and 19 of the ESM Treaty provide that: 'the Board of Governors is entitled to amend certain provisions of the ESM Treaty through a simplified proce- dure, thus obviating the need to submit the amended Treaty to a full process of ratification. This is notably the case for changes to the autho- rized capital stock and to the maximum lending volume as well as the review of the type of instruments of assistance available to the ESM' (De Gregorio 2012: 1623).

The Eurogroup has thus acquired greater discretion under the ESM as EMU finance ministers – formally on their own – dispose of the decision- making power to change the scope and firepower of the ESM. The Board of Directors (i.e. the EWG), for its part, has benefited from the ESM's financial tools' diversification and is now involved in a broader array of decision-making procedures. On top of the approval of financial assistance facility agreement and the disbursement of tranches, as foreseen already by the EFSF, the BoD is also entrusted with decision powers on the mainte- nance of a credit line of precautionary financial assistance (art. 14) and is in charge of adopting 'the detailed guidelines on the modalities for imple- menting' (art. 14–4) the latter. A similar role is foreseen for the BoD on the primary market support facility (art. 17) and the secondary market support facility (art. 18). In addition, the ESM Treaty also foresees that the BoD approves the ESM budget annually (art. 26).

Going forward, it can be argued that the informal lock-in of the Eurogroup over financial assistance is likely to be lasting. The ESM rules not only foresee a role for the two bodies in the disbursement of funds, in both its initial (BoG) and subsequent tranches (BoD), it also ensures a regular check of the BoG (i.e. the Eurogroup) on existing loans with a regular review of the adjustment programme conducted by the country under assistance to keep being able to benefit from the funding. Projections of the duration of the ESM outstanding loans (ESM 2018) go beyond the year 2050 and will only pass below the figure of € 100 bn in 2036.

In any case one can assume that the Eurogroup and the EWG will remain closely tied to the ESM. Yet, the ESM's institutional evolution is far from certain. An involved interviewee summarized the situation in those words: 'for the foreseeable future, they will administer the programme but once we get into the payment phase: question mark...'.[43] This statement is consistent with a broader institutional soul-searching that lies ahead of the ESM: it turns out to have 'ambitions which go beyond the back office'.[44] Expectedly, interviews conducted with ESM officials did not lead to the gathering of supporting evidence of those ambitions. However, they pointed at a high responsiveness of ESM staff to the wishes of their shareholders, EMU's Member States: 'if our shareholders ask us we do our best to service them'.[45] This brings up a bigger question on the future role of the ESM in the wider EMU architecture: 'everybody is conscious of the issue but nobody can give a definitive answer'.[46] What is clear is that the ESM will have to face a basic dilemma over the years to come: 'either you mothball 2/3 of the staff or you have a new range of activities'.[47]

THE CONVERSION OF THE EUROGROUP AND OF THE EWG

The Eurogroup is an informal body that gathers Finance Ministers of the euro area in a monthly meeting held over dinner. As Chap. 2 uncovered however, its members have extended the body's scope and functions since its creation in 1997. This task expansion process occurred in a sequence of three steps: the Eurogroup experienced an incremental institutionalization through layering (via the acquisition of a prominent role of peer reviewing in fiscal surveillance and an increased involvement in economic policy coordination – see also Puetter 2014) and then consolidated its power during the early euro crisis management. However, the creation of the new financial mechanisms in 2010–2011 marked a decisive and disruptive phase in the institutional conversion of the Eurogroup.

The Eurogroup has exploited what Streeck and Thelen (2005: 31) have characterised as 'gaps between rules and enactment'. Notoriously, the Eurogroup's original mandate is broad and ambiguous, a fact that allowed the institution to redeploy itself further to 'changing contextual conditions' (Streeck and Thelen 2005: 31). As a result, ever since its creation in December 1997, the Eurogroup has incrementally layered new tasks. Its first conquest has been to establish itself as the 'political centre of fiscal policy coordination under the Stability and Growth Pact (SGP)' (Puetter

2014: 158), for which the Eurogroup has crafted 'an underlying working consensus' (Puetter 2014: 158). Yet, the body has also repeatedly resisted the formalization of its decision-making (Puetter 2014: 158). The Eurogroup's subordinate and preparatory group, the EWG followed in its footsteps.

The Eurogroup's task expansion ran in parallel to an institutional building that saw a constant reform of its working methods (Puetter 2014: 155). For example, a look at the Eurogroup Work Programme for the first half of 2016[48] reveals the ample scope of policy issues (from the European Semester and the enforcement of the SGP to the review of the financial assistance programmes in various countries onto the Banking Union) which the body deems to be falling under its contemporary remit (Eurogroup 2015). The larger umbrella term under which euro area finance ministers consider their function, i.e. 'co-ordinating policy responses at the Eurogroup level' (Eurogroup 2015: 1) is in line with this broad scope. This self-interpretation of their mission runs in sharp contrast to the institutional characterisation of the Eurogroup provided for by the Lisbon Treaty's Protocol 14. The latter refers to an 'enhanced dialogue between the Member States whose currency is the euro' (Lisbon Treaty, Protocol 14).

Following the precedent of the European Council, the institutionalization of the Eurogroup has been legally recognised, albeit ambiguously by the Lisbon Treaty's Annexed Protocol 14 whose article 1 states that 'Ministers of the Member States whose currency is the euro shall meet informally' [...] 'to discuss questions related to the specific responsibilities they share with regard to the single currency' and specifies that 'such meetings shall take place, when necessary' (Lisbon Treaty 2009). The October 2011 Euro Summit statement was the latest milestone in the Eurogroup's institution-building. It included two provisions of key relevance for its future development. It mentioned that the Euro Working Group[49] would have its chairman appointed full-time and become Brussels-based, a reflection of the growing power of this body which has been particularly active during the critical moments of the crisis and which morphed into a secretariat function (Kasel 2012).

This institutional change continued well into the euro crisis period which from its very beginning, provided the ground for these informal institutions to occupy centre stage in euro crisis management. As recalled by Tuori (2012: 47), the 'Euro Group, as well as the President and the Working Group of the Eurogroup have gained in importance' with the euro crisis. By the same token, they also moved out of the shadow of the official structures of which they are originally a mere informal spin-off: the Treaty-based ECOFIN Council (for the Eurogroup) and the EFC for the EWG. Despite being informal, they progressively acquired decision-making powers. For example, Eurogroup decisions as encapsulated in statements 'provided the basis for the release of credit tranches by the European Financial Stability Facility (EFSF) and the European Stability Mechanism (ESM)' (Puetter 2014: 159). They did not take the form either of ECOFIN Council official acts, like for the GLF and the EFSM, nor of ESM Board of Governors decisions.

Yiangou et al. (2013: 233) explain that 'the effect of these changing incentives is already visible in the agenda and practice of the Eurogroup, where discussions on economic developments in vulnerable countries have become a regular feature'. As an EU official interviewed by Puetter (2014) recognised already in early March 2009: 'the Eurogroup worked very well in the crisis. Everything was discussed and reviewed by ministers: bailout, banking system; people pre-discussed domestic approaches' (Puetter 2014: 157). The crisis thus seems to have accelerated the body's transformation from an informal deliberative body to a genuine executive and decision-making EMU institution. In the words of Salines et al. (2012: 676): 'the set-up of the ESM has put in motion a process of redirection of existing EU institutions'. The post-euro crisis Eurogroup is therefore equipped with all the functional attributes of a proper and formal institution. At the organizational level, it disposes of a permanent president, of a secretariat[50] and of an implementing arm, the EWG. It meets on a monthly basis but its webpage recognises that 'if necessary, additional meetings or teleconferences can also be held' (Eurogroup 2015).

Administratively speaking, it sets a yearly work programme, organizes its discussions using an official agenda, and summarizes the latter discussions in confidential minutes directly sent to Finance Ministries by the Eurogroup's secretariat. From a communication perspective, the Eurogroup increasingly publishes statements and press releases while its President participates, at times, in Eurogroup official press conferences. Lastly, it disposes of an official and quite well furnished webpage and of its own logo (which features a € symbol instead of the starting E). If abstraction is made from its legal status, the Eurogroup thus qualifies as an official institution.

Despite these clear features of institutionalization, sceptics might argue that the institutional change experienced by the Eurogroup and the EWG is nothing but old wine in new bottles as the history of several Council working groups which have become institutionalized over the years (e.g. the Antici group, the Mertens group) reveal. Another related instance of working group reliant process is Comitology which throve because of Member States' unwillingness to 'loosen their intergovernmental grip on the implementation process in favour of supranational institutions' (Joerges and Neyer 1997: 276), a driver that is comparable to the instance under study. Joerges and Neyer's reasoning (1997: 279) that 'in the gap between the EC structure and its tasks, comitology has provided a forum for the development of novel and mediating forms of interest formation and decision-making', leading to some form of 'deliberative supranationalism' (Joerges and Neyer 1997: 273) seems to capture the nature of the EMU institution-building.

Under this light, the Eurogroup plausibly appears to have been an 'institutional response to the deep-seated tensions between the dual supranational and intergovernmentalist structure of the Community on the one hand, and its problem solving tasks on the other' (Joerges and Neyer 1997: 273). The key differences with Comitology are however twofold: whereas Comitology has been traditionally applied to rule-making, i.e. a policy-making activity of a legislative or administrative nature, the Eurogroup and the EWG operate in the realm of executive politics. Secondly, while the Comitology process is chaired by the Commission, it is the opposite in the case of the Eurogroup/EWG, as they are chaired by a Member State representative.

Since its creation in 1997 as a spin-off of the EFC, the EWG acts as the preparatory body of the Eurogroup. It gathers once a month the most senior public officials of finance ministries whose countries participate in the euro – usually Treasury directors – to prepare the discussions of the Eurogroup. The EWG typically meets a week before the Eurogroup is set to take place. With time, the EWG gradually evolved and slowly went out of the shadow of the EFC to constitute an institution on its own. The frequency of meetings of the EWG has evolved over the years, as the below Fig. 4.1 elaborated by the ECB indicates. In 2008, i.e. before the euro crisis hit the continent, it reached an average of around 10 meetings a year. In spite of this, the EWG retained its informal status, like the Eurogroup.

The *new intergovernmentalism* literature has spotted an evolving role for European expert groups in policy coordination. Puetter (2014) notes a 'proliferation of new senior expert committees, which are primarily or solely charged with supporting policy coordination within the Council of

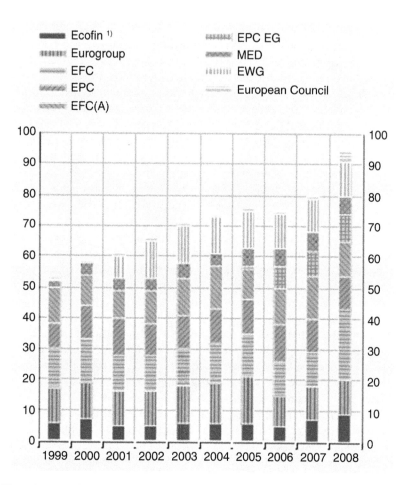

Fig. 4.1 Evolution of meetings attended by ECB staff over the period 1999–2008. (Source: ECB 2011)

Ministers rather than legislative decision making' (Puetter 2014: 172). The Euro Working Group fits within this trend as it emerged as an expert, high-level support group. However, its centrality in crisis management and its conversion, with the creation of the ESM, to an almost stand-alone body, makes it distinctive. As far as its internal dynamics are concerned, the EWG is close to what has been characterised in the literature as an 'epistemic community' (Haas 1992; Verdun 2002). It is an expert forum in which participants share values, world views and feel themselves both intellectually and personally close to each other. The forum is homogenous in that its members usually have a similar academic/intellectual background being all economic and financial experts with sound experience in international economic policy-making. Compared to the COREPER, 'people come directly from national Treasuries, they are not diplomats'.[51] Interviews conducted confirm these characteristics, as EWG members were found to display a 'shared knowledge, a shared understanding' of the issues[52] and to be forming a closed circle: 'these people know each other'.[53]

Another dimension of the EWG is the fact that it usually regroups the highest-ranked officers of EMU finance ministries, and thus dispose both of a proximity to finance ministers but also of strong domestic bureaucratic resources. This twin strategic and operational characteristics has turned Treasury directors into trusted and valued advisors of finance ministers during the euro crisis: they are 'close to ministers and have the expertise'.[54] As a result of this convenient position, 'they know where the compromise can be found'[55] and they also have the domestic institutional capacity to prepare decisions, through human competences and data. The EWG's approach to policy-making is thus made up of both expertise and political realism: 'they should design the technically efficient solutions given political constraints'.[56] In other words, 'you accommodate for the red lines, the EWG spent hours on that during the crisis'.[57] It would thus be wrong to understand the EWG as a purely technical structure because its political dimension is highly salient too. This led an interviewee to explain that 'the EWG is a semi-political institution', in the EU landscape 'it is considered as political'.[58]

This alchemy of skills made EWG members indispensable to the euro crisis management: 'these guys were the best placed to deal with it'.[59] While an expert support group would stick to making recommendations, the euro crisis management required the EWG experts to move more centre stage. Actors involved on a daily basis in the Brussels policy-making confirm the centrality of the EWG in crisis management: 'of course the EWG has been decisive'[60]; 'the EWG has been central to euro crisis management',[61] the 'EWG is an absolutely central actor'.[62] It acted 'like the board of directors of the euro area' (Kasel 2012) and had to deal with the most pressing issues under tight time constraints: 'the hot potatoes landed on their desk because they are an effective set up'[63] and 'they do excellent work'.[64] Overall, as the euro crisis transformed the Eurogroup, it also transformed the EWG into a more operational set-up. Asked to confirm this change, an interviewee replied: 'of course, because it became operational'.[65] The interviewee then added that: 'looking back before the crisis, the EWG had very abstract discussions, there was nothing operational'. It was closer to an OECD Working Group. Instead, the post 2008 context 'produced a totally different working culture and working method, with different levels of engagement'. One could thus argue that it has evolved from a discussion group into a working college.

Willingly or unwillingly, EWG members participated in this change of role. Acting as good soldiers to their finance ministers, they showed their readiness to play their part in crisis management and proved available also on short notice: 'these people are the people who can mobilize through *conf'calls*'.[66] Another interviewee remembers for example that sometimes the EWG 'had 3 or 4 conference calls per week lasting each 3 or 4 hours'.[67] Yet, a remarkable characteristic of the EWG is that despite its self-empowerment, its members seem to realize that there is an institutional red line which the EWG cannot cross: 'they are clever enough to keep it for themselves'.[68] It is there that its subordination to the authority of the Eurogroup is the most visible: 'in the end, the people have to answer to their politicians'.[69] In that light, 'its role is key in consensus-building'.[70] Because of the opacity of their deliberations and decision-making, the delineation of the powers held by the Eurogroup and the EWG remains however blurry. One therefore finds some interviewees who insist on the EWG's autonomy ('the EWG is running the show while the Eurogroup is the one which is signing off'[71]) from the Eurogroup while other stress their subordination ('it is correct that the EWG is quite central in this process but it would be wrong to say that the Eurogroup only rubber-stamps, that's not how things happen'[72]). What is clear however, is that the EWG seemed to be more influential on the crisis management decision-making than on rule-making: 'it is a very strong crisis management group but less so on economic governance'.[73]

This balance between staying central while retaining a low political profile is however not always easy to maintain. Asked about the evolving role of the EWG and its increased political dimension, an interviewee explained to have been 'surprised to read about the EWG in the press'.[74] Referring to the EWG's traditionally informal and low-profile nature, the same interviewee added: 'you know when the EWG meets and this is new'.[75] A new feature of the EWG is the fact that as of January 2012, following the October 2011 euro area summit statement, the EWG disposes of a permanent, full-time and Brussels-based President, who is also chairing the

Economic and Financial Committee. According to interviews conducted, this institutional novelty played a noteworthy role in helping the process of crisis management: 'it helps that you have a full time person'; 'it's a good solution'; 'it makes sense to have a Brussels person'.[76] Another interviewee went further and declared that the full-time presidency of the EWG 'was a game changer'.[77] For instance, 'it just happened that it was the EWG drawing up the ESM treaty'.[78] Because of this supranational attribute and the fact that socialization forces are at play within the WG, it would thus be restrictive to narrow down the EWG to an institution that is only intergovernmental. From its pure membership constitution, the EWG grants the Commission and the ECB an observer status for example. And on substance 'the role of the Commission (and of the ECB) in the EWG is quite large'.[79] Talking about the Eurogroup, an interviewee thus characterised it as a form of 'semi-intergovernmental method for the euro area'.[80]

Conclusion

This chapter isolated a crucial difference in institutional empowerment between the newly created financial assistance instruments: the GLF and the EFSM on the one hand and the EFSF and the ESM on the other. While the Eurogroup has been the principal of all instruments from the very beginning of the financial mechanisms' creation, its implementing agents have been changing as the EWG gradually took over tasks from the Commission which in turn was dwarfed into a secretariat role.

The chapter has also claimed that the ESM, despite its lack of formal subordination to any existing institutions, is an informal Eurogroup instrument. The ESM's creation, in a feedback loop has thus resulted in the conversion of Eurogroup into the executive arm of the Economic and Monetary Union. The establishment of the ESM marked indeed the latest step of the institutionalization of the Eurogroup and of its subgroup, the EWG. The empowerment of these informal bodies should be situated in the broader context of the euro crisis during which 'new official, semi-official and unofficial bodies have abounded; some of them with formal decision-making powers, others without any formal competence but still exercising considerable influence' (Tuori 2012: 46). The pattern of centralization of financial assistance capacity building during the crisis displayed a crucial feature: compared to the Maastricht Treaty's intrinsic link between the centralization of the monetary policy instrument and the delegation of that instrument given to a single institution (the ECB), the euro crisis saw no similar one-to-one correspondence between the creation of the instruments and their formal subordination to an institution. Instead, this progressive informal process saw a clear shift, as the magnitude of the fiscal capacity of the new instruments increased, from an empowerment of the Commission to an empowerment of the Eurogroup and the EWG. In summary, both an existing executive actor (the Commission) and existing informal and non-executive actors (the Eurogroup and the EWG) were flanked with the operation of new financial assistance instruments, which in turn led to a fundamental fragmentation of this power at EU level.

The institutionalization of both the Eurogroup and the EWG with the ESM occurred because of a solid path-dependence that was present in the system. As explained by Verdun (2015: 231), 'institutions were built on previous institutions or were inspired by structures that had been created before'. This fact led, in a feedback loop, to an institutional redirection of the Eurogroup and the EWG which have experienced a disruptive change in their functions.

The establishment of the ESM along with its conversion effect it had on both the Eurogroup and the EWG, are opening the way for lasting institutional implications and are likely to bring the EU and EMU to evolve in two separate directions. Indeed, the main reason why the Eurogroup has resisted formalization for so long is that EU leaders were reluctant to unleash differentiation dynamics between EU and EMU. It was retained that a single polity had to be maintained to safeguard the unity of the European project. However, the adoption of the Lisbon Treaty proved to be a genuine watershed in this regard as it 'signifies retreat from the principle of European unity' (Tuori 2012: 8), both because of the newly created article 136 which provides an autonomous legal basis for the adoption of secondary legislative acts only applicable to EMU countries and because of the formalization of the Eurogroup. As Tuori explained (2012: 8): 'the Lisbon Chapter on the euro area reflects resignation in front of a lingering bifurcation of the Union into the euro area and non-euro area Member States'. The implications of this analysis confirm and extend the differentiation argument as it can be argued that the creation of the ESM and the conversion of the Eurogroup-EWG into the executive arm of EMU have durably put a wedge between the EU and the EMU institution-building. The future of the ESM is therefore intrinsically linked to the evolution of EMU as an institutional order.

What remains a cause for concern is that the new financial assistance functions are subject to inefficiency and suboptimal institutional parallelism between the Eurogroup and the ESM on the one hand and the Commission on the other. This entails an inherent instability. This fact has been implicitly recognised by the '5 Presidents Report on the future of EMU' which called for the ESM Treaty's absorption into EU law and overall envisages institutional consolidation. Proposals have been made by expert observers along those lines, for instance, by turning the ESM into a European Monetary Fund (Gros and Mayer 2010). In a similar functional spirit, others have argued that the ESM or more generally the financial assistance mechanisms would be the backbone of a European Treasury (De Gregorio 2012: 1645) or of a European Finance minister (Enderlein and Haas 2015). The informal institutional fusion that the ESM and Eurogroup embody, makes it indeed more likely to situate the future European treasury within the Eurogroup's institutional landscape, as opposed to making it rest within the Commission. Chapters 7 and 8 elaborate further on the above aspects.

NOTES

1. Interviewee 50 – European Stability Mechanism official.
2. Interviewee 4 – European Commission official.
3. Financial provision to non-euro area members was already a fact of life in the EU since 2002 through the Balance of Payments Facility (BoP).
4. Interviewee 38 – European Central Bank official.
5. Interviewee 4 – European Commission official.
6. Interviewee 38 – European Central Bank official.
7. Interviewee 38 – European Central Bank official.
8. *The Guardian*, 11 April 2010.
9. Interviewee 12 – European Commission official.
10. Ibid.
11. http://ec.europa.eu/economy_finance/eu_borrower/efsm/index_en.htm
12. Interviewee 27 – Finnish Ministry of Finance official.
13. Interviewee 12 – European Commission official.
14. Interviewee 4 – European Commission official.
15. Interviewee 9 – EU Council official.
16. Interviewee 49 – European Stability Mechanism official.
17. *Financial Times*, 9 February 2012, 'Germany and Europe: A very federal formula'.

18. EWG Chairman.
19. German Interior Minister, representing German Finance Minister Wolfgang Schäuble who was ill upon arrival in Brussels and unable to negotiate for Germany.
20. Interviewee 1 – EU Council official.
21. Interviewee 4 – European Commission official.
22. Yet it retained a key administrative role in terms of preparing the Memorandum of Understanding and monitoring the compliance of 'conditionality'.
23. *Financial Times*, 12 May 2010, 'Paris seen as trumping Berlin at the EU table'.
24. Ibid.
25. Interviewee 27 – Finnish Ministry of Finance official.
26. Interviewee 1 – EU Council official.
27. The EFC president and the EWG president are the same persons.
28. *Questions & Answers section of the EFSF website*, consulted on 31 January 2016.
29. *Financial Times*, 27 September 2010, 'Eurozone Needs a permanent bail-out fund', by Peter Bofinger, Henrik Enderlein, Tommaso Padoa-Schioppa and André Sapir.
30. Interviewee 34 – European Central Bank official.
31. Interviewee 34 – European Central Bank official.
32. Interviewee 34 – European Central Bank official.
33. Interviewee 27 – Finnish Ministry of Finance official.
34. Interviewee 50 – European Stability Mechanism official.
35. Interviewee 4 – European Commission official.
36. Interviewee 27 – Finnish Ministry of Finance official.
37. Interviewee 43 – European Central Bank official.
38. Interviewee 43 – European Central Bank official.
39. Interviewee 32 – European Central Bank official.
40. Interviewee 40 – EU Council official.
41. Interviewee 1 – EU Council official.
42. Interviewee 12 – European Commission official.
43. Interviewee 40 – EU Council official.
44. Interviewee 43 – European Central Bank official.
45. Interviewee 50 – European Stability Mechanism official.
46. Interviewee 40 – EU Council official.
47. Interviewee 40 – EU Council official.
48. https://www.consilium.europa.eu/media/21468/eurogroup-wp-ii-2016.pdf
49. Also called at times 'Eurogroup Working Group'.

50. In truth the Eurogroup disposes of two secretariats, one located in the Council's Secretariat General and another one located in the Commission's DG ECFIN.
51. Interviewee 43 – European Central Bank official.
52. Interviewee 18 – Italian Ministry of Finance official.
53. Interviewee 18 – Italian Ministry of Finance official.
54. Interviewee 10 – EU Council official.
55. Interviewee 18 – Italian Ministry of Finance official.
56. Interviewee 18 – Italian Ministry of Finance official.
57. Interviewee 22 – Italian Ministry of Finance official.
58. Interviewee 27 – Finnish Ministry of Finance official.
59. Interviewee 10 – EU Council official.
60. Interviewee 20 – Independent analyst.
61. Interviewee 1 – EU Council official.
62. Interviewee 13 – European Parliament official.
63. Interviewee 10 – EU Council official.
64. Interviewee 10 – EU Council official.
65. Interviewee 40 – EU Council official.
66. Interviewee 18 – Italian Ministry of Finance official.
67. Interviewee 22 – Italian Ministry of Finance official.
68. Interviewee 22 – Italian Ministry of Finance official.
69. Interviewee 18 – Italian Ministry of Finance official.
70. Interviewee 22 – Italian Ministry of Finance official.
71. Interviewee 32 – European Central Bank official.
72. Interviewee 30 – Finnish Ministry of Finance official.
73. Interviewee 32 – European Central Bank official.
74. Interviewee 22 – Italian Ministry of Finance official.
75. Interviewee 22 – Italian Ministry of Finance official.
76. Interviewee 18 – Italian Ministry of Finance official.
77. Interviewee 50 – European Stability Mechanism official.
78. Interviewee 10 – EU Council official.
79. Interviewee 22 – Italian Ministry of Finance official.
80. Interviewee 12 – European Commission official.

References

Beukers, T., & De Witte, B. (2013). The Court of Justice Approves the Creation of the European Stability Mechanism Outside the EU Legal Order: Pringle. *Common Market Law Review, 50*(3), 805–848.

Bickerton, C. J., Hodson, D., & Puetter, U. (2015). *The New Intergovernmentalism: States, Supranational Actors, and European Politics in the Post-Maastricht Era.* Oxford: Oxford University Press.

Buti, M., & Carnot, N. (2012). The EMU Debt Crisis: Early Lessons and Reforms. *Journal of Common Market Studies, 50*(6), 899–911.

De Gregorio, A. M. (2012). Legal Developments in the Economic and Monetary Union During the Debt Crisis: The Mechanisms of Financial Assistance. *Common Market Law Review, 49*(5), 1613–1645.

Dutch Court of Auditors. (2016). Dedicated webpage of the Dutch Court of Auditor on Financial Assistance Mechanisms. http://www.rekenkamer.nl/english/Publications/Topics/EU_governance_to_combat_the_economic_and_financial_crisis/Financial_stability_instruments/Financial_instruments/Greek_loan_facility. Visited on 31 Jan 2016.

Enderlein, H., & Haas, J. (2015, October). *What Would a European Finance Minister Do? A Proposal* (Policy Paper N°145). Jacques Delors Institut Berlin.

ESM. (2018, March). European Financial Stability Facility and European Stability Mechanism. *Investor Presentation.*

ESM Treaty. (2012). *Treaty Establishing the European Stability Mechanism.*

EU Council. (2010, May 9/10). Extraordinary Council Meeting, Economic and Financial Affairs. *Press Release.* Brussels.

Euro Area Statement. (2010, May 7). *Statement by the Heads of State and Government of the Euro Area.* Brussels.

Eurogroup. (2015, December 7). *Work Programme for the Eurogroup for the First Half of 2016.*

European Central Bank. (2011, September). *Beyond the Economics of the Euro: Analysing the Institutional Evolution of EMU 1999–2010* (ECB Occasional Paper Series No. 127).

European Commission. (2010, May 9). *Proposal for a Council Regulation Establishing a European Financial Stabilization Mechanism.*

Eurostat. (2011, January 27). New Decision of Eurostat on Deficit and Debt: The Statistical Recording of Operations Undertaken by the European Financial Stability Facility. *Eurostat News Release.*

Gocaj, L., & Meunier, S. (2013). Time Will Tell: The EFSF, the ESM and the Euro Crisis. *Journal of European Integration, 35*(3), 239–253.

Gros, D., & Mayer, T. (2010, February). *How to Deal with Sovereign Default in Europe: Create the European Monetary Fund Now!* (CEPS Policy Brief No. 202).

Haas, P. M. (1992). Introduction: Epistemic Communities and International Policy Coordination. *International Organization, 46*(1), 1–35.

Hodson, D. (2013). The Little Engine that Wouldn't: Supranational Entrepreneurship and the Barroso Commission. *Journal of European Integration, 35*(3), 301–314.

Jansen, R. (2011). The European Financial Stability Facility and the European Stability Mechanism: A Legal Overview. *European Banking and Financial Law Journal EUREDIA, 4,* 417–423.

Joerges, C., & Neyer, J. (1997). From Intergovernmental Bargaining to Deliberative Political Processes: The Constitutionalisation of Comitology. *European Law Journal, 3*(3), 273–299.

Kasel, A. (2012). La présidence de l'Eurogroupe et la gouvernance économique de la zone euro. In V. Charlety (Ed.), *Le Système présidentiel de l'Union Européenne après Lisbonne*. Paris: ENA.

Lisbon Treaty. (2009). *Treaty on the Functioning of the European Union (Consolidated Version)*.

Louis, J. V. (2011). Guest Editorial: The No Bail-Out Clause and Rescue Packages. *Common Market Law Review, 47*(4), 971–986.

Micossi, S., Carmassi, J., & Peirce, F. (2011, March 8). *On the Tasks of the European Stability Mechanism* (CEPS Policy Brief No 235). Brussels.

Olivares-Caminal, R. (2011). The European Stability Mechanism: Some Notes on a New EU Institution Designed to Avert Financial Crises. In J. La Brosse, R. Olivares-Caminal, & D. Singh (Eds.), *Financial Crisis Containment and Government Guarantees*. Edward Edgar: Cheltenham/Northampton.

Puetter, U. (2014). *The European Council and the Council: New Intergovernmentalism and Institutional Change*. Oxford: Oxford University Press.

Salines, M., Glöckler, G., & Truchlewski, Z. (2012). Existential Crisis, Incremental Response: The Eurozone's Dual Institutional Evolution 2007–2011. *Journal of European Public Policy, 19*(5), 665–681.

Streeck, W., & Thelen, k. (Eds.). (2005). *Beyond Continuity: Institutional Change in Advanced Political Economies*. Oxford: Oxford University Press.

Tuori, K. (2012). *The European Financial Crisis – Constitutional Aspects and Implications* (EUI Working Papers). Department of Law, 2012/28.

Van Rompuy, H. (2012, May 4). *Speech by Hermann Van Rompuy, President of the European Council at the Stockholm School of Economics*. Stockholm.

Verdun, A. (Ed.). (2002). *The Euro: European Integration Theory and Economic and Monetary Union*. Lanham: Rowman and Littlefield Publishers.

Verdun, A. (2015). A Historical Institutionalist Explanation of the EU's Responses to the Euro Area Financial Crisis. *Journal of European Public Policy, 22*(2), 219–237.

Yiangou, J., O'keeffe, M., & Glöckler, G. (2013). 'Tough Love': How the ECB's Monetary Financing Prohibition Pushes Deeper Euro Area Integration. *Journal of European Integration, 35*(3), 223–237.

CHAPTER 5

Developing an EMU Lending of Last Resort Capacity

INTRODUCTION

The European Central Bank (ECB) has been the decisive manager of the euro crisis. Its strategic yet conditioned interventions have been essential in avoiding a currency break-up and in safeguarding the financial stability of the euro area. The crisis pushed the ECB to go beyond its strict, inflation-combating monetary policy mandate as originally defined by the Maastricht Treaty and become a *de facto* lender of last resort (Winkler 2016), a role that entails a fiscal dimension. Compared to other instances of fiscal centralization during the crisis, the case of the ECB is particularly illuminating because this capacity-building process occurred through an informal and covert self-empowerment of the Bank. Acting outside of its traditional comfort zone, the ECB had however to preserve its monetary dominance over both fiscal and financial actors. For that, the ECB set what I term 're-insurance conditions' from sovereigns. Its strategic interventions were indeed always preceded by the elaboration of a stricter controlling framework which acted as anchoring conditions for its engagements. Overall, its actions can be considered as intrusions in the political realm. As an interviewee explained: 'the ECB bailed out political circles'.[1] For this precise reason, the ECB behaved strategically (Torres 2013), and always selected critical junctures of the euro crisis to intervene, sometimes much later than what would have been in Europe's general interest.

© The Author(s) 2019
P. Schlosser, *Europe's New Fiscal Union*,
https://doi.org/10.1007/978-3-319-98636-4_5

With hindsight, it was far from obvious that the ECB would take over the role of lender of last resort less than 15 years after its creation; particularly so as 'it is quite clear that the Maastricht Treaty was not made to have the ECB as lender of last resort'.[2] The original Treaty that established EMU had indeed primarily tasked the ECB with the independent conduct of monetary policy. It had narrowly assigned the Bank with the core and priority mandate of maintaining price stability over the medium term and had set prohibitions on bail-out and monetary financing in this regard. In truth, the Bank's original mandate was perceived as so limited that it has been even characterised as the embodiment of a simple monetary rule (Folkerts-Landau and Garber 1992), 'the rule in question being that the money supply should be regulated so as to ensure low and stable inflation' (Eichengreen 2012: 130). The prohibitions provided by Maastricht derived from a strong concern to ensure the separation of monetary and fiscal policies in EMU and thereby eliminate inflation biases. Treaty designers overlooked however the implicit fiscal liabilities that could stem from weak systemic banks. Should a 'too big to fail' bank from a large EMU country become illiquid and risk being insolvent and its host country be unable to support it, the ECB would then have to step in to provide liquidity to the bank. The recognition of this dangerous and underestimated loop which would lead to 'financial dominance', was one of the reasons why the ECB felt obliged to go beyond its natural comfort zone and reluctantly embraced an unprecedented integrationist approach (as I will underline in further detail below), compared to its past lukewarm posture (Hodson 2011).

The ECB's quasi-fiscal intervention took the form of a series of measures. It first acted through a maturity increase of its Long-Term-Refinancing Obligations (LTRO). As pressure gathered pace, it then performed sovereign bond purchases, first in limited form as part of the Securities Market Programme (SMP) and then with the potentially unlimited Outright Monetary Transaction (OMT) instrument, thereby exposing its balance sheet to higher credit risks. The central OMT instrument followed the declaration by Mario Draghi on 26 July 2012 to do 'whatever it takes to preserve the euro' (Draghi 2012). Yet it remains, so far, an untested instrument. Crucially, the ECB also ensured, for example through its promotion of the Fiscal Compact that its interventions would not usher in governments "sitting back", as this would have weakened its monetary dominance. Another condition to exert the function of last resort was to avoid financial dominance by having a more 'intimate knowledge of the

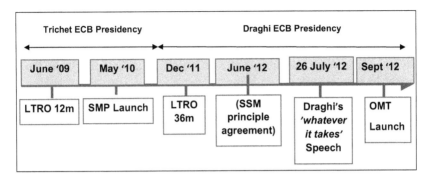

Fig. 5.1 Timeline of the ECB's strategic interventions (2009–2012)

exact situation of the banks for which it is supposed to act as a lender of last resort' (Ioannidou 2015: 11), hence the ECB's advocacy (De Rynck 2016) to establish the Single Supervision Mechanism (SSM), as an agency of the ECB. As an illustration of the wealth of instruments deployed or supported by the ECB to safeguard the integrity of the euro, Fig. 5.1 below captures the diversity of the ECB strategic interventions over the period 2009–2012.

Against this background, the purpose of this chapter is to document the key crisis management actions performed by the ECB, to characterise the logic of the ECB's intervention and to determine the nature and extent of the ECB's informal self-empowerment to a temporary role of lender of last resort.

The ECB's Fiscal Deamons Awaken

While it is widely common in advanced economies to have a clear separation between monetary and fiscal policies, this distinction is in reality only valid in 'good times'. In 'hard times', when central banks are burdened with enhanced responsibility to credibly restore confidence in the financial system, some of the tasks performed by the monetary authority enter into a grey area, 'blurring the boundary with fiscal policy' (BIS 2014: 1). The lending of last resort function, 'perhaps the most controversial role in a central bank' (BIS 2014), is a perfect illustration of such type of ambiguity. For this reason, the economic literature on the subject generally finds that lending of last resort entails a fiscal dimension (see e.g. Illing and König 2014: 24). While virtually all monetary policy decisions have fiscal implications (De Grauwe 2013), one can reasonably argue that lending of last resort operations, with the enhanced credit risks that they involve, can potentially have a significant fiscal impact on tax-payers money as the sovereign will have to recapitalize the central bank in case the latter faces severe losses.

Because of its proximity to fiscal policy, lending of last resort thus almost always involves a dialogue or a coordination between the central bank, the Treasury and, at times, also private banking actors to determine the adequate fiscal burden-sharing. In a study 'based on sample survey of 104 bank crises cases in 24 industrialized countries in 1993, Goodhart and Schoenmaker (1995) found for instance that out of 27 rescue programmes in which central banks were engaged, they were the sole contributor in just two cases' (Hu 2015: 629) while the Treasury was involved on its own in 18 cases and together with others in 28 cases (Goodhart and Schoenmaker 1995: 552). In crisis times, central bankers are thus torn between their expected function to 'provide emergency liquidity assistance to financial institutions' (BIS 2014: 1) on the one hand, and on the other, legitimate considerations that 'LOLR is seen as very risky, potentially creating moral hazard on a massive scale, exposing the central bank to large financial risks' (BIS 2014: 1). As monetary and fiscal policies come closer to another, it is logical that central bankers become increasingly concerned about the implications of their action both for their independence and for the enhanced responsibility that it implies.

Two solutions to this traditional power conflict between monetary and fiscal policy have been identified by the literature while a third one, which recognises the impact of the growing power of the banking system on central bank independence, is now emerging. The first, coined, *monetary dominance,* is a situation 'in which fiscal policy is passive and monetary policy is active' (Walsh 2010: 143). The preservation of monetary dominance can be ensured through the granting of independence to the central bank, thereby shielding monetary policy from fiscal pressures and by the same token solving the time inconsistency issue (Kydland and Prescott 1977; Sargent and Wallace 1981). The constitutional independence of a central bank considerably reduces the risk of debt monetization pressure and thus institutionalizes monetary dominance (Sargent and Wallace 1981). This model rests on a full de-politicization of the central bank. It has been the approach underpinning the German Bundesbank. Since the Bundesbank model strongly influenced the Maastricht negotiations, the principles of monetary dominance are also enshrined in the Maastricht

Treaty (art. 103, 105 and 130 TFEU) and underpin the regime of the ECB.[3]

The second regime, coined *fiscal dominance*, is a situation in which 'the monetary authority... must try to finance with seigniorage any discrepancy between the revenue demanded by the fiscal authority and the amounts of bonds that can be sold to the public' (Sargent and Wallace 1981: 2). Fiscal dominance is a regime under which fiscal actors directly or indirectly exert pressure on the central bank to use the printing press to ensure the sustainability of debt levels. It arguably made its come-back with the euro crisis. As documented by Blommestein and Turner (2012: 220): 'general government debt increased from 69.8% of debt/GDP ratio in 2000 to 73.1% in 2007 and to an estimated 97.6% at the end of 2020. It is fairly certain that government debt/GDP ratios in major countries will continue to rise, setting the stage for a new period of fiscal dominance[4]'. The third regime, called *financial dominance*, is a more recent recognition. It has been defined as a situation in which 'macro-prudential policy is too lax and the financial sector does not absorb losses to a sufficient degree, monetary policy may be forced to become too accommodative so as to reduce private sector debt and shore up bank balance sheets' (Lewis and Roth 2015: 2). It has been understood only recently that financial dominance could also weigh on the independence of central banks.

The hindrance of fiscal dominance has been institutionally ensured by granting independence to modern-day central banks. Absent a track record, the young ECB clang to its independence to establish its credibility. In reality, the nature of the ECB's independence is such that the Frankfurt institution has even openly contested to be an EU institution in the first place. As reminded by Hodson (2011: 26), the ECB argued in the OLAF European Court of Justice case that 'it could not be counted as an institution, body, office, or agency of the Community' as the Bank was first and foremost defined by its independence from governments and its price stability mandate. A similar, ideological argument was then voiced by the ECB in the case of the Convention on the Future of Europe whose draft was 'listing the ECB as an EU institution' (Hodson 2011: 27). This extreme independence conception runs however counter to historic evidence on the importance, for central banks, to be 'embedded' in a polity. As McNamara (2013) outlines 'no currency union has ever succeeded without being embedded within a broader political union with a robustly centralised fiscal system'. At a more conceptual level, one could hypothesize that the ECB's self-conception as an independent body within EMU was inherited from the economic literature's insistence on monetary dominance. The latter was understood to be reinforced in a situation in which discretionary coordination with fiscal authorities was absent and fiscal liabilities of the central bank would be excluded *ex ante* through constitutional rules.

Whereas the ECB features quite some variation from other Western central banks, it proved to be a distinctive body also among EU institutions. A salient singularity of the ECB was indeed its long-lasting reluctance to embrace *per se* the idea of an 'ever closer union'. In contrast to the Commission and to the Parliament which typically 'prefer more Europe which is to say that they are characterised by a common preference for greater competences for themselves and for the European Union as a whole' (Pollack 2003: 39; Hodson 2011: 22), the ECB is first and foremost conditioned by its high independence. In other words, 'the precision of the ECB's price stability mandate, as Heisenberg and Richmond (2002: 204) recognize, makes it harder for the ECB to justify a competence-maximizing strategy, particularly when steps towards further integration cannot be easily reconciled with the pursuit of price stability' (Hodson 2011: 23). In fact, the ECB 'enjoys a higher degree of statutory independence and attaches more weight to the pursuit of price stability than most other monetary authorities' (Hodson 2011: 21). Biased by its price stability concerns, the ECB 'has proven to be a reluctant EU institution that has, in many cases, resisted attempts to enhance the Community dimension of EMU' (Hodson 2011: 22). In sum, 'the Bank's preference for 'more Europe' has traditionally been contingent on its overriding commitment to price stability' (Hodson 2011: 22).

THE LACK OF AN EMU FISCAL ACTOR PUTS THE ECB AT CENTRE STAGE

Lending of last resort implies an increase in the central bank's risk exposure and a corresponding increase in the likelihood of the central bank's recapitalization by its sovereign. In normal jurisdictions, central banks are recapitalized by the Treasury in case they take on excessive risks. Anticipating such a burden-sharing *ex ante*, lending of last resort usually entails the capacity to broker a risk-sharing deal with the fiscal authority. This is why the lending of last resort function is highly controversial. It is the case in established national democracies, and is all the more so the case in EMU, a supranational and technocratic construct in which a central fiscal authority is missing.

In EMU, fiscal burden-sharing – or indeed re-insurance mechanisms – were missing pre-crisis. Some moral hazard-centric contributions have stressed that the absence of a large scale recapitalization mechanism would be the best guarantee to avoid that the ECB 'is forced into risky financial operations' (Belke 2009: 13) thereby assuming a role it shouldn't obtain (Belke 2009). Yet, the crisis showed that such absence did not prevent the Bank to act. What differed, is that in the absence of a central fiscal authority in the EU, the ECB had to set the red lines between monetary policy and fiscal policy on its own by designing strict, fiscal and banking supervisory frameworks as pre-condition for its interventions. The euro crisis that hit Europe has thus openly revealed the shortcomings in EMU's architecture (Eichengreen 2012; Giavazzi and Wyplosz 2015) and also showed the need to 'have a common political backing to these shared risks'.[5] Early supporters of a minimalist EMU reliant on market discipline thus proved with hindsight to be rather naïve.

Yet the ECB itself could be portrayed as having been plagued by a certain ingenuousness too. The dominant narrative that presents the ECB as a decisive player in extinguishing the crisis fire minimizes the fact that the ECB dragged its feet from May 2010 to June 2012. The ECB also did several mistakes when it decided to raise interest rates in July 2008 and time and again in early 2011 (Honohan 2017). Over several months the Frankfurt body resisted the design of a 'big bazooka' able to crush the self-fulfilling expectations over a euro break-up and alleviate the existential pressure on the sustainability of the currency. For a long time, the ECB hoped indeed that 'heads' would take action to restore financial stability. However, this never happened. Leading by default, the ECB had to set up the necessary risk-sharing mechanisms that heads of state and government were not prepared to openly agree on: 'the ECB did most of the job, always playing it carefully'.[6] Because 'heads' resisted formalisation pressures to overtly reform EMU's crisis management arsenal again at the height of the crisis, the ECB lost the 'chicken game'. It had to make up for the formally missing top-down functions and had to rely on covert integration dynamics for that. Given the inaction of euro area governments, the ECB inherited the implicit mandate of 'saving the euro' – a provision which obviously did not feature in the Maastricht Treaty. These changing circumstances, in turn, dramatically forced the ECB to reconsider its preference on European integration and also on its own role within the EU polity. While it is logical that the ECB would be ready to go down with the euro, ECB leaders ultimately did not shy away from their responsibilities. As an interviewee witnessed: 'what the ECB has done is courageous'.[7]

Giavazzi and Wyplosz (2015: 727) have recalled that 'the absence of a fiscal authority at Eurozone level is a well-recognized inherent characteristic of EMU'. 'The euro is unique in that it is a currency without a sovereign' (Bénassy-Quéré 2016: 63), or to follow the earlier words of Tommaso Padoa-Schioppa, it is 'a currency without a state' (Padoa-Schioppa 1999b). However, such absence was an intentional choice made in Maastricht: 'fiscal policy was deliberately left non-unionised so as to safeguard the independence of the ECB' (Schelkle 2012: 33). The unintended consequence of this was that when the euro crisis hit: 'there was no fiscal actor who could take responsibility' (Schelkle 2012: 33). The absence of an EU or EMU level fiscal authority implied indeed that 'the ECB has no fiscal back up. There is no guarantee, insurance or indemnity for any private credit risk it assumes' (Buiter 2009: 8). More concretely, there is 'no single fiscal authority, facility or arrangement which can re-capitalise the ECB/Eurosystem when [it] makes capital losses that threaten its capacity to implement its price stability and financial stability mandates' (Buiter 2009: 5) and means also that there is 'no single fiscal authority, facility or arrangement which can re-capitalise systematically important border-crossing financial institutions in the EU or the Euro Area, or provide them with other forms of financial support' (Buiter 2009: 5). In other words, when the ECB embarks on lending of last resort functions, it increases its own credit risk at its own peril and acts without mutualized safety nets.[8] This explains why for a long time, the ECB 'lacked the will to play the role of the LLR' (Hu 2015: 631). Such a behaviour came in sharp contrast to the reaction of other 'major central banks who expanded liquidity provision on an unprecedented scale and scope' (BIS 2014: 2).

EMU's initial architecture featured no lender of last resort mandate to the ECB. As a result, the ECB did 'not have the power to provide unlimited liquidity' (Hu 2015: 631). The Bank 'declared on many occasions that it will not provide unlimited liquidity because no measures could be at the cost of the objective of maintaining price stability' (Hu 2015: 631). Emergency Liquidity Assistance (ELA) which many see as the instrument that is closest to standard lending of last resort remains a decentralized responsibility: 'it is the competent national central bank that takes the decision concerning the provision of ELA to an institution operating in its jurisdiction. Such a decision is under the responsibility and at a cost of the national central bank in question (or by a third-party acting as a guarantor)' (Nieto 2015: 94). Absent strong liquidity provision instruments, 'there were growing calls for the establishment of the LLR facility in the Eurozone, and for the ECB to assume this role' (Hu 2015: 630).

Since its existence, the ECB has been guided by a deep concern for fiscal dominance. It is for this reason that the ECB is constitutionally independent from governments and that it is also prohibited from conducting monetary financing of government debt. The Maastricht Treaty thus rests on a strict separation of monetary and fiscal policy: 'the economic constitution of EMU is based on a historically 'unprecedented divorce between the main monetary and fiscal authorities'' (Schelkle 2012: 28; Goodhart 1998). This is illustrative of central bankers' success over the ultimate design of EMU (Mcnamara 1999) where 'monetary dominance' was asserted (Praet 2015). The ECB's preoccupation with fiscal dominance also took another form. The institution constantly argued against any constitution of a fiscal authority at the EU level even in the form of an enhanced coordination. In some areas 'where plans to strengthen economic governance are perceived as a threat to price stability, the ECB has made clear its opposition' (Hodson 2011: 29). 'A case in point is the Bank's consistent stance against giving the Eurogroup a greater say in euro area governance' (Hodson 2011: 29). On this, the ECB's behaviour revealed 'a concern for price stability [which was] never far from the surface' (Hodson 2011: 30). The ECB feared that 'coordination between finance ministers results in political pressure on the ECB to loosen monetary policy' (Hodson 2012: 9; Beetsma and Bovenberg 1995). Its dogmatic approach to the independent conduct of a price stability oriented monetary policy revealed that the ECB had an interest in prolonging the 'status quo of an asymmetric EMU' (Hodson 2012).

Moreover, obsessed with fiscal dominance, Treaty designers overlooked the effects that financial dominance would have had on the ECB's independence. Some early observers had identified this beforehand. Giavazzi and Wyplosz (2015: 724) restated their initial claim (Begg et al. 1991) that in its original form, 'EMU might not be able to deal effectively with the insolvency of a large financial institution – either closing it down or using tax-payers' money to re-capitalize it – so that such a default might reverberate throughout the Euro area'. And this is exactly what occurred during the crisis. As Schelkle specifies: 'it was not collusion between the central bank and governments that created this heterodox role for the proudly independent institution in Frankfurt. Rather, the unforeseen feedback loop between bank balance sheets and government finances 'fiscalized' the monetary policy of the ECB […]. It was ultimately the concern for the stability of the banking system that created a fiscal union through the back door of monetary policy' (Schelkle 2012: 29).

In other words, 'the financial-fiscal feedback loop, not a weak and broken Stability Pact, has proven to be the Achilles heel for independent monetary policy' (Schelkle 2012: 29). As recalled by Praet (2015: 5): 'this financial dominance problem has now been acknowledged by elevating governance of the banking sector to the European level through Banking Union'. Before the crisis however, the Maastricht consensus rested on the belief that banking supervision could remain decentralized. This sharply went against some key claims advanced at the times of the Maastricht Treaty: 'the idea of entrusting the ECB with supervisory powers has been floating in policy circles for more than 20 years' (De Rynck 2016: 125). The Bundesbank, in particular, argued at the time 'that a prudential task 'could be misinterpreted as a lender of last resort function'' (James 2012: 292). Critics of this decentralized regime such as Tommaso Padoa-Schioppa promoted instead the creation of a 'collective euro area supervisor that would work as effectively as 'within a single nation'' (Padoa-Schioppa 1999b).

Paradoxically, it was the minimalist mandate of the ECB combined with its absence of discretion due to the existence of numerous rules to protect the Bank that forced the ECB to do more (Yiangou et al. 2013; Schelkle 2012) and to expand its role. On top of changing the nature of the ECB from a technocratic actor to a political actor (Chang 2016: 494), the crisis also turned the ECB from an independent institution into an EU institution which now engages with other EMU actors. Forced to accept new tasks which go beyond price stability to avoid the implosion of the currency, the crisis has led to the ECB's higher institutional embeddedness which goes against its initial depoliticized nature. Put more extremely, the euro crisis transformed the ECB from a rule (Folkerts-Landau and Garber 1992) into a genuine EU institution. Its competence accumulation is however also a cause for concern. As an interviewee highlighted: 'it is problematic to have a single institution having so many powers, some of which being possibly conflicting; at the same time, it is the institution that kept the euro alive'.[9]

Trichet's Cautious Stance

During the crisis, the ECB reverted to a vast array of reformed or completely new instruments to safeguard the stability of the euro area. On top of the conventional cut of interest rates, the Bank also successively relied on the extension of collateral types, on the buy-out of covert bonds, on forward guidance, on refinancing operations, and last but not least, on bond-buying programmes. Under a first phase that precisely corresponds to Jean-Claude Trichet's mandate (which expired in end-October 2011), the ECB followed an incrementalist approach that limited the ECB's liabilities increase. Trichet's mandate was characterised by a conservative stance which resulted in the design of non-balance sheet expanding actions.

Further to a significant provision of liquidity in August 2008, the ECB muddled-through until the very end of 2011 and kept its balance sheet in check. This came in sharp contrast to the action pattern of the US FED and of the Bank of England who grew their balance sheet considerably and consistently. The ECB's intervention pattern was thus conditioned by a strong concern for the containment of its balance sheet expansion, with two exceptions. On the one hand, an existing instrument – the Long Term Refinancing Operations (LTRO) – was redirected to new purpose to inject additional liquidity to banks, and on the other, an entirely new instrument, the Securities Markets Programmes (SMP) was created, officially to ensure the real transmission of monetary policy but unofficially to ensure that pressure recedes on the bond markets of troubled euro area countries (i.e. Greece, Portugal, Ireland, Spain and Italy).

The LTRO's first extension to 12 months on 7 May 2009 was not a one-off event. Its design, which encompassed the *ex ante* announcement of several allotment dates over a period of more than 6 months was meant to drive expectations of financial actors by providing them with more certainty. This is why the LTRO was at the time considered to be a step change from the previous, hyper-cautious ECB approach that mainly consisted in a revision and extension of its collateral policy, or put in the technical words of the ECB: 'the list of assets eligible as collateral in Eurosystem credit operations'. The LTRO extension also implied a significant expansion of its balance sheet which moved from '5% of GDP before the crisis to about 10% of GDP in 2009–2010' (Pisani-Ferry and Wolff 2012: 1). The LTRO was considered a convenient instrument for swift liquidity injection because it was a solution that did not lead to too much uproar in

Germany (De Grauwe 2012: 2). It however also had the downside of relying on financial institutions and its 'panicked bankers' (De Grauwe 2012:
2) to influence the yield curve. Thus, LTRO only affected the borrowing
conditions of Southern sovereign countries (and Ireland) to the extent
that financial institutions used this cheap liquidity to buy sovereign bonds.
When a year later the ECB noticed that this leverage was insufficient, it
designed a new instrument aimed at the buy-out of sovereign bonds on
secondary markets (the direct purchase of bonds from their emitters, i.e.
government's being banned by the Treaty): the Securities Markets
Programme (SMP).

The SMP – launched on 9 May 2010 – formed part of the broad basket
of big bazooka instruments, i.e. of the Greek Loan Facility, the European
Financial Stabilization Mechanism (EFSM) and of the European Financial
Stability Facility (EFSF) agreed over the famous May 2010 week-end of
intense negotiations. Under the SMP programme, 'the ECB buys government bonds in secondary markets only, while private bonds can be bought
in primary and secondary markets. This is in line with the Treaty constraints, which does not allow the ECB to buy Treasury bonds from sovereign debtors directly' (Schelkle 2012: 30). Justifying its new instrument,
the ECB explained that the SMP was meant to 'ensure depth and liquidity
in those market segments that are dysfunctional' [...] 'in view of the current exceptional circumstances prevailing in the market' (ECB 2010: 1).
On top of this market failure argument, the ECB also explained that such
tensions were preventing the fulfilment of its monetary policy mandate
which thus required to 'restore an appropriate monetary policy transmission mechanism' (ECB 2010: 1). Despite the invention of this innovative
instrument, the ECB was keen to limit the damage that the SMP would
have on its balance sheet and therefore 'sterilised' the programme through
corrective monetary actions that ensured that its monetary base would not
increase significantly as a result of SMP operations.

The SMP came in two waves. One that started in May 2010 and lasted
around 3 months followed by another one, of higher intensity, which
started in early August 2011 (still under Trichet) and lasted until January
2012 (under Mario Draghi). A crucial feature of the SMP, besides its 'ster-
ilisation' was the fact that its design was both limited in time and in scope.
While the first Spring SMP use was focussed on Portugal and Ireland, the
second use focussed on Spain and Italy. This is in line with the rising market pressure on the bond markets and with the contagion of the

phenomenon at the time. The SMP was thus responsive to immediate market pressures.

Between its creation in May 2010 and the 17 February 2012 (i.e. a few months away from its termination), it had accumulated a volume of 219 billion euros. As Schelkle (2012: 30) reported, the ECB has always claimed that: 'intervening in secondary markets only, while not announcing a target bond yield, means that the ECB lets market forces decide what interest rates sovereign borrowers have to pay at each auction. Sterilization ensures at the same time that there is no money creation directly from the ECB's outright purchase of securities, i.e. the Bank does not increase its balance sheet, but reduces its lending to banks to that extent'. However, the SMP appeared to be a much more contentious instrument upon release than the LTRO. Regardless of this, it also proved to have had a 'fairly limited success [...], by announcing that these purchases would be strictly limited and discontinued as soon as possible, it lacked credibility' (Illing and König 2014: 33). This explains partly why, when taking over the ECB early November 2011, Mario Draghi selected the LTRO as an instrument to build upon for the future, instead of the SMP.

Draghi Leads the ECB into the Grey Area

On 1 November 2011, Mario Draghi took over the presidency of the ECB. He became the successor of Jean-Claude Trichet who had been the longest serving President since the ECB creation. While Mario Draghi had academic credentials that Trichet did not have, he however lacked the institutional authority that Trichet had built up over those years. His long tenure as President made it arguably very hard during his last years in office to contradict him in the Governing Council.[10] Conscious of the emergency of the situation, Mario Draghi saw it however as its first priority to slowly build up consensus within the Governing Council for a more interventionist approach. In this task, he was assisted by his fellow colleagues from the ECB's Executive Board and in particular by three newly nominated members who supported the consensus building actions, mostly in Berlin and Paris: Belgian-national Peter Praet (nominated in June 2011), French-national Benoît Coeuré (nominated in November 2011) and German-national Jörg Asmussen (nominated in January 2012).

The very first action conducted by the new Executive Board was to advocate the creation of a new credible fiscal framework for euro area countries. During his first public appearance in front of the European

Parliament just a month after his nomination, Mario Draghi campaigned in favour of a 'Fiscal Compact'. Whereas several measures were already adopted as part of the Six Pack, he knew that supporting the Compact would put the ECB in line with German preferences. With hindsight, given the symbolic nature of the Fiscal Compact (see also Chap. 3), Draghi's move in its favour can be interpreted as a reputation-building manoeuvre. Alternatively, it can also be argued that it derived from a genuine call for the definition of a fiscal anchor by Member States as a precondition for the provision of further liquidity. If the second interpretation is correct, this would also imply that the Fiscal Compact has to be understood under the logic of an ECB seeking re-insurance before it embarked on risky operations. Enhanced liquidity was in reality provided only a few days later, in the form of an extension of the LTRO. It marked the start of a phase of disruptive institutional changes that saw the ECB becoming the euro area's banking supervisor and *de facto* lender of last resort. But the ECB's progressive activism should also be seen as a reluctant behaviour, it was constrained by the absence of any central fiscal actor. As an interviewee insisted: 'you need the government alongside the bank to take the big risks, the ECB would have needed a government'.[11]

LTRO Extension to 36 months (Dec 2011)

On 8 December 2011, the ECB announced 'measures to support bank lending and money market activity' (ECB 2011). These measures included a reduction of the reserve ratio, an 'increase of collateral availability' and most crucially, the enacting of an extension of the LTRO programme to 36 months in two allotments. The LTRO extension resulted in the provision of an impressive amount of liquidity to the euro area banking system. Wyplosz (2012: 1) indicates that already 'by the end of December [2011], 'LTROs had injected €250 billion of fresh cash''. Indeed, 'the difficult balance sheet situation of many Eurozone banks was reflected in the high volumes of liquidity allotted during these two operations, which, overall, amounted to around € 1 trillion' (Drudi et al. 2012: 890). The instrument explicitly targeted a restoration to health of the banking system but, also, had as a secondary objective the function of 'stabilising the government bond markets in the eurozone' (De Grauwe 2012: 1). The same author argued that 'these injections were necessary to save Europe's banking system' (De Grauwe 2012: 1) but also that these 'lender of last resort operations' were 'ill-designed' (De Grauwe 2012: 1). De Grauwe claimed notably that 'the ECB chose not to intervene at the source of the problem – the sovereign bond markets – and thereby allowed the crisis to become a banking crisis. And when the latter emerged, it delegated the power to buy government bonds to the banks, trusting they would buy these bonds' (De Grauwe 2012: 1).

Another criticism made was that the LTRO programme, despite its attempt to use banks as a back-door channel to ensure a higher liquidity on bond markets, also reinforced the link between banks and sovereign. As the FT reported: 'Spanish and Italian banks, the heaviest users of the LTRO, borrowed from the ECB and used a chunk of it to buy government bonds. The result is the LTRO has increased the links between governments and their banks just as the regulatory framework is encouraging banks to hold more sovereign debt due to the preferential way it is treated on a bank's balance sheet' (FT 2012: 1). In other words, 'the ECB took a stopgap action to reduce market pressure, knowing that the nexus between banks and sovereigns would intensify' (De Rynck 2016: 128). An interviewee contested however that the nexus was reinforced in a significant and intentional way.[12]

Swift Agreement on the Single Supervisory Mechanism (June 2012)

Nevertheless, the late realization of the full implications of the nexus between bank and sovereign by European leaders is precisely what drove the sudden appearance of the Banking Union on the agenda.[13] As reported by De Rynck (2016: 123): 'the June 2012 eurozone summit and European Council signified a breakthrough for transferring bank supervision to the ECB. It asked finance ministers to agree on this urgently, given that effective European supervision was a precondition for the European Stability Mechanism (ESM) to directly recapitalize fragile banks without further liability for the sovereign (European Union 2012), which was at the time most crucial for Spain'. Regardless of the fact that the ESM direct bank recapitalisation instrument was ultimately 'designed in a way that it will be probably never be used',[14] the Banking Union train was launched and could no longer be stopped.

From an institutional perspective, the design of the SSM was much more straightforward and subject to less bargaining among EMU executive actors than in the other more overtly fiscal areas analysed (i.e. fiscal surveillance, financial assistance, banking resolution). The chief reason for this is that the Maastricht Treaty foresaw the possibility to delegate this task to the ECB. The resulting negotiation was thus constrained by the existence of article 127 (6). As an interviewee recalls, there was a '*passerelle* in the treaty, without treaty change the ECB could do it',[15] since it was 'credible and legally possible' to assign this task to the ECB 'there was no choice'. Some members of the European Parliament would have preferred to assign this task to a stand-alone institution or agency so as to 'avoid excessive concentration of powers' and have sufficient 'checks and balances in place',[16] yet they also came to realise after a while that the ECB 'was the *least worse* option'.[17] Another source puts it in more controversial terms: 'Member States didn't want the Commission to do this so the ECB became the natural option'.[18] Also, because of its systematic insistence on the use of bail-outs during the crisis, the Commission had lost some credibility in the eyes of Member States: 'we didn't trust the Commission'.[19]

In the words of an interviewee, there was a need for 'someone independent and without conflict of interest'[20] and the Treaty foresaw that the ECB could be in charge of micro-prudential policy, but this did not necessarily mean that the ECB would be in favour of obtaining the SSM: 'the ECB was not pressuring to get the SSM'.[21] Nevertheless, the 'ECB can thank Tommaso Padoa-Schioppa'[22] for his efforts in putting this enabling clause in the Treaty. The new powers of the ECB are supervisory in nature. However, to the extent that the creation of the SSM also implies a much closer watch by the ECB over the build-up of vulnerabilities on bank balance sheets which have traditionally also deteriorated the public finances situation of the concerned Member State, it thus also limits the implicit fiscal liabilities of euro area governments as a whole. As reminded by ECB's chief economist and executive board member Peter Praet, 'the Single Supervisory Mechanism reduces the risk of supervisors showing excessive forbearance towards insolvent banks' (Praet 2015: 5). The powers deriving from the SSM hence amount to what one could term 'fiscal prevention powers'.

Of which type are those powers in practice however? Stefaan De Rynck, who participated in the negotiation of the SSM (De Rynck 2016: 123–124), reminds us of the key new competences of the ECB on banking supervision: 'first the ECB will be exclusively in charge of issuing and withdrawing licenses to operate a bank […]. Second, the ECB replaces national supervisors for the direct and exclusive supervision of approximately 120 institutions, which represent 85 per cent of bank assets' […]. 'Third the ECB gets all micro-prudential powers with full access to bank data and the possibility for conducting inspections' [...] 'Fourth, the ECB can impose measures to prevent the deterioration of a balance sheet, such as divestments or remuneration limits. It can dismiss managers and trigger resolution whereby the new Single Resolution Board will have to restructure or wind down a bank'.

When comparing the initial and final Commission proposal on the SSM similarities are thus striking as are the very limited amendments which were conducted during a quite uncontroversial negotiation. More precisely, the rather quick negotiation of the SSM 'which was given fast-tracked treatment by the Commission' (Dehousse 2015: 16) never called into question the fact that the ECB was the best placed to perform the job – because of its credibility and independence. The EP contested the use of the legal basis, as article 127 (6) formally excluded the EP from the negotiation while the classic internal market legal basis (art. 114) was retained as irrelevant. Moreover, the ALDE Group within the Parliament suggested that an independent agency should be tasked with the banking supervision. However, given the broad discretion that banking supervision involved, it was accepted that one 'cannot give such power to an agency'[23] and so the ECB naturally became the default option. In sum, apart from the EP who had an interest in disputing the relevant legal basis as article 127(6) excluded the EP from the negotiation, no actor disputed the logic of attributing this task to the ECB. What gained traction in the debate was rather how to engineer Chinese walls to ensure that the ECB would not be trapped in conflicting interests (price stability vs. financial stability). Another central negotiation element was the scope of the mechanism, initially envisaged to be covering 'all banks in the euro area, with the ECB at the heart of the system' (Rehn 2012: 2) while the adopted mechanism is only covering the most systemically important ones, on the insistence of Germany.

In a similar way that the design and adoption of the Fiscal Compact preceded an extension of the LTRO facility as a *quid pro quo* between control and liability (Wyplosz 2012), the creation of the SSM preceded the announcement of a new facility, the OMT, whose credibility and firepower would be enough to deter self-fulfilling dynamics on Southern European bond markets fuelled by the uncertainty over the integrity of the euro. As I have argued, the creation of the SSM should thus be regarded as an instrument that provides crisis prevention and limits the fiscal liability of the ECB. Under this perspective, to the extent that the 'single Supervisory Mechanism reduces the risk of supervisors showing excessive forbearance towards insolvent banks' (Praet 2015), its creation contributes to restoring monetary dominance. As Praet (2015) explained: 'this financial dominance problem has now been acknowledged by elevating governance of the banking sector to the European level through Banking Union'.

'Whatever It Takes' and the OMT

While the euro area summit and the European Council meetings of June 2012 reached a clearly termed mandate on the creation of a Single Supervisory Mechanism, the wording of the outcome reached on the other central element of the negotiation, the design of a 'scudo anti-spread' (i.e. an "anti-spread-missile") in the words of Mario Monti[24] was much more ambiguous and open for diverging interpretations. The principle put on the table for discussion was to achieve the reduction of spreads on Italian and Spanish bonds. 'In view of the possible obstacles facing the ECB, the Italian authorities elaborated a proposal to set up a market stabilization program to be implemented with bond purchases financed with resources provided by the EFSF/ESM. The ECB could act as an agent of the ESM […]. In the end the proposal was not adopted because of the German opposition. However, some results were achieved: a different attitude vis-à-vis the rising spreads was gaining ground; sovereign bond spreads were no longer considered as the unappealable judgment of an infallible court, but rather as a market dysfunction that required treatment' (Saccomanni 2016: 122). After the SSM deal, market stabilization was suddenly on the policy agenda.

For a few weeks, the ECB waited that the heated debate on the exact implications of the June Summit meetings ebbed down, but then it took action. Its subsequent intervention took a quite peculiar form as it merely consisted in a first step, in mere words; words that came out of the mouth of its President Mario Draghi however. The ECB President, speaking at a Global Investment Conference organised on 26 July 2012 in London, declared in his speech to investors, reading a few remarks which appeared to have been inserted in a last minute as they do not flow naturally from what the previous paragraphs contain: 'but there is another message I want to tell you. Within our mandate, the ECB is ready to do whatever it takes to preserve the euro. And believe me, it will be enough' (Draghi 2012: 3). Those few lines of Draghi's speech proved powerful enough to surprise markets who seemed to have interpreted his declarations as a credible commitment to save the currency. Anticipating that if necessary, further ECB interventions would occur, market pressure receded.

The Draghi speech was hence an extremely cheap strategy to eradicate a big tail-end risk: the collapse of the euro. And indeed, no one else could have saved the euro: the ECB was the only actor capable of eliminating the self-fulfilling expectations of the euro break-up. Within less than 6 weeks, yields on 10-year Spanish government bonds went down from almost 8% to close to 6% while Italian bond yields decreased from more than 6% to around 5%. The announcement of the Outright Monetary Transactions (OMT) – the instrument that substantiated Draghi's declaration – on 6 September had a significant effect on bond markets: 'it provided comfort to the market that there is a buyer'.[25] By the end of 2012, Spanish 10 year bond yield thus had reached around 5% while Italian bonds had reached almost 4%. As ECB executive board member Asmussen summarized in front of the German Federal Constitutional Court: 'I am firmly convinced that introducing the OMT programme was the right thing to do to ensure price stability in the euro. After all, a currency can only be stable if its continued existence is not in doubt' (Asmussen 2013: 7).

On 6 September 2012, the OMT programme was launched by the ECB, following on its President's promise. The OMT's key feature is that it is unlimited in scope and in time and that its provision is conditional on the request of financial assistance under the ESM. As the constitution of the SSM was driven by the expectation that Spain was at risk, its adoption in principle implicitly cleared the way for Draghi's 'whatever it takes' speech which was followed up by the OMT instrument in September 2012. The claimed goal of unconventional monetary instruments have been to support the 'monetary transmission mechanism' (Cour-Thiman and Winkler 2013: 5), i.e. aiming at 'ensuring the proper transmission of the ECB's interest rates to the euro area economy and the singleness of its monetary policy' (Cour-Thiman and Winkler 2013: 5). In practice however, the OMT served the purpose of last resort lending. As an interviewee indicated: 'I think that the OMT programme can be described as a de facto lender of last resort function'.[26] Another interviewee confirmed that 'the OMT has helped programme countries but with a much stronger link with conditionality'.

Compared to the SMP, the OMT is unlimited in time and quantity ('no *ex ante* quantitative limits are set on the size of Outright Monetary Transactions[27]') but remains limited in scope. Indeed, 'the prohibition of monetary financing prevents the ECB from purchasing government bonds in the primary market and limits its intervention in the secondary market to serving specific monetary purposes consistent with its primary objective of price stability' (Cour-Thiman and Winkler 2013: 5). A few design features ensure that the OMT does not lead to fiscal dominance: (1) 'OMTs are limited to transactions in secondary markets for sovereign bonds: the money goes to investors, not to the sovereign issuer; (2) the transactions are focused on short-term maturities' and lastly (3) 'OMTs require explicit conditionality attached to an appropriate EFSF/ESM programme, to ensure that government make the necessary efforts to restore the sustainability of public finances' (Cour-Thiman and Winkler 2013: 5).

As explained by Hu (2015: 633): 'within this framework, once a troubled country satisfies the conditions for EFSF/ESM bond-buying in the primary market, the ECB can purchase unlimited amount of one-to three year government bonds in the secondary market. The ECB also has a final say on the launch, duration and suspension of the bond-buying and regularly discloses information on OMTs bond-buying. The bonds bought by the ECB will be fully sterilized'. The fact that OMT activation is made conditional on a request for ESM assistance by itself limits the risk exposure of the ECB: 'to the extent that bank failures do still spill over to sovereigns and threaten their market access, the position of the ECB vis-à-vis governments is protected by the design features of Outright Monetary Transactions (OMT), where the requirement for an ESM programme preserves monetary dominance' (Praet 2015: 5). However, as a matter of fact, the OMT was never used: 'perhaps best of all, the ECB has never had to activate the facility. It has not actually bought any bonds under the program. Its promise to act was enough to calm markets' (Eichengreen 2013: 1).

The ECB Reluctantly Filling the Political Vacuum?

Together with Mario Draghi's 'whatever it takes speech', the OMT proved to be a way out of the European Council's institutional deadlock. The intergovernmental institution, paralyzed by the unanimity rule was caught in a 'joint-decision trap' (Scharpf 1988). Pressured by their Parliaments to follow a hard-line on debtor countries, i.e. by not granting them with additional money, creditor governments preferred to revert to 'covert institutionalization' (Héritier 2000) that minimized political conflicts (Héritier 2013). Surreptitious institutional change was thus preferred as a device to end the crisis as huge political capital was already invested in particular in 2010 on financial assistance mechanisms and in June 2012, on the design of a Banking Union. As an interviewee explained: 'it is said that in the 1960s the ECJ stepped up to fill a vacuum; well the ECB filled the vacuum of decision-making during the crisis'.[28] This implicit delegation of a temporary fiscal power to the ECB proved convenient for the governments both in case of success and of failure: 'if it works, we avoid a painful debate in parliament; if it doesn't, well, we have someone to blame'.[29] The inaction of euro area governments left the ECB with the choice between 'the extremely painful and the absolutely impossible'.[30] As an interviewee suggested, 'if it wasn't for the ECB, we could not have avoided the worst'.[31]

Ex post, the ECB's action was legitimated by its results. As an interviewee highlighted, 'they say that the best way to legitimize a war is to win it, and the ECB won it'.[32] The ECB was also confirmed in its line of action by the implicit mandate of euro area politicians and by the ECJ in its *Gauweiler*[33] ruling. However, it would be misleading to rationalize the ECB's success *ex post* as a sign of the institution's decisiveness. The ECB was hesitantly dragged into this: 'the ECB was reluctant to take many steps it did take'; 'there was an appreciation of the legal order and the mandate'.[34] As Eichengreen (2012: 131) outlined: 'the decision to go ahead with the ESM reflected a recognition that it was undesirable for the ECB to constantly be placed in the position of policy-maker of last resort – for it to have to purchase the debt of financially troubled governments because there was no other way of containing and resolving their problems'.

An interviewee remembers that the ECB repeatedly urged Member States for further action in 2011 and 2012 and explained in Eurogroup and EWG meetings that 'this is fiscal policy, we can't go there'[35] to which governments responded 'we will see what happens'.[36] Put differently, this was a disguised way of saying that they would do nothing about the problem and would simply go down the road of 'politically induced procrastination' (Giavazzi and Wyplosz 2015: 727). To make their commitment to inaction credible, 'many made the credible claim that their Parliament would never accept it'.[37] While hard evidence on the exact nature of those discussions and on whether governments forced the ECB to act on their behalf is likely to be missing for decades, it is for now reasonable to side with Illing and König (2014: 16) who suggest that the ECB 'felt forced to do so because the euro area did not have a fiscal institution capable of stopping the crisis worsening and preventing a break-up of the European Monetary Union'. An interviewee confirmed that 'the ECB was reluctant to take many of the steps it did take'.[38] The fact that EMU governments did not oppose the OMT (Dehousse 2015: 6) indicates the existence of a soft consensus for it among governments. Another indication of the ECB's reluctance to lead is the fact that it only progressively and cautiously took on additional risks, as illustrated by the slow but persistent rise in the default probabilities of its collateral from 0, 02 to 0,14 in 2013 (ECB 2013). Moreover, the 'rather late introduction of the OMT program during the crisis revealed the structural design flaws of the euro area and the inefficient delays associated with the activities of the European Central Bank as lender of last resort. Its current institutional design reinforced the ECB's tendency to initially act in a reserved and timid manner' (Illing and König 2014: 28).

The crisis forced the ECB to do more than it wanted because EMU did not feature any pre-existing fiscal centre. By saving the euro, the ECB inexorably exposed itself to higher credit risks. Despite the ECB's successes, 'it is questionable whether such activities are included in the ECB's mandate. The European Stability Mechanism (ESM) would, in principle, be better suited to act as a lender of last resort for governments should future crises occur' (Illing and König 2014: 16). Fiscal measures needed to be negotiated 'on the fly' and one by one, against the background of an ever diminishing appetite for political compromise. Redistribution consequences were clearly visible to everyone, it was obvious who would benefit and lose from fiscal mutualisation. This fact, reportedly, transformed the discussion on how to save the euro into a 'discussion about transfer of wealth'.[39] This leads Illing and König (2014: 23) to claim that 'as long as there is no central authority in the euro area with sufficient fiscal sovereignty, any attempt to split the burden-sharing between individual governments will entail huge coordination problems'.

CONCLUSION

Absent a central EMU fiscal and political authority, euro crisis events assigned ECB with the ultimate responsibility of saving the euro. Dragged into assuming the role of EMU's lender of last resort by the conscious passivity of euro area governments, the ECB had to take action beyond its historic and strict price-stability mandate. It did so through strategic yet conditioned actions. It invested time and efforts to determine the contours of its responsibilities and secure guarantees for its patchwork of actions. Becoming increasingly conscious of its 'institutional loneliness'

(Padoa-Schioppa 1999a), the ECB's task expansion also accelerated the Bank's awareness that it should be more 'institutionally embedded' (Matthijs and Blyth 2015) in the European political system. I argued that this move away from the ECB's original depoliticized nature occurred as part of an enhanced recognition that its responsibility was a heavy burden to bear.

The ECB's actions have allowed to prevent the realisation of a self-fulfilling prophecy about the end of the euro as a currency. What seems not to have been taken seriously enough when designing EMU in Maastricht was indeed the fact that in a monetary union, 'it is necessary to prevent countries from being pushed into bad equilibria by self-fulfilling fears of liquidity crises' (Eichengreen 2012: 520). Yet, assuming the role of *de facto* lender of last resort also implied to blur the responsibilities between monetary and fiscal policies. Schelkle (2012), for instance, claimed that a fiscal 'crypto-union, created involuntarily by the ECB, has prevented a second financial collapse and is the paradoxical consequence of trying to prevent a European fiscal union' (Schelkle 2012: 28). The tension between Member States' reluctance to create a full-fledge fiscal union (relying instead extensively on rules) and the fact that to support the euro, credible capabilities needed to be adopted swiftly (rules had led to instability has been fuelling uncertainty) was very strong. Rising tension pushed the ECB to adopt a more activist approach to crisis resolution. However, the ECB's decisive task expansion was not an evident and linear process. While it became soon obvious to EU leaders that the EFSF/ESM scheme was not sufficient to restore confidence in the currency, EU leaders were reluctant to mutualize new fiscal resources in an overt way. This over-reliance on the ECB faced public criticism all the same. It was ultimately supported by the ECJ in its *Gauweiler* ruling and by the mere fact that it was successful to bring calm back to bond markets, thereby dispelling the fear of euro break-up.

In this context, the ECB was implicitly allowed to embark on an informal self-empowerment, broadening its field of actions through strategic interventions. Heads of state and government thus relied on covert integration patterns and chose to assign the mandate of 'saving the euro' to EMU's benevolent actor who contained the damages of the euro crisis. Acting as a leader by default throughout the crisis, the ECB was thus placed as a buffer between market and political dynamics. One could argue that its role has been one of filling the vacuum of decision-making as the ECB intervention provided a way out of the European Council's joint-decision trap (Scharpf 1988) and allowed governments to minimize domestic political conflict. Indeed, 'integration of core state powers in the EU has frequently occurred not manifestly in the formal central political arena but rather in a process of covert integration without being explicitly mandated by formal political actors' (Héritier 2013: 230). In other words, 'the blockade effect of the joint-decision trap has not brought integration to a standstill but to an increasing reliance on conflict preventing mechanisms. This constant attempt to avoid the joint-decision trap give the EU its specific institutional form which is characterized by delegation to independent institutions, incomplete contracts, and a strong preference for integration by regulation' (Héritier 2013: 8).

The crisis has also transformed the ECB. The absence of a central 'fiscal backing' (Buiter 2009) in the original architecture of EMU, radically turned the ECB from the dogmatic implementer of a monetary rule into an actor, a true principal that should at the same time define and respect its own rules. This development could have dangerous consequences: 'the central bank can act as a fiscal agent of the government. It should not act as a fiscal principal, outside the normal accountability framework' (Buiter 2009: 8). In the end, the high concentration of powers that characterises the post-crisis ECB is therefore a cause for concern. As an interviewee concluded: 'the ECB is the only fire-fighter and that's not a sustainable solution'.[40] Potentially, the euro crisis could force upon the ECB the recognition that the absence of a fiscal centre, rather than being a guarantee of its independence, jeopardized its own independence as separation from fiscal policies proved insufficient to protect its independence After all, 'a central bank with a clear macroeconomic mandate is in fact only independent if it can take any measure necessary to meet its mandate' (Illing and König 2014: 24).

Ironically, the euro crisis hence re-politicized an institution whose originally strict divorce with fiscal policy was precisely 'meant to depoliticize monetary policy completely and thus ensure price stability even against intense popular pressure for stimulus' (Schelkle 2012: 28). As Schelkle (2012: 28) has argued, 'the crisis has thus revealed that the separation, far from strengthening the central bank through splendid isolation, creates a paradoxical weakness. The ECB was drawn into bailing out sovereign debtors and insolvent banks precisely because EMU lacks fiscal backing for a joint monetary policy, unlike the central banks in the United States or Britain (Buiter 2009)'. The institutional result of the euro crisis as far as a credible lending of last resort in EMU is concerned is still unsettled: 'the

ECB without the ESM, can hardly fulfil the role of the LLR in the long run, while the ESM, without the ECB, lacks the ability to boost market confidence' (Hu 2015: 637). Long-term this calls for a reform of the ECB's mandate as I will argue in the final chapter of this book.

Notes

1. Interviewee 32 – European Central Bank official.
2. Interviewee 45 – Independent analyst.
3. The ECB's monetary dominance is even enhanced by the fact that there is no single European or Eurozone fiscal policy, unlike in classic economic constituencies.
4. A strand of the monetary economics literature, called 'Fiscal Theory of the Price Level' led by economists (see for example, Leeper 1991; Sims 1994; and Woodford 1994), argue that, despite the independence of a central bank, fiscal dominance can still exist if governments do not internalise the inter-temporal budget constraint. If they are committed in ignoring this stability constraint, the central bank will have no options left but to adjust, thereby being trapped in a position of dominance.
5. Interviewee 22 – Italian Ministry of Finance official.
6. Interviewee 20 – Independent analyst.
7. Interviewee 44 – European Commission official.
8. The Lisbon Treaty's Protocol 4 on the ECB, in its article 28, foresees a procedure for the capital increase of the ECB which can be increased by qualified majority subject however to conditions and limits determined by the Council. In this light, the Council has introduced a cap of 5 bn for the future increases of the ECB's capital in the adopted COUNCIL REGULATION (EC) No 1009/200 0 of 8 May 2000. And since the ECB has decided in 2010 to increase its 'subscribed capital by € 5 billion, from € 5.76 billion to € 10.76 billion', with effect from 29 December 2010, no further capital increase could be performed after this date without a prior revision of the 2000 Council Regulation. https://www.ecb.europa.eu/press/pr/date/2010/html/pr101216_2.en.html
9. Interviewee 22 – Italian Ministry of Finance official.
10. Interviewee 30 – Finnish Ministry of Finance official.
11. Interviewee 42 – European Commission official.
12. Interviewee 30 – Finnish Ministry of Finance official.
13. Chapter 6 retraces the emergence of the idea of the Banking Union in more detail.
14. Interviewee 27 – Finnish Ministry of Finance official.
15. Interviewee 41 – Independent analyst.
16. Interviewee 11 – European Parliament official.

17. Interviewee 11 – European Parliament official.
18. Interviewee 12 – European Commission official.
19. Interviewee 29 – Finnish Financial Stability Authority official.
20. Interviewee 41 – Independent analyst.
21. Interviewee 30 – Finnish Ministry of Finance official.
22. Interviewee 9 – EU Council official.
23. Interviewee 9 – EU Council official.
24. *La Repubblica*, 'Monti: Bene lo scudo anti-spread ma l'Italia non intende uttilizarlo', 29 June 2012.
25. Interviewee 26 – Finnish Ministry of Finance official.
26. Interviewee 26 – Finnish Ministry of Finance official.
27. ECB *Press Release*, Technical Features of Outright Monetary Transactions, 6 Sept 2012.
28. Interviewee 30 – Finnish Ministry of Finance official.
29. Interviewee 30 – Finnish Ministry of Finance official.
30. Interviewee 30 – Finnish Ministry of Finance official.
31. Interviewee 20 – Independent analyst.
32. Interviewee 30 – Finnish Ministry of Finance official.
33. Judgement of the European Court of Justice of 16 June 2015, *Peter Gauweiler and others vs. Deutscher Bundestag.*
34. Interviewee 30 – Finnish Ministry of Finance official.
35. Interviewee 30 – Finnish Ministry of Finance official.
36. Interviewee 30 – Finnish Ministry of Finance official.
37. Interviewee 30 – Finnish Ministry of Finance official.
38. Interviewee 30 – Finnish Ministry of Finance official.
39. Interviewee 30 – Finnish Ministry of Finance official.
40. Interviewee 45 – Independent analyst.

REFERENCES

Asmussen, J. (2013, June 11). *Introductory Statement by the ECB in the Proceedings Before the Federal Constitutional Court by Jörg Asmussen.* Member of the Executive Board of the ECB, Karlsruhe.
Bank for International Settlements. (2014, September). *Re-thinking the Last Resort* (BIS Papers No 79).
Beetsma, R. M. W. J., & Bovenberg, A. L. (1995). *The Interaction of Fiscal and Monetary Policy in a Monetary Union: Balancing Credibility and Flexibility* (Discussion Paper 1995–101). Tilburg University, Centre for Economic Research.
Begg, D., Chiappori, P.-A., Giavazzi, F., Mayer, C., Neven, D., Spaventa, L., Vives, X., & Wyplosz, C. (1991). *The Making of Monetary Union, Monitoring European Integration* (Vol. 2). London: CEPR.

Belke, A. (2009, March 15). How Much Fiscal Backing Must the ECB Have? The Euro Area Is Not the Philippines. *Note*, European Parliament Committee on Economic and Monetary Affairs.

Bénassy-Quéré, A. (2016, April). Fixing a Sovereign-less Currency. *VoxEU Column*, 8, www.voxeu.org

Blommestein, H. J., & Turner, P. (2012, May 1). *Interactions Between Sovereign Debt Management and Monetary Policy Under Fiscal Dominance and Financial Instability* (OECD Working Papers on Sovereign Borrowing and Public Debt Management, No. 3). OECD Publishing.

Buiter, W. (2009, March 21). Fiscal Dimensions of Central Banking: The Fiscal Vacuum at the Heart of the Eurosystem and the Fiscal Abuse by and of the Fed. *FT Blogpost*, Willem Buiter's maverecon.

Chang, M. (2016). The (Ever) Incomplete Story of Economic and Monetary Union. *Journal of Contemporary European Research, 12*(1), 486–501.

Cour-Thiman, P., & Winkler, B. (2013, April). *The ECB's Non-Standard Monetary Policy Measures: The Role of Institutional Factors and Financial Structure* (ECB Working Paper Series, No. 1528).

De Grauwe, P. (2012, March 23). *How Not to Be a Lender of Last Resort*, CEPS Commentary.

De Grauwe, P. (2013, February). *Design Failures in the Eurozone: Can They Be Fixed?* LSE 'Europe in Question' (Discussion Paper Series, LEQS Paper No. 57/2013). London.

De Rynck, S. (2016). Banking on a Union: The Politics of Changing Eurozone Banking Supervision. *Journal of European Public Policy, 23*(1), 2016.

Dehousse, R. (2015, August 26–29). The New Supranationalism. *Paper for Presentation at the ECPR General Conference Panel P298*. Reflections on the Euro-crisis and the Future of Representative Democracy Montreal.

Draghi, M. (2012, July 26). *Speech by Mario Draghi, President of the European Central Bank*. Global Investment Conference, London.

Drudi, F., Durré, A., & Mongelli, F.-P. (2012). The Interplay of Economic Reforms and Monetary Policy: The Case of the Eurozone. *Journal of Common Market Studies, 50*(6), 881–898.

Eichengreen, B. (2012). European Monetary Integration with Benefit of Hindsight. *Journal of Common Market Studies, 50*(s1), 123–136.

Eichengreen, B. (2013, September 8). The ECB Grows Up. *Il Sole 24 Ore*.

European Central Bank. (2010, May 10). *Press Release, ECB Decides on Measures to Address Severe Tensions in Financial Markets*.

European Central Bank. (2011, July). The European Stability Mechanism. *ECB Monthly Bulletin*.

European Central Bank. (2013, July). *ECB Monthly Report*.

European Union. (2012, June 29). *Euro Area Summit Statement*. Brussels.

Financial Times. (2012, June 19). Banks Wrestle with Tough Funding Options. http://www.ft.com/cms/s/0/30221076-b921-11e1-9bfd-00144feabdc0. html#axzz4HJfs0y30

Folkerts-Landau, D., & Garber, P. M. (1992, March). *The European Central Bank: A Bank or a Monetary Policy Rule*. (NBER Working Paper No. 4016).

Giavazzi, F., & Wyplosz, C. (2015). EMU: Old Flaws Revisited. *Journal of European Integration, 37*(7), 723–737.

Goodhart, C. (1998). The Two Concepts of Money: Implications for the Analysis of Optimal Currency Areas. *European Journal of Political Economy, 14*(3), 407–432.

Goodhart, C., & Schoenmaker, D. (1995). Should the Functions of Monetary Policy and Banking Supervision Be Separated? *Oxford Economic Papers*, New Series, 47(4), 539–60.

Heisenberg, D., & Richmond, A. (2002). Supranational Institution-building in the European Union: A Comparison of the European Court of Justice and the European Central Bank. *Journal of European Public Policy, 9*(2), 201–218.

Héritier, A. (2000, June). Overt and Covert Institutionalization in Europe. *Preprints from the Max-Planck-Project Group on the Law of Collective Goods*. Bonn.

Héritier, A. (2013). Covert Integration of Core State Powers: Renegotiating Incomplete Contracts. In P. Genschel & M. Jachtenfuchs (Eds.), *Beyond the Regulatory Polity? The European Integration of Core State Powers*. Oxford: Oxford University Press.

Hodson, D. (2011). *Governing the Euro Area in Good Times and Bad*. New York: Oxford University Press.

Hodson, D. (2012). Managing the Euro: The European Central Bank. In J. Peterson & M. Shackleton (Eds.), *The Institutions of the European Union* (pp. 199–218). Oxford: Oxford University Press.

Honohan, P. (2017). Central Banking in Europe Today: Over-Mighty or Under-Powered? *Lecture*, 26 November 2018, European University Institute, Florence.

Hu, K. (2015). The Institutional Innovation of the Lender of Last Resort Facility in the Eurozone. *Journal of European Integration, 36*(7), 627–640.

Illing, G., & König, P. (2014). The European Central Bank as Lender of Last Resort. *DIW Economic Bulletin, 9*, 16–28.

Ioannidou, V. (2015). A First Step Towards Banking Union. *Voxeu Column*, 16 October 2012. www.voxeu.org

James, H. (2012). *Making the European Monetary Union*. Cambridge: Harvard University Press.

Kydland, F., & Prescott, E. (1977). Rules Rather than Discretion: The Inconsistency of Optimal Plans. *Journal of Political Economy, 85*(3), 473–492.

Leeper, E. (1991). Equilibria Under 'Active' and 'Passive' Monetary Policies. *Journal of Monetary Economics, 27*(1), 129–147.

Lewis, V., & Roth, M. (2015, May 09). Interest Rate Rules Under Financial Dominance. *KU Leuven, Centre for Economic Studies, Discussion Paper Series.*

Matthijs, M., & Blyth, M. (Eds.). (2015). *The Future of the Euro.* Oxford: Oxford University Press.

Mcnamara, K. R. (1999). *The Currency of Ideas: Monetary Politics in European Union.* Ithaca: Cornell University Press.

Mcnamara, K. (2013). *Currency Unions in Historical Perspective: What Can We Learn?* Paper Presented at the Council for European Studies 2013 Conference, Amsterdam.

Nieto, M. (2015). Regulatory Coordination in the Banking Union: The Role of National Authorities. In L. M. Hinojosa & J. M. Beneito (Eds.), *European Banking Union, the New Regime.* Spain: Wolters Kluwer.

Padoa-Schioppa, T. (1999a, December 29). Europas Notenbank ist einsam ('Europe's Central Bank Is Lonely'). Interview with *Die Zeit.*

Padoa-Schioppa, T. (1999b, February 29). EMU and Banking Supervision. *Lecture by Tommaso Padoa-Schioppa,* Member of the ECB Executive Board, London School of Economics, Financial Markets Group, London.

Pisani-Ferry, J., & Wolff, G. (2012). Voxeu.org: http://voxeu.org/article/ltro-quantitative-easing-disguise

Pollack, M. (2003). *The Engines of European Integration: Delegation, Agency and Agenda-Setting in the EU.* Oxford: Oxford University Press.

Praet, P. (2015, March 11). Public Sector Security Purchases and Monetary Dominance in a Monetary Union Without a Fiscal Union. *Speech by Peter Praet,* Member of the Executive Board of the ECB, at the Conference, The ECB and its Watchers XVI, Contribution to the Panel on Low-Interest-Rate Policy and Non-standard Monetary Policy Measures: Effectiveness and Challenges, Frankfurt am Main.

Rehn, O. (2012, September 3). Towards a Genuine Economic and Monetary Union. *Speech,* European Parliament ECON Committee.

Saccomanni, F. (2016). Policy Cooperation in the Euro Area in Time of Crisis: A Case of Too Little, Too Late. In T. Bayoumi, S. Pickford, & P. Subacchi (Eds.), *Managing Complexity: Economic Policy Coordination After the Crisis* (p. 2016). Brookings: Institution Press.

Sargent, T., & Wallace, N. (1981). Some Unpleasant Monetarist Arithmetics. *Federal Reserve Bank of Minneapolis Quarterly Review, 5*(3), 1–17.

Scharpf, F. (1988). The Joint-Decision Trap. Lessons From German Federalism and European Integration. *Public Administration, 66*(2), 239–278.

Schelkle, W. (2012). European Fiscal Union: From Monetary Back Door to Parliamentary Main Entrance. *CESifo Forum 1/2012, 13*(1), 28–34.

Sims, C. A. (1994). A Simple Model for Study of the Determination of the Price Level and the Interaction of Monetary and Fiscal Policy. *Economic Theory, 4*(3), 381–399.

Torres, F. (2013). The EMU's Legitimacy and the ECB as a Strategic Political Player in the Crisis Context. *Journal of European Integration, 35*(3), 287–300.

Walsh, C. E. (2010). *Monetary Theory and Policy* (3rd ed.). Cambridge: The MIT Press.

Winkler, A. (2016). The ECB as Lender of Last Resort: Banks vs. Governments. *Jahrbücher für Nationalökonomie und Statistik, 235*(3), 329–341.

Woodford, M. (1994). Monetary Policy and Price Level Determinacy in a Cash-in-Advance Economy. *Economic Theory, 4*(3), 345–380.

Wyplosz, C. (2012, July). The Role of the ECB in Fiscal Adjustment Programmes. In *The Role of the ECB in Financial Assistance Programmes*. Study for the ECON Committee, Monetary Dialogue.

Yiangou, J., O'keeffe, M., & Gloeckler, G. (2013). Tough Love: How the ECB's Monetary Financing Prohibition Pushes Deeper Euro Area Integration. *Journal of European Integration, 35*(3), 223–237.

CHAPTER 6

Centralizing Banking Resolution

INTRODUCTION

Around forty European banks show substantial activity across European borders (EBA 2013). And yet, the resolution of European banks has for long remained a decentralized competence in Europe. The 'regulatory gap between transnational banks and national resolution regimes' (Kudrna 2012: 291), formulated by Mervyn King by the telling image 'global banks are international in life but national in death'[1] was in truth not considered as an apparent contradiction. As a result, central European banking resolution regime, understood as a set of procedures, financial capacity and decision-making powers to deal with distressed banks outside of the court system, was thus unavailable when the euro crisis hit the continent, in late 2009. Banking supervision, for its part, had seen the constitution of a minimalist European architecture revolving around committees of national supervisors (the so-called Lamfalussy process).

Instead, the European resolution framework was only constituted by a set of minimal rules of non-binding nature, encapsulated in a Memorandum of Understanding on Cross Border Financial Stability[2] and by the more general but binding provisions on EU state aid. Central resolution instruments or actors were however inexistent. To fill this void and safeguard Europe's financial stability, the Commission came up with a series of largely unnoticed communications (Commission 2009, 2010b, c) on 'crisis management' in the early days of the euro crisis. Operating in an area where powers were clearly decentralized, the Commission, quickly realized

© The Author(s) 2019
P. Schlosser, *Europe's New Fiscal Union*,
https://Doi.org/10.1007/978-3-319-98636-4_6

133

however that they could have no further ambition than defining a 'common understanding'[3] on crisis management. As an involved interviewee witnessed, it was 'as far as we could go'.[4]

This situation changed radically during the crisis. After a series of bank bail-outs, Europe's political class slowly began to realize the unsustainability of the single-handed bail-out approach. The regulatory pendulum therefore moved back to its command and control extremity and aimed at restoring market discipline and safeguarding tax-payers' money. The notion of bail-in – i.e. the process through which an ailing bank would first see its loss being born by its shareholders and creditors – gained traction. The implementation of this paradigm shift took two steps. The first, one might say, *regulatory* step was the elaboration and adoption of the Bank Recovery and Resolution Directive (BRRD) which has been amply documented in the literature (Wojcik 2016; Binder and Singh 2016; Micossi et al. 2014). The BRRD goes a long way in establishing a new regulatory regime falling on banks and revolves around a bail-in logic as opposed to bail-outs. The second step, which this chapter focuses on, was the *institutional* creation of the Single Resolution Mechanism (SRM) which revolved on the one hand on the creation of a new agency (the Single Resolution Board) and on the other, on the constitution of a fund, the Single Resolution Fund.

The adoption in April 2014 of the SRM was a breakthrough. The creation of the SRM entailed a significant transfer of fiscal powers to the EU level. While the SRB was empowered to resolve ailing banks, the financial capacity of the EU's crisis management was complemented by a € 55 bn bank resolution fund financed through a levy falling on banks. Some have argued that the creation of a Banking Union has acted as a substitute for a genuine fiscal union (Gros 2013; Rey 2013). But the SRB is also characterised by numerous checks and balances and its autonomous authority is, being an agency and not an institution, rather weak. This could already be observed during the singular negotiation process through which the new resolution regime came about. Initiated under the framework of a single piece of EU legislation, the negotiation ended up sliced into two pieces: an EU Regulation and an Inter-Governmental Agreement (IGA). A central consideration in this split was how far the Treaty was allowing the EU to centralize financial resources.

In this light, this chapter retraces the negotiation that led to the adoption of the SRM and documents the fragmentation logic which lies at the core of its institutional design. The case of the SRM is particularly illuminating as its emergence asks the larger question of the centralization of executive and fiscal powers in the EU. The degree of centralization became indeed a predominant element in the debate on the design of the SRM. However, despite ultimately resulting in the creation of an independent resolution agency (the SRB), the agency's autonomous decision-making power proves to be weak as its actions is subject to multiple vetoes. This design goes against the classic decisive and resolute features of such a 'fire-extinguishing' body which ought to be able to dispose of strong executive powers to orderly wind down or resolve a bank over the course of a week-end.

WHEN AGENCIES TAKE OVER POWERS 'DESTINED' TO THE COMMISSION

The creation of a Single Resolution Mechanism has implied the delegation of resolution tasks to the SRB, a new central body which takes the legal form of an EU agency. What is particularly intriguing in this instance is that despite the high number of existing European bodies that could have been tasked with the banking resolution mission (e.g. European Commission, European Banking Authority, and European Stability Mechanism), co-legislators (EU Council and EP) retained as more appropriate to delegate this task to a newly created agency, confirming a past trend in European integration of regulatory agencies creation (Thatcher 2002; Majone 1996). An academic literature has tried to explain the proliferation of EU agencies over the last decades and connected the phenomenon to the rise of an 'executive centre formation at the EU level' (Rittberger and Wonka 2012: 7). A key question in this 'agencification' (Pollitt et al. 2001) process is 'why then, instead of delegating more authority to the Commission, were new European agencies created?' (Kelemen 2002: 94). While functional benefits seem to have driven the development of EU agencies in a first phase (Dehousse 1997), other types of considerations have come to the fore in explaining the prevalence of agencies over other institutional alternatives: the 'coordination of the multiple organizations involved in EU regulation' (Dehousse 1997) and a response to 'institutional fragilities' of EU regulation, including the weakening of the Commission's independence from governments and hence ability to offer credible commitments (Majone 2000).

In the light of awwn increasingly polycentric EU polity (Dehousse 2013), one more recent explanation provided is offered by the 'role of inter-institutional politics and power games in the EU' (Rittberger and Wonka 2012: 3). Independent agencies appear to be relevant problem-solving entities as they can perform similar tasks than the Commission without leading to a formal empowerment of the latter. This is convenient for Member States. Relying on agencies allows them to limits risks of bureaucratic or agency drift, i.e. 'the ability of an agency to enact outcomes different from the policies preferred by those who originally delegated power' (Epstein and O'Halloran 1999: 25). Agencies represent an alternative to the Commission, and are 'said to represent a 'compromise' reflecting the interests of their multiple principals' (Rittberger and Wonka 2012: 7). *A contrario*, Kelemen (2002) has argued that 'as conflict between principals increases, delegation to executive agencies is less likely to occur and, where it does occur, is more likely to be subject to constraints on discretion. To the extent that opponents of regulation have an opportunity to shape the design of a new agency, they will attempt to saddle the agency with a weak, fragmented structure and a vague, non-enforceable mandate' (Kelemen 2002: 96). As regards the consequence that these sweeping changes imply for the EU, Genschel and Jachtenfuchs (2016) conclude, referring to Bickerton et al. (2014) that 'to the extent the integration of core state powers involves the creation of new supranational capacity, the Member States often prefer vesting it into task-specific de novo EU bodies and not the Commission' (Genschel and Jachtenfuchs 2016: 47).

The Road Towards the Banking Union

Pre-crisis, the EU framework addressing the potential resolution of a bank in financial difficulty was kept 'minimal in scope and substance' (Commission 2009: 7). This approach, strongly inspired by subsidiarity concerns, stemmed from the fact that bank resolution almost inevitably implies the disbursement of money to banks, a fundamentally 'unpopular'[5] task. For this reason, the political sensitivity on the mutualisation of banking resolution capacities has always been higher than on banking supervision. It is no coincidence that the most renowned international expert group on banking supervision, the Basel Committee on Banking Supervision, made it a point never to discuss resolution (Goodhart 2011; Quaglia 2015). Such a minimalist integrationist line survived almost all the euro crisis period, until things suddenly changed in Spring 2012, when

EU leaders regarded more centralization on both supervision and resolution as inevitable, mostly due to the deteriorating situation of Spanish banks. The Commission, for its part, had an ambivalent behaviour towards banking resolution, being stuck in an inconclusive middle way between acknowledging the need for more central resolution and the lack of ambition to work towards achieving such a centralisation process. In the following years, the Commission's preference would also shift from a coordinated model to an integrated model, at times oscillating back (Kudrna 2012). This hesitation is documented by the incredibly long period of consultation that preceded legislative proposals on resolution (see Fig. 6.1 below).

In a first Communication released in October 2009, the Commission regretted the 'lack of an effective crisis management for cross border financial institutions' (Commission 2009: 2). It stressed that earlier resolution patterns (e.g. Fortis, Lehman Brothers, Icelandic banks) consisting of ring-fencing bank's assets in their domestic jurisdiction and mobilizing national resolution devices instead of acting at a group level would be likely to repeat themselves. This would be also emphasized much later to defend the *raison d'être* of a new bank resolution regime by EU Commissioner Barnier: 'the cumbersome decision-making process which led to the orderly resolution of Dexia is not an example to follow' (Commission 2013b: 1). The Commission's key message was to underline 'how damaging the absence of an adequate resolution framework can be

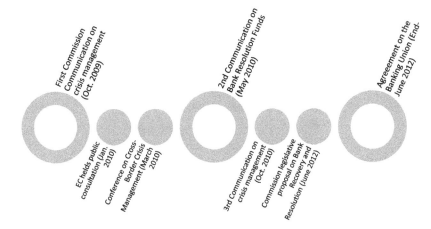

Fig. 6.1 Consultation milestones on banking resolution in the run up to the June 2012 Euro Area Summit which founded the Banking Union

for financial stability of the whole EU banking system' (Commission 2009: 2). Absent such a framework, the behaviour of Member States was only constrained by voluntary agreements such as the minimal non-binding rules of the 2008 Memorandum of Understanding – which was blatantly violated during the financial crisis – and by flexibly interpreted EU state aid rules. In early June 2012, the Commission came forward with a proposal on bank recovery and resolution (the so-called BRRD) in order to establish the central requirements of a new and centralized banking resolution regime. Figure 6.1 below reconstructs the key milestones preceding the formal proposal made by the Commission. The proposal anticipated by only a few weeks the crucial Euro Area Summit meeting that marked the genesis of the Banking Union.

The idea of creating a Banking Union, understood as a central supervision and resolution regime suddenly stuck on the agenda in June 2012: 'it emerged from nowhere to gain traction almost immediately' (Hadjiemmanuil 2015: 11). Pressure to act on the banking side gathered momentum after that policy responses to the euro crisis had mainly targeted the restoration of fiscal discipline, the set-up of financial firewalls under strict conditionality and the design of a plethora of new liquidity instruments by the ECB. The crucial trigger of this change of context was the persistent rise of spreads in euro area heavy weights Spain and Italy from end-2011. This market development focussed the minds of policymakers on systemic interlinkages.

Arguably, it is already at this time that German Finance Minister Schäuble insisted on the need for a new *quid pro quo* following the now famous symmetry pre-requisite between liability and control that structured much of Europe's crisis response (Boone and Johnson 2011). It is in this same moment that 'perceived or real'[6] evidence on the nexus between sovereigns and banks on bond markets came to the fore, exposing the vulnerability in particular of Southern banks to bond market movements. Garicano (2013: 1) provided evidence that the holdings of Spanish government bonds by the Spanish financial system more than tripled over the period 2008–2013. Those developments were particularly worrying for European policymakers because it was obvious that the existing EU capability did not include a sufficiently strong EU instrument which would be able to confront the rising pressure on Spanish and Italian bond markets. There was a 'feeling that the institutions already built by then could not sustain the euro'.[7]

Cyprus, one of Europe's smallest Member States, provided another blow to the credibility of then available European crisis management tools.

Its banking system collapsed in March 2012 and the country was granted a € 10 bn financial assistance from the EU and the IMF to restore its financial stability. The lack of clarity surrounding the conditions of both bail-out and bail-in and the effects they would have for the Cypriot banking system and their depositors led however to a general confusion. Remarks by Eurogroup President Dijsselbloem[8] that the Cyprus bail-out and partial bail-in of depositors was a model to follow fuelled the crisis further. It also left some observers with 'serious doubts on the ability of the group to make decisions to push Europe forward to financial stability and economic growth' (Pissarides 2014: 2). The Cyprus crisis, because of its 'use of ad hoc solutions' (ECB 2013a: 3) generated an uncertainty that thus played a role in revealing the lack of a credible and institutionalized regime to deal with banking crisis at European level. How to directly address, at the EU level, banks bearing financial stability risks was hence a question gathering pace in Spring 2012. In parallel, a slow but firm international consensus had emerged for more action on crisis supervision and management in particular among European leaders as they gathered in May 2012 in Camp David (USA) at the G8 and in June 2012 in Los Cabos (Mexico) for the G20. The IMF, through its Managing Director Christine Lagarde, made itself very vocal on this issue too in April 2012.[9]

The true trigger for the Banking Union came however from the Spanish banking sector (De Rynck 2016; Gloeckler et al. 2017). On 25 June, the Spanish government asked for a direct refinancing under the European Stability Mechanism for a loan of up to € 100 bn. The day after, the so-called Four Presidents Report written under the leadership of European Council President Van Rompuy was released. It provided the backbone of a Banking Union. These two developments occurred only days before what later came to be considered as the critical juncture in the creation of the BU: the Euro Area Summit of 29 June 2012. The summit's conclusions are indeed the first EU official document that recognises the 'imperative need to break the vicious circle between banks and sovereigns' (European Union 2012: 1). Crucially, it also entails the mandate to the European Commission to come up with a proposal on the constitution of a single supervisory mechanism (SSM) and, not incidentally, restates the agreement reached on the provision of financial assistance to Spanish banks through the EFSF/ESM vehicles. Compared to the swift adoption of the SSM, the negotiation of the Single Resolution Mechanism was however much more tedious: an interviewee remembers that the 'SRM dynamics were a bit confusing when compared to the SSM', 'the SSM was quite easy'.[10]

Negotiating the SRM

While EU leaders could rely on an enabling clause to allocate the SSM to the ECB, in the case of the SRM, their June 2012 commitment to establishing the SRM had 'left out where to set it and how it should be organized'.[11] Exploiting this ambiguity, the Commission's regulation proposal on the SRM (July 2013) had a clear centralization twist. It foresaw the delegation of resolution powers to both the Commission and to an EU independent agency. However, during the negotiation, a conflict line over the design of the new European resolution authority emerged between two camps. When the negotiation entered its most heated phase and the exchange of arguments turned into a clash between the Commission and the Council over the legal basis used to justify the SRM, the original model of a swift and effective resolution regime started to tumble. Germany and its allies played a crucial role in taming town the Commission's proposal and in reducing its ultimate role in the Single Resolution Mechanism.

While the imperative need 'to break the link between sovereign debt and bank debt' (Commission 2012) was very present during the early months of the negotiations of the first pillar of the Banking Union (the Single Supervisory Mechanism), the discussions around the design of the SRM occurred against a background of receding market pressure and of a lower political urgency to act. Draghi's *coup* of July 2012 had produced lasting effects. In a similar vein than on fiscal surveillance where the discussions over the Six-Pack took centre stage while the subsequent Two-Pack received more limited attraction (Laffan and Schlosser 2016), some actors seemed to believe that past actions were enough to restore market confidence. Surely, this was the stance chosen by Germany. Notwithstanding this reality, the Commission was keen to keep a symmetry in the institutional structure of the Banking Union and forcefully argued that 'in the banking union, bank supervision and resolution need to be exercised by the same level of authority' (Commission 2014: 7). In this spirit, the Commission astonishingly suggested that a new resolution agency should be created. Interestingly, the Commission thus excluded from the beginning the possibility of hosting the mechanism in-house (i.e. inside the Commission, replicating the past semi-autonomous models of DG COMP or OLAF for example[12]).

Anticipating Member States' conservatism, the Commission argued early on that a central mechanism 'would be more efficient than a network of national resolution authorities, in particular in the case of cross-border failures, given the need for speed and credibility in addressing bank crises' (Commission 2012: 9). The arguments developed in the Commission proposal to justify the added-value of the SRM focussed on the need to 'overcome the current financial fragmentation', break the link between sovereigns and banks and 're-launch cross-border activity in the internal market' (Commission 2013a: 2). More specifically, the expected purpose of the SRM was to avoid 'disorderly liquidation' and 'to put an end to finance the process with public resources' (Commission 2013a: 3). This sudden change towards bail-in proved to be a paradigmatic shift. However, the fact that the key provisions on bail-in were laid out in another, earlier piece of legislation, the Bank Recovery and Resolution Directive made things more complicated too: 'it was a bit difficult. We just had agreed on the BRRD, so there was a need to write the same things as in the BRRD'.[13]

When it comes to the institutional dimension, the proposal entailed three key features. It first foresaw that a 'strong central decision-making body' would be set up 'to ensure speed and effectiveness in resolution decisions with a view to avoiding uncoordinated action' (Commission 2013a: 3–4). The body would constitute 'a centralised pool of bank resolution expertise and experience' (Commission 2013a: 4) and would 'contribute to minimizing the costs of resolution both since it can attain significant advantages in terms of economies of scale over a network, and because it is instrumental to the enforceability and optimality of the resolution decision' (Commission 2013a: 5). In other words, 'the SRM will bring significant economies of scale and will avoid the negative externalities that may derive from purely national decisions and funds' (Commission 2013a: 7).

Secondly, the Commission envisaged to entrust the preparation and implementation of resolution tasks to a 'Single Resolution Board'. The Board would take the form of an EU agency, whose design would however 'depart from the model of all other agencies of the Union' (Commission 2013a: 21). The latter would 'determine when to recommend to the Commission to place a bank or a group under resolution' (Commission 2013a: 12), define which instruments to proceed with the resolution (within the framework set by the Commission) and execute the resolution plan. Its role would also be to 'monitor the execution by the national resolution authorities of its decisions at the national level' (Commission 2013a: 9). However, the discretionary power to both determine the menu of resolution instruments and to formally decide on the resolution of a bank would be attributed to the Commission itself, partly because of the Meroni doctrine.[14] In this model, 'the Commission was assigned the ultimate decision-making power on whether or not to initiate a resolution' (Howarth and Quaglia 2014: 133).

While the Commission would have – following an opinion by the ECB – the power to initiate a resolution procedure 'based on a recommendation by the Resolution Board or on its own initiative' (Commission 2013a: 9), it would furthermore get to decide on the framework of the resolution tools. The new agency was hence merely meant to act as the Commission's implementation agent. It is therefore fair to claim that despite the proposed independent agency, the Commission proposal granted itself a free hand to resolve banks by turning the agency into an empty shell. This self-aggrandizing approach was also illustrated in the suggested composition of the executive board of the SRB in which only Commission and ECB representatives would feature extensively. The underlying reason for the envisaged exclusion from Council representatives in the Board was, to cut the link between sovereign states and decisions related to the fate of banking assets, i.e. to 'separate the decision-making on the most efficient resolution strategy from the direct distributive consequences for the Member State involved' (Kudrna 2012: 292).

Thirdly, the Commission envisaged that the mechanism would be supported by the creation of a 'Single Bank Resolution Fund' to avoid the chaotic management that the deployment of national funds would imply (Commission 2013a: 4). The Fund would be financially underpinned by a levy falling on banks. As it emphasized earlier, the Commission's intent was leaning towards the application of the "polluter pays" principle, in the banking sector (Commission 2010a: 3). The SBRF's chief objective was to guarantee financial stability through the provision of 'short-term funding to an institution under resolution or guarantees to potential buyers of an institution under resolution' (Commission 2013a: 13). Being financed by a levy on banks (the aim was to reach a target size of '1% of covered deposits in the banking system of the participating Member States' (Commission 2013a: 14)), the idea was that the fund would work as an insurance mechanism (Commission 2013a: 14).

Altogether, the fund would thus collect an amount of € 55 bn. However, the Fund constitution would occur over 'a transitional period of 10 years' (Commission 2013a: 14). The initial proposal remained blurry when it came to the ultimate role played in resolution by European tax-payers and did not exclude their ultimate involvement. While it is recognized that 'as a principle, the cost of resolution will be borne by bail-in and the banking sector' (Commission 2013a: 8), the proposal also specified that the 'use of extraordinary public support is minimized' (Commission 2013a, b: 8), i.e. bail-out is not completely excluded. In reality, discussions around the design of bank resolution frameworks ran in parallel to wider consider-ations on the pertinence and feasibility of bail-in regimes in Europe com-pared to the use of a fiscal backstop. On this last aspect, the Commission proposal remained however silent. It did not formulate any role for a fiscal backstop that would grant the SRM with a firepower that would provide it with more intervention credibility (Schlosser 2017).

Broad Alignment Among Commission, ECB and EP

During the negotiation on the SRM major divergences of views on the SRM came to the fore 'between the German government and a few north-ern European Member States, on the one hand, and the EU institutions, France and euro area periphery Member States on the other' (Howarth and Quaglia 2014: 2). The three EU institutions (the European Commission, the ECB, and the European Parliament) showed indeed broad alignment on the need for a centralized SRM, supported by a cen-tral fund.

As one can anticipate, the Commission proposal was broadly in line with its institutional interest. Interviews held generally confirmed this view. A Commission interviewee explained that the Meroni doctrine led to the fact that 'it had to be an institution' taking care of resolution decisions and that as a consequence 'on the SRB we were the only ones left'.[15] Under this perspective the reason why the agency is located outside of the Commission is that 'the SSM model was followed'[16]; this way authorities 'could talk to each other while the integrity of the state aid regime would be preserved'.[17] Another, non-institutional interviewee, provided a more cynical perspective and stated that 'the SRB was a way for the Commission to get back what it lost in the SSM'.[18] This was partly confirmed by an ECB interviewee who stressed that the 'Commission wouldn't have minded doing it[19]' (i.e. operating the SRM).

Both the ECB and the EP converged on the key provisions entailed by the initial Commission proposal. The ECB came out strongly in favour of a centralized resolution mechanism which it deemed to act as a natural complement to the already existing Single Supervisory Mechanism, now falling under the ECB's competence. ECB executive board member Yves

Mersch explained in April 2013 that the SRM and the SSM were 'two sides of the same coin' (Mersch 2013) while Benoît Coeuré, another ECB executive board member, dramatically declared a month later that 'from the ECB's point of view, only if the SSM is complemented by a Single Resolution Mechanism with a common backstop can the negative feedback loop between sovereigns and banks be broken' (ECB 2013a: 4). In its opinion issued in November 2013 on the SRM, the ECB explicitly states that 'a strong and independent single resolution authority (SRA) should be at the centre of the SRM (…) as the levels of responsibility and decision-making for resolution and supervision have to be aligned' (ECB 2013b: 3). It underlines that 'a decision-making process should allow for timely and efficient decision-making, if necessary, within a very short time, such as a few days or, where necessary, a few hours.' (ECB 2013b: 3). The Frankfurt institution also showed eagerness to see to have the SRM 'fully operational by 1 January 2015' (ECB 2013b: 3). However, despite the ECB's impatience to see this new tool up and running, the ECB showed no interest in operating the instrument: 'the ECB did not want it'[20]; the 'ECB did not want it because it is un-popular, the fiscal implications aspect comes later'.[21]

The European Parliament, for its part, has been similarly 'pushing for a stronger, more centralised authority' (FT 2014a: 1). In a report issued already in 2010 by the ECON Committee, the EP asked for the set-up of 'an effective EU crisis management framework' (EP 2010: 5). The Parliament also explained that this mechanism 'should evolve in the medium or long term towards a universal regime covering all cross-border financial institutions in the Union and this should include a harmonised EU insolvency regime' (EP 2010: 7). During the negotiation, the EP proved relentless in its efforts to shape the Banking Union and to ensure that a central SRM entrusted with a genuine capability would be designed. It could harness some leverage out of the fact that the SRM was set to be negotiated in the run up to new European Parliament elections, held in May 2014. The Parliament used timing as a bargaining instrument.

Pre-crisis, France was keen to push for more centralization on bank resolution. As evidenced by a policy-maker involved in the early crisis management frameworks: 'France was ahead of the curve at the time'.[22] During the crisis, in line with other actors, its attention focussed on the design and conditions of financial assistance to programme countries. As the Banking Union project started to stick on the policy agenda from early June 2012 onwards, France's newly elected François Hollande became convinced by the project, and formed an *ad-hoc* coalition with Spain and Italy while trying its best not to antagonize Germany. Its efforts led France as far as claiming paternity for the Banking Union project.[23] Throughout 2013 the French government remained consistent on its preference: 'we want a full banking union and we want it fast' explained French Finance Minister Moscovici (FT 2013a: 2). This contrasts with Germany's ambivalent approach, being pro-active on the establishment of a Single Supervisory Mechanism but reluctant on the constitution of a Single Resolution Mechanism.

'Germany was a key actor in the SRM negotiation',[24] being decisive both in promoting and in impeding the emergence of the Banking Union. Berlin had to face the unintended consequence of the process it had initiated itself when linking the mobilization of ESM funds to banks with the reinforcement of the EU's controlling capacity over banks (Howarth and Quaglia 2014: 129). On the SRM, Germany thus acted as a 'reluctant midwife' (FT 2013a). It resisted the creation of the SRM using all the means at its disposal. Once it understood the full implications of the Banking Union project, it did its best to prevent the creation of a central resolution mechanism with strong powers and attempted to tame down the autonomy of the resolution authority. Teaming up with France, Germany had already made a contribution in May 2013 where it had outlined its preference for a resolution board based on a network of national authorities. Why was Germany such a fierce opponent to the SRM? Moral hazard grounds and the reluctance to assume future liabilities surely counted. But so did short term material considerations. Germany realized that very few of its own banks would be likely to benefit from the SRM in the first place (see Howarth and Quaglia 2014: 127–129). As highlighted by Howarth and Quaglia (2014), one feature of the German banking landscape is indeed its low concentration which ensures that comparatively few German banks fall under the Single Supervisory Mechanism and are thus also likely to be supported under the Single Resolution Mechanism.

A LEGAL AND INSTITUTIONAL BATTLE

As usual in European negotiations, the positioning of every actor involved in the legislative process started way before the Commission came out with the formal proposal in July 2013. However, in the instance of the SRM, conflicting views were also extensively voiced in the public realm, which is a rarer phenomenon in European politics. On first observation, the chief conflict lied between Germany and the Commission. The latter had argued internally that it would be 'the best placed institution to adopt all relevant decisions related to resolution with a discretionary nature' (FT 2013b) while Germany clearly expressed its preference over the ultimate SRM design: 'we don't want a European authority or European fund' (FT 2013a). In essence, Germany defended the following concepts: a 'network of national resolution authorities', a 'coordination of national resolution funds' and a 'eurozone's bail-out fund acting as backstop principally for member states, not banks' (FT 2013a). While Germany was the most vocal advocate of this approach, Finland and the Netherlands had similar positions.

The publication of the Commission's SRM proposal on 13 July 2013 stirred a complicated negotiation, visually summarized on Fig. 6.2 below. Two particular issues gained salience during the negotiation: the legal basis issue and the centralization of decision-making authority. The legal conundrum centred on the question whether the EU Treaty allowed the creation of a central Single Resolution Mechanism at the EU level in the first place. Anticipating this legal tug of war, the Commission had stated in its proposal that the 'SRM must be created within the EU legal and institutional framework (…) in order to protect the democratic and institu-

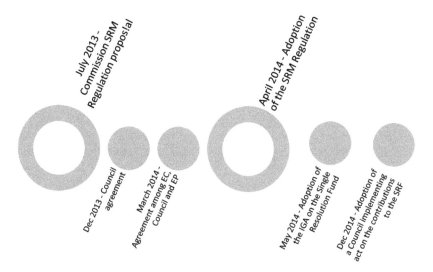

Fig. 6.2   Legal process leading up to the adoption of the SRM

tional order of the EU' (Commission 2013a: 4). It also claimed that 'ad hoc inter-governmental tools outside the EU framework', while necessary 'to tackle exceptional market circumstances', 'threaten the democratic quality of the EU decision-making' (Commission 2013a: 4). This preventive deterrence is a quite uncommon formulation in a Commission proposal. At other moments in the introduction of the SRM Proposal, references were made to the fact that the SRM 'must entail decision-making structures which are legally sound and effective in times of crisis' (Commission 2013a: 8).

The choice of the legal basis was a source of conflict among Member States and between the Commission and Member States. It entailed high stakes because of the voting rule that a Community legal basis would provide (Qualified Majority Voting) compared to an Inter-Governmental Agreement (unanimity). The Commission was confident that the SRM could rest on article 114 TFEU (the so-called 'single market article'), i.e. the 'classical legal basis for the adoption, through the ordinary legislative procedure, of measures for the functioning of the internal market' (Zavvos and Kaltsouni 2015: 9). Germany, on the other hand, disagreed, and argued that such a centralization step would require Treaty change as the SRM would ultimately usher in additional fiscal liabilities for participating states, regardless of the fact that the proposal formally entailed a levy on private banks, not a tax. Jurists have claimed that 'the scope of article 114 TFEU has been considerably extended over the years by the case law of the ECJ. It is now common ground that this provision authorizes the setting up of centralized mechanisms to ensure uniform application of EU law in the Member State at both normative and administrative level' (Messori and Barucci 2015: 44). What is directly required from the use of art. 114 is that the measures taken 'provide a concrete contribution to remove hindrances to the functioning of the internal market' (Messori and Barucci 2015: 46), in this case, the fragmentation of European financial markets. From a legal point of view, the Commission thus felt to be on solid ground as an interviewed Commission official confirmed: 'on article 114, we had three legal opinions saying yes'.[25]

The Commission proposal also provoked a clash with the EU Council as it had foreseen that most resolution powers would have been concentrated in the hands of the Commission. This came in conflict with the views of Germany and of its allies who preferred a softer centralization of resolution. Finland, for example, was distrustful of granting the Commission with resolution powers as it would have amounted to entrust the leaders of the bail-out mantra with the enforcement of bail-in: the Commission and in particular 'DG ECFIN wanted to use a lot of money to solve the crisis, it's old school'.[26] The burning phase of the negotiation took place in autumn 2013. From the start of the bargaining, Germany took on a significant role, with the support of its creditor allies. It put itself always on the defensive and dragged its feet (Schild 2015).

Germany's objective was to limit the exposure of German tax-payers by substantially constraining the firepower of the new instrument (i.e. 'no backstop') and reducing the role of the Commission in the mechanism to a minimum, or even to leave it out altogether (FT 2013b). Constituting a central mechanism under EU law was thus for Germany 'a red line that could not be overcome at all'.[27] This led to a significant stalemate in the Council which lasted over the whole autumn 2013 period. The coalition led by Germany involved the Netherlands and Finland, precisely those countries which, in September 2012, had issued a statement 'backtracking on June EU summit commitments' (Euractiv 2012: 1) on the use of the ESM as a direct bank recapitalisation facility. To escape this deadlock, a Dutch proposal was brought forward in December 2013 to split the negotiation in two parts. One part would be negotiated under EU law within the discussion on the Single Resolution Mechanism proposed by the Commission while controversial aspects – (mainly related to the levies to be collected in the Fund) would be taken out of the text and negotiated within an Inter-Governmental Agreement (IGA) that Member States committed to finalise by 1 March 2014 (EU Council 2013: 1). With this split in sight, Germany seemed to back down in its attempt to prevent the Commission from acquiring any resolution powers at all.

On substance, the interim ECOFIN Council agreement forged a week later, on 18 December 2013, also foresaw 'broad powers' for the SRB (EU Council 2013: 2). The powers envisaged for the SRB were indeed larger than the ones initially suggested by the Commission. In this concept, the SRB could also trigger a resolution procedure and would also be in charge of 'determining the application of resolution tools and the use of the single resolution fund' (EU Council 2013: 2). However, as a complement, the Council also provided for a higher intrusion for itself in the resolution decision. The deal envisaged that within 24 hours of the resolution scheme adoption by the SRB, the Council could object to it or ask for modifications, iteratively. As regards the appointment of the Single Resolution Board's members, the Council completely reshuffled the casting of the Board and excluded the ECB and the Commission from it. The

December deal only foresaw that the SRB would be composed of 'an exec-utive director, four full-time appointed members' (EU Council 2013: 2). As a result of these amendments, the Council reaffirmed itself as 'the ulti-mate EU resolution authority' (FT 2013a, b, c). Commenting on the interim Council compromise found on the SRM, Andrea Enria, the Chairman of the European Banking Authority explained: 'you need European decision mechanisms rather than having always a committee-type of decision in a crisis. Committees in a crisis don't work' (FT 2013c).[28]

As the negotiation took a drastic turn, the Commission would face severe criticisms by the Parliament for its handling of the negotiation pro-cess, despite their original preference alignment. The EP first contested the December deal to split the negotiation in two and resort to an inter-governmental agreement. In January 2014, European Parliament President Schulz wrote a fierce letter to Commission President Barroso in which he regretted that the Council decided on 18 December 2013 to strap some elements out of the Single Resolution Mechanism Resolution and regulate on them in an Inter-Governmental Agreement (IGA). He confidently stressed that 'there is no legal need for an intergovernmental agreement' (Schulz 2014: 1). The Parliament argued that the 'side-pact breaches fundamental EU law' (FT 2014a). In another letter, sent this time to the Greek Council Presidency, the EP's ECON Committee kept on defending the Community method and regretted that the circumven-tion of the ordinary legal procedure as illustrated by the elaboration of an IGA would go against the principles of 'sincere cooperation (art. 4(3) TEU), the principle of institutional balance and the principle of democ-racy, which are all part of the core constitutional principles of EU legal order' (EP 2014: 1).

As an interviewed European Parliament official highlights: 'we have opened up the SRM to intergovernmentalism, thereby distorting the pro-posal'.[29] And indeed, one can wonder why the Commission and the Parliament did not work more hands in hands in this matter being both losers of the introduction of an IGA which has been suggested precisely 'in order to eliminate EP involvement on these matters and minimize the Commission's role' (Howarth and Quaglia 2014: 135). The same inter-viewee thus wondered: 'why didn't the Commission withdraw the text?'. However, one should recall that the context of the time was marked by 'an electoral phase in which both José Manuel Barroso and Michel Barnier did not support us [i.e. the EP]'.[30] Michel Barnier, EU Commissioner on Financial Services, in particular, had the political ambition to be nominated as *Spitzenkandidat* for the European People's Party in March 2014. Despite the efforts of the Parliament to re-communitarize the SRM debate, the two-step approach went its way forward and successfully passed the winter.

On substance, the Parliament regretted a very complex framework, too much intrusiveness by the Council in the resolution process and insisted on giving the ECB 'final say about whether a bank fails' (Münchau 2014: 1). The negotiation reached its most acute phase in March 2014 as a still very conflict-prone European Parliament showed no willingness to surrender to the Council, putting the Greek Council presidency under severe time pressure. The adoption of the SRM regulation was indeed heavily conditioned by the nearing end of the EP's mandate with new elections due in May 2014. Apart from the legal dimension of the proposals, divergences were still to be found between the EP and the Council on: the transition phase of the fund (the EP advocated a swifter transition), the 'lack of a truly single fund' because of the proposed national compartmentalization of the fund in the transition phase (EP 2014: 2) and 'serious impediments to the speed and efficient functioning of the decision-making process and the implementation of the decisions' (EP 2014: 2). Fearing that an agreement would not be reached during the upcoming trilogue meeting[31] set to be held on 19 March 2014, the Greek presidency invited Eurogroup President Jeroem Dijsselbloem to join the trilogue negotiations, an unusual move not foreseen by official Council procedures. The latter accepted and from this moment 'took centre stage' (Schild 2015). As an interviewee recalls: 'the Greek minister was not on top of the issues. Dijsselbloem was'.[32] Jeroem Dijsselbloem ultimately crafted the deal. Once the agreement was in reach, he 'called Schäuble and Moscovici at 5 a.m.'[33] to inform them about it and get their green light for finalizing the negotiation.

GERMANY AND ITS VETO GAMES

Germany proved particularly stubborn during the negotiations on the SRM: 'Germany had more influence on the design of banking union than other eurozone Member States' (Howarth and Quaglia 2014: 128). An interviewee notes that while 'countries not completely happy with it voted in favour; Germany kept their position regardless of the fact that all the other countries were of the other view'.[34] Of course Germany plays a crucial role in many European negotiations. However, what appears distinctive in this instance was the capacity of Germany to exert a veto right in a process ruled by co-decision, i. e. in which the Council adopts legal acts in qualified majority voting: 'we were in QMV, we could outvote Germany'.[35] Most interviewees tended however to play down and depoliticize the fact that Germany managed not to be outvoted: 'it's not a question of hege-mony'[36]; 'they believed in what they said even though they were wrong'.[37] Another interviewee from the Commission insisted on the need to agree to broker a compromise to make the new regime sustainable: 'it's like a wedding, you don't want to impose it'[38]; 'it was important that everyone was happy about the outcome'.[39] Another Commission interviewee was more nuanced. He explained that 'antagonizing the Germans was not the way to go, we had to give in'[40] but stressed also that 'the IGA was a big blow for the Commission, it was a tough one to swallow'.

The strategy pursued by Germany to block the SRM relied mostly on the mobilization of legal arguments which 'framed the talks' (FT 2013b). The essence of the German argument was that the legal basis provided by the EU Treaty for the creation of an EU resolution authority was too thin. More specifically, it was retained that because of the vulnerability of reso-lution decisions to court challenges (resolution decisions involve a clear reallocation of property rights), there was a credibility issue at stake: 'if there is an activity that needs a solid legal base, it is resolution' (Schäuble 2013) explained the German Finance Minister. He thus regretted that what was emerging was 'a timber-framed, not a steel-framed, banking union' (Schäuble 2013) and called for a limited treaty change to provide 'a safe legal basis for a European resolution authority' (Schäuble 2013).

In a second step, the legal argumentation was made more sophisticated. It also entailed the instrumentalization of a domestic dimension, meant to act as a constraint in framing the negotiation, in an illustration of a suc-cessful two-level game (Putnam 1988). The claim was made that the SRM proposal would be incompatible with the German Constitution and with the role it foresees for the *Bundestag*, the German Parliament: 'German taxpayers would be required to step in to support the SRM without con-stitutionally required parliamentary approval' (Howarth and Quaglia 2014: 130). The shadows of the German fundamental law and its enforcer, the Karlsruhe Constitutional Court, were therefore cast over the negotia-tions. The German Court was indeed taken very seriously by the German government at the time and by its partners, as the Court was formulating its judgement on the ECB's Outright Monetary Transactions (OMT) dur-ing the last stages of the SRM negotiation. Judges asked themselves whether the ECB instrument constituted a fiscal transfer among EU countries. The German negotiators were thus 'scared that the Karlsruhe judges would block it'.[41]

Yet, all three legal services of EU institutions were aligned – a fact which seldom occurs – on the compatibility of the proposal with the TFEU, lending support to the claim that Germany was simply bluffing: 'they used it as an argument[42]' observed an interviewee. Another interviewee confirmed this interpretation: 'yes it was legal but before the legal it was a political position'.[43] A convincing evidence that supports this view is the absence of any formal expert analysis that was provided by Germany to make its case: 'there has never been a written proof'[44] in support of the German argument. In all likelihood, Germany thus instrumentalized its Constitution and the Karlsruhe Court as a domestic veto player. In the end, Germany had its way and the IGA was thus accepted as an idea to accommodate Germany's concerns. Germany also managed to shape the policy process according to its needs. On top of circumventing the Community method with the IGA, Germany also brokered a bilateral deal with European Council President Van Rompuy to ensure that informal discussions between staff from the German Constitutional Court and the EU Council's legal service could be held to fine-tune the wording of the texts: 'it's the first time that there were meetings with the Karlsruhe lawyers' in Brussels.[45] This atypical process was confirmed by another interviewee who casually declared '*yeah yeah... there were discussions*'.[46]

OUTCOME AND IMPLICATIONS OF THE BAROQUE DESIGN OF THE SRM

Guided by the concern to keep a better institutional balance than the one foreseen by the pro-Council interim agreement of December 2013, the compromise reached by Council, Parliament and Commission in March 2014 puzzled many observers nonetheless (Münchau 2014; FT 2014a, b, c). The outcome reveals that multiple vetoes prevail over both the resolution decision and the composition of the SRB, which turns the SRB into an agency that displays a rather weak autonomy. Due to the high number of actors involved, and the amount of conditions to be met for a smooth operation, the enforceability of the new banking resolution regime thus becomes questionable. In light of the above, it is logical to ask why legislators decided to entrust the resolution of banks to a separate agency thereby discounting the empowerment of existing institutions.

In March 2014, Council and Parliament reached a compromise on the design of the SRM. The adopted SRM Regulation and of the Inter-Governmental Agreement ended up granting more powers in the resolution process to independent actors (the ECB and the SRB), rather than to the Commission. Below Table 6.1 provides a comparison of the original and adopted proposals in its key features.

The ECB is now the formal triggering authority of the SRM while the SRB is able, under certain conditions, to initiate a resolution procedure on its own initiative too. This has been portrayed by an interviewee as a 'safety valve against potential procrastination'[47] by the ECB. The activation of resolution is no longer 'fully dependent'[48] on the Frankfurt institution. Because it has the triggering authority, the ECB is however the central actor of the resolution process: 'will the SRB ever have the same level of information than the ECB?'[49] asked rhetorically an interviewee. In contrast to the December 2013 pro-Council compromise, the Commission in the end retains a decision role in the resolution process: it is 'given a formal

Table 6.1   Original proposal vs. adopted SRM regulation

Features	Initial proposal	Final outcome
Triggering authority for the start of a resolution procedure	Commission	ECB and SRB
Possibility of autonomous resolution initiative by the Commission	Yes	No
Formal resolution decision	Commission	Commission and Council
Veto power	Only Commission	Commission and Council
Membership of the Executive Session of the SRB	Representatives from Commission, ECB, and national resolution authorities	Chair + 5 experts + Commission and ECB as permanent observers only
Appointment procedure of the SRB	Commission proposes, Parliament is consulted, Council appoints	Commission proposes, Parliament approves, Council appoints
Level of autonomy of the SRB	Low	Medium
Fund size	€ 55 bn	€ 55 bn
Transition period	10 years	8 years
Legal basis of the SRM	Art. 114 TFEU	Art. 114 TFEU + Inter-Governmental Agreement
Scope of application	All EU banks	Only SSM banks

role to approve resolution decisions recommended' (FT 2014c) by the SRB although this remains subject, in some of its features, to a veto by the Council. The Commission thus remains a central actor of the procedure. It needs to assess the compatibility of the SRB's resolution proposal with the state aid rules and should evaluate whether the decisions proposed by the SRB are adequate. Therefore, 'any resolution action involving SRF financing can only be undertaken with the approval of the Commission, exactly as if it were a form of state aid' (Hadjiemmanuil 2015).

However, since the agreement does not grant the Commission any autonomous initiative to trigger a resolution procedure (unlike what was foreseen in the original SRM Regulation proposal), the leverage that the state aid regime provides to the Commission amounts more to a veto right than to a discretionary power over the resolution of banks. Overall, the Commission has thus seen its prerogatives considerably tamed down during the negotiation. The Council, in turn, has managed to obtain a 'quite significant interference in SRM activity' (Messori et al. 2015: 18) and has acquired a *de facto* veto power. It can block the resolution proposal, but only under the condition that two features are affected: if the 'amount of resources drawn from the Single Fund is modified or if there is no public interest in resolving the bank' (Commission 2014). The appointment procedure of the SRB is another illustrating example of the Council's power in the resolution process. In the final agreement, the Single Resolution Board members are shortlisted and proposed by the Commission, approved by the Parliament and ultimately appointed by the Council. On paper, the three institutions have thus an equal veto in the selection process. However, the result of the recruitment process in December 2014 is unambiguous as to the ultimate authority retained by the Council in the appointment process. The first SRB of its time is chaired by Elke König, a German national while the Vice-Chair position is occupied by Timo Löyttyniemi (a Finnish national). The other board members which were appointed are of French, Spanish, Italian and Dutch nationality. This led an interviewee to claim that the SRB is 'controlled by the Council'[50] and another one to explain that 'the board of the SRB is now under political control'.[51] Moreover, while the Board represents the most prominent members of the two coalitions which collided over the institutional design of the SRM, it is the German-led coalition that prevailed in the top level attributions.

The inter-institutional negotiation seems to have ushered in a satisfaction of all power considerations: 'every single institution wants to have a say when it comes to sharing the costs'.[52] This ambiguity has been claimed to be intentional by the same Commission interviewee: 'we achieved what we wanted, clear checks and balances'.[53] The above interpretation assumes however that the checks and balances are clearly delineated and that they do not lead to a gridlock. I content instead that the executive resolution powers end up been blurrily spread among actors: to such an extent that it becomes impossible to tell who has the final authority over resolution. Europe's resolution authority is fundamentally and purposely divided. All executive institutions involved in the process can mutually offset each other.

These scattered and partly overlapping powers blur the line as to who retains the final authority over resolution under the new regime. Interviews conducted confirmed what a Commission interviewee suggested: 'if you talk to those institutions, people will tell you that of course they have the resolution authority'.[54] Logically however, if all actors are seriously convinced that they are in charge of resolution, it means that no one is ultimately responsible for it. Indeed, when asked who has the final word on resolution, interviewees came up with different answers with some pointing at the ECB, the SRB, the Commission or the Council. The most honest and wisest reply probably came from a senior expert who admitted: 'I don't know'; 'experience will tell'; 'there are potential conflicts but let's see how it works'.[55] When compared to the supranational and centralized Single Supervisory Mechanism, the SRM's ultimate institutional shape is characterised by a limited and weak centralization which 'suggests that the Commission's objective of aligning the exercise of banking supervision and bank resolution at the same level of governance in the EU has not been met' (Kern 2015: 158).

The involvement of so many actors and the fragmentation underpinning the SRM bear the risks of ultimately undermining the resolution regime's credibility and effectiveness. Compared to the original objective of setting up a swift and centralized resolution process, the final outcome is plagued by the multilateral nature of the SRM. A necessary condition for a swift resolution is therefore that all bodies involved[56] (ECB's Single Supervision Board, SRB's executive session; SRB plenary session; Commission college; Commission DG COMP; EU Council) align their views on the need for resolving a bank and on the relevance of the resolution tools chosen. In other words, a crucial factor for the SRM to work is that 'the players act in mutual trust and a spirit of cooperation' (Messori et al. 2015: 98).

Taking some distance from the agreement, it becomes questionable, based on its numerous inherent constraints and its lack of firepower credibility, whether the Single Resolution Fund will be mobilized at all. This interpretation goes against the very spirit of the negotiations which attributed a central and credible role to the Single Resolution Fund. However, interviews conducted revealed that the expectations of involved actors as to the use of the fund are quite low. One interviewee explained for example that 'the idea of the SRF is to pay for costs (e.g. electricity, employees, etc), it's not really to rescue a bank'.[57] The same interviewee then contended that 'in practice, the SRF will not be used'.[58] Another interviewee insisted on the last resort character of the SRF and stressed that there are 'lots of steps before the SRF can be tapped'.[59]

These concerns echo reservations voiced during the SRM negotiations. Asked in January 2014 about the proposed SRM instrument, US Treasury Secretary Lew declared: 'we don't think it's big enough. We don't think it's fast enough' (FT 2014a: 1), thereby summarizing two distinctive caveats of the interim agreement which are nonetheless still valid to characterize the finally adopted mechanism. A crude conclusion of a Member State official involved in the negotiations is particularly telling: 'instead of a resolution, you get a resolution process. It reminds me of the Middle East: you don't have peace but you have a peace process'.[60] The lack of credibility of the mechanism's enforcement reminds one of the corrective arm of the Stability and Growth Pact, another procedure whose *raison d'être* lies more with its deterrence rather than with the likelihood of its use. All this comes on top of the fact that in respect of the BRRD principles and its cascade of measures to address ailing banks,[61] the mobilization of the SRM/SRF will come very late in the process, with many safety valves being activated before the SRM can intervene at all.[62] Overall, the consensus among policy-makers on the new resolution regime seems to be that its credibility is uncertain. One interviewee explained: 'the new resolution regime? I would say that it is more predictable: is it much better or just better than before, I don't know, *on verra...*'.[63] Along similar lines, another interviewee stressed that it is 'hard to see in advance[64]' whether the new regime is credible. A key reason for this is that the SRB is among others tasked with ensuring the paradigm shift from bail-out to bail-in which proves to be much more radical as many anticipated.

Against the background of the SRM's highly fragmented structure and diffused authority and given its low credibility as an effective and swift resolution instrument, one can wonder why the agency solution kept being pursued by EU actors while functional equivalents were available. Why was it necessary to make the SRB sit on top of an independent agency if this agency – because of the Meroni doctrine – would be only partly in charge of resolution and would not be completely independent in the first place? The SRB could have been attributed to the Commission herself as a stand-alone Directorate General. The Commission's DG Competition, for instance, operates in relative independence from the politicized College of Commissioners and has, over the years, developed a culture of confidentiality and objectivity in its assessment of the cases on which it rules. It is thus fair to speculate that a similar set-up focussed on the resolution of banks would have been likely to lead to a similar balance between independence and politicization.

One might argue as Genschel and Jachtenfuchs (2013) do, that the more money is involved, the more likely it is that intergovernmental arrangements will prosper. Yet, a genuinely intergovernmental agreement, the European Stability Mechanism, was also available and could have hosted the Single Resolution Board. Chinese walls could have been used to ensure that the various functions of the Mechanism would have been kept separate – they currently exist between the ESM's funding team and the rest of the ESM staff for example. Interviewees suggested that the option of entrusting the ESM with banking resolution was discussed and that the ESM even showed interest in hosting the SRB: 'the ESM wanted to be in charge of resolution at a certain point'.[65] An interviewed ESM official confirmed that this scenario 'was in the cards for several months. As an institution we never pushed for it, but if Member States wanted us to do it…'.[66] Retracing the discussion of the time, the same interviewee explained that the idea of attributing banking resolution to the ESM was based on 'functional arguments, but that politically it was toxic to have a new role'.[67] The interviewee concluded that the political reasoning was retained as valid and added 'even if this is somewhat inefficient. For us it would have meant hiring a few more people'[68] but the burden would have been much lower than setting up a new agency from scratch. Feeling that it would be coherent to provide this task to an actor who is in charge of financial stability, the Commission was even conditionally supportive of this solution: 'on the ESM, we thought that we need a treaty change and it becomes the resolution authority'.[69] However, the ESM as a banking resolution authority option was not retained as relevant, for two main reasons: 'people did not want to mix things up'[70] and 'they did not want to re-open the ESM Treaty'.[71]

Conclusion

This chapter retraced the process through which the new banking resolution regime came into being. The constitution of the Single Resolution Mechanism, built around the Single Resolution Board and supported by a fund of € 55 bn, marked a clear departure from the previously decentralized regime on the crisis management of banks in the EU. The analysis has shown that strong institutional design contests surfaced when the detailed features of the proposal began to be discussed. Institutional interests and the shadow of agency drift clearly conditioned the negotiations on the SRM. These challenges revealed the tensions inherent in the constitution of central fiscal capacities and exhibited a tendency for the fragmentation of powers among executive institutions. A pervasive and crumbling dynamic was indeed at play and it led all the way to a marked centrifugal twist of resolution powers at the EU level.

This centrifugal turn is illustrated by the creation of an agency – another infant of the euro crisis – in charge of resolution, the Single Resolution Board. While institutional alternatives (i.e. the Commission, the EBA, the ECB, the ESM) existed, it was retained as the most appropriate option to entrust resolution tasks to a brand new EU agency, confirming a past trend of 'agencification' in European integration. The original SRM proposal had foreseen an executive and discretionary power for the Commission to conduct the resolution of banks, yet the ultimate agreement disempowered the Commission. Instead, it satisfied almost every EMU executive actor by involving them all in the process (ECB, EU Council, and Commission) and by granting veto powers to both Commission and EU Council over the resolution of banks and to the Parliament, the Commission and the Council on the appointment of the Single Resolution Board.

Against this backdrop, the chapter has argued that the SRM's ultimately fragmented and rather weak autonomy fuels the claim that the mechanism is not credible enough or on its own, to make a vital contribution to financial stability. The ultimate governance and capabilities of the SRB seems to be in line with the predictions of Kelemen (2002: 96), which stressed how opponents of power delegation would attempt to 'saddle the agency with a weak, fragmented structure and a vague, non-enforceable mandate' (Kelemen 2002: 96). The resolution process involves many actors and is consequently likely to be too slow to be decisive in resolving a very large systemic bank over a week-end. While it is quite clear that the ECB – being the triggering authority – disposes of a strong resolution prerogative, the high dilution of powers within the SRM makes it difficult to determine who disposes of the ultimate authority over the resolution of banks at the EU level.

The analysis of the negotiation of the SRM also revealed a reluctance by the Council, on the insistence of Germany but with the support of Finland and the Netherlands, to the delegation of a new executive power with fiscal dimension to the European centre. It lined out the crucial contributions made by Germany and its allies in hampering the SRM development, attenuate the centralization of fiscal prerogatives that it would involve and tame down the Commission control in the process. The veto power exercised by Germany and its allies on the legal basis of the SRM was a decisive moment in the SRM negotiation. Yet, Germany did not prevent the SRM and the Single Resolution Fund to be agreed upon as it only led to a legal split between the institutional aspects of the wider SRM and elements pertaining to the transfers and mutualisation of funds of the SRF. This move was welcomed by the German Constitutional Court, but also by the Council's legal service as providing 'maximum legal certainty' (EU Council 2014). Despite clearing the way for the use of art. 114 also for the SRF, the latter had warned legislators of the risk of a constitutional challenge.

The case of the SRM, lastly, informs about the institutional impediments that are inherent when moving from a rules-based coordination regime to the creation of a common central institution. Whilst the initial resolution regime was constituted by a complex set of rules (i.e. the MoU on Financial Stability and the EU state aid rules that set the terms of cross-border cooperation in case of a systemically relevant failure of a bank), the SRM now coexist with an even broader set of rules – the BRRD – and is centred around a new agency. Yet, the enforcement capability of the new resolution regime remains largely untested, also because the ultimate executive and discretionary power over banking resolution was never really settled. Only time will tell whether the inter-institutional politics that presided over the negotiation on the SRM design will in the future usher into a hub of relationships based on trust and confidence. Meanwhile, it can be postulated that despite its blatant fragilities, the existence of the Single Resolution Mechanism has accelerated the move from a rules-based EMU towards an EMU based on common institutional capacities.

Notes

1. *The Economist*, http://www.economist.com/news/special-report/215 87378-2008-global-financial-integration-has-gone-reverse-too-much-good-thing
2. https://www.ecb.europa.eu/pub/pdf/other/mou-financialstability2008en.pdf
3. Interviewee 16 – European Commission official.
4. Interviewee 16 – European Commission official.
5. Interviewee 35 – European Central Bank official.
6. Interviewee 26 – Finnish Ministry of Finance official.
7. Interviewee 19 – Italian Ministry of Finance official.
8. http://blogs.ft.com/brusselsblog/2013/03/26/the-ftreuters-dijsselbloem-interview-transcript/
9. http://www.imf.org/external/np/speeches/2012/041712.htm
10. Interviewee 28 – Finnish Financial Stability Authority official.
11. Interviewee 29 – Finnish Financial Stability Authority official.
12. Interviewee 48 – European Commission official.
13. Interviewee 29 – Finnish Financial Stability Authority official.
14. The Meroni Doctrine derives from a famous ECJ case law of 1956 (10/56) in which the Court argued that 'delegation of powers to *ad hoc* bodies, not envisaged by the ECSC Treaty, was possible only subject to strict conditions, and that, in any event, the delegation of broad discretionary powers was not permitted' (Dehousse 1992: 389).
15. Interviewee 42 – European Commission official.
16. Interviewee 42 – European Commission official.
17. Interviewee 42 – European Commission official.
18. Interviewee 41 – Independent analyst.
19. Interviewee 38 – European Central Bank official.
20. Interviewee 29 – Finnish Financial Stability Authority official.
21. Interviewee 35 – European Central Bank official.
22. Interviewee 16 – European Commission official.
23. *Le Monde* – 'L'Union Bancaire est. une avancée politique pour tous les peuples d'Europe', 20 December 2013.
24. Interviewee 11 – European Parliament official.
25. Interviewee 48 – European Commission official.
26. Interviewee 48 – European Commission official.
27. Interviewee 19 – Italian Ministry of Finance official.
28. *Financial Times,* Interview of Andrea Enria, Chairman of the European Banking Authority, 17 November 2013.
29. Interviewee 5 – European Parliament official.
30. Interviewee 5 – European Parliament official.

31. Trilogue meetings gather Commission, Council and Parliament negotiating teams to craft compromises in view of 1st reading, fast-track legislative adoption among EU co-legislators.
32. Interviewee 11 – European Parliament official.
33. Interviewee 11 – European Parliament official.
34. Interviewee 19 – Italian Ministry of Finance official.
35. Interviewee 9 – EU Council official.
36. Interviewee 48 – European Commission official.
37. Interviewee 40 – EU Council official.
38. Interviewee 48 – European Commission official.
39. Interviewee 48 – European Commission official.
40. Interviewee 42 – European Commission official.
41. Interviewee 9 – EU Council official.
42. Interviewee 17 –European Parliament official.
43. Interviewee 19 – Italian Ministry of Finance official.
44. Interviewee 13 – European Parliament official.
45. Interviewee 9 – EU Council official.
46. Interviewee 40 – EU Council official.
47. Interviewee 26 – Finnish Ministry of Finance official.
48. Interviewee 26 – Finnish Ministry of Finance official.
49. Interviewee 41 – Independent analyst.
50. Interviewee 41 – Independent analyst.
51. Interviewee 35 – European Central Bank official.
52. Interviewee 19 – Italian Ministry of Finance official.
53. Interviewee 48 – European Commission official.
54. Interviewee 48 – European Commission official.
55. Interviewee 29 – Finnish Financial Stability Authority official.
56. On this, see Howarth and Quaglia (2014).
57. Interviewee 38 – European Central Bank official.
58. Interviewee 38 – European Central Bank official.
59. Interviewee 28 – Finnish Financial Stability Authority official.
60. Interviewee 19 – Italian Ministry of Finance official.
61. See for example Wojcik (2016) for an overview on bail-in in the BRRD.
62. On this see for example Micossi et al. (2014).
63. Interviewee 40 – EU Council official.
64. Interviewee 28 – Finnish Financial Stability Authority official.
65. Interviewee 35 – European Central Bank official.
66. Interviewee 50 – European Stability Mechanism official.
67. Interviewee 50 – European Stability Mechanism official.
68. Interviewee 50 – European Stability Mechanism official.
69. Interviewee 48 – European Commission official.
70. Interviewee 35 – European Central Bank official.
71. Interviewee 35 – European Central Bank official.

References

Bickerton, C. J., Hodson, D., & Puetter, U. (2014). The New Intergovernmentalism: European Integration in the Post-Maastricht Era. *Journal of Common Market Studies, 53*(4), 703–722.

Binder, J., & Singh, D. (Eds.). (2016). *Bank Resolution: The New Regime*. Oxford: Oxford University Press.

Boone, P., & Johnson, S. (2011, July). Europe on the Brink. *Policy Brief,* Peterson Institute for International Economics, N°PB11–13, Washington, DC.

De Rynck, S. (2016). Banking on a Union: The Politics of Changing Eurozone Banking Supervision. *Journal of European Public Policy, 23*(1), 1–17.

Dehousse, R. (1992). Integration v. Regulation? On the Dynamics of Regulation in the European Community. *Journal of Common Market Studies, 30*(4), 383–402.

Dehousse, R. (1997). Regulation by Networks in the European Community: The Role of European Agencies. *Journal of European Public Policy, 4*(2), 246–261.

Dehousse, R. (2013). *The Politics of Delegation in the European Union*. Paris: Centre d'Etudes Européennes de Sciences Po, Cahiers européens de Sciences Po.

Epstein, D., & O'Halloran, S. (1999). *Delegating Powers: A Transaction Cost Politics Approach to Policy-Making Under Separate Powers*. Cambridge: Cambridge University Press.

EU Council. (2013, December 18). Economic and Financial Affairs, Council of the European Union. *Press Release*, Brussels.

EU Council. (2014, July 14). Press Release, *Council Adopts Rules Setting Up Single Resolution Mechanism*, Brussels.

Euractiv. (2012, September 26). *Germany, Finland, Netherlands Begin to Unravel EU Banking Union Plans*. Available Under http://www.euractiv.com/euro-finance/germans-finns-dutch-unravel-eu-p-news-515027

European Banking Authority. (2013, January 23). *Recommendation on the Development of Recovery Plans*.

European Central Bank. (2013a, May 23). *Speech* by ECB Executive Board Member Benoît Coeuré, Member of the Executive Board of the ECB, on 'The Single Resolution Mechanism: Why It Is Needed' at the ICMA Annual General Meeting and Conference 2013, Organised by the International Capital Market Association, Copenhagen.

European Central Bank. (2013b, November 6). *ECB Opinion* on the Single Resolution Mechanism.

European Commission. (2009). An EU Framework for Cross-Border Crisis Management in the Banking Sector. *Commission Communication*, COM/2009/0561 Final.

European Commission. (2010a, June 30). Enhancing Economic Policy Coordination for Stability, Growth and Jobs and Tools for Stronger EU Economic Governance. *Commission Communication*, COM(2010) 367/2 Final.

European Commission. (2010b, May 26). Communication on Bank Resolution Funds. *Commission Communication*, COM/2010/254 Final.

European Commission. (2010c, October 20). Communication on a New EU Framework for Crisis Management in the Financial Sector. *Commission Communication*, COM/2010/579 Final.

European Commission. (2012). Communication 'A Roadmap Towards a Banking Union'. *Commission Communication*, COM/ 2012/0510 Final.

European Commission. (2013a, July 10). *Commission Proposal for a 'Regulation Establishing Uniform Rules and a Uniform Procedure for the Resolution of Credit Institutions and Certain Investment Firms in the Framework of a Single Resolution Mechanism and a Single Bank Resolution Fund and Amending Regulation (EU) No 1093/2010 of the European Parliament and of the Council'.* COM(2013) 520 Final.

European Commission. (2013b, July 10). Commission Proposes Single Resolution Mechanism for the Banking Union. *Press Release.*

European Commission. (2014, March 20). European Parliament and Council Back Commission's Proposal for a Single Resolution Mechanism: A Major Step Towards Completing the Banking Union. *Press Release.*

European Parliament. (2010). European Parliament Resolution of 7 July 2010 with Recommendations to the Commission on Cross-Border Crisis Management in the Banking Sector (2010/2006(INI)).

European Parliament. (2014, January 15). *ECON Committee Letter to the Greek Presidency.*

European Union. (2012, June 29). *Euro Area Summit Statement.* Brussels.

Financial Times. (2013a, April 29). EU Split Over Plans for Bank Resolution. *Financial Times.*

Financial Times. (2013b, June 3). Brussels Bank Resolution Blueprint Sets Up Clash with Germany. *Financial Times.*

Financial Times. (2013c, November 17). Euro Bank Watchdog Attacks Unwieldy Governance.

Financial Times. (2014a, January 16). European Parliament Challenges Plan for €55bn Bank Rescue Fund. *Financial Times.*

Financial Times. (2014b, March 11). The German Veto on EU Banking Regulation. *Financial Times*, Brussels Blog.

Financial Times. (2014c, March 20). EU Reaches Deal on Final Piece of Banking Union.

Garicano, L. (2013). In Spain, the Diabolic Loop Is Alive and Well. In F. Allen, E. Carletti, & J. Gray (Eds.), *Political, Fiscal and Banking Union in the Eurozone?* Philadelphia: European University Institute and Wharton School, University of Pennsylvania.

Genschel, P., & Jachtenfuchs, M. (Eds.). (2013). *Beyond the Regulatory Polity? The European Integration of Core State Powers.* Oxford: Oxford University Press.

Genschel, P., & Jachtenfuchs, M. (2016). More Integration, Less Federation: The European Integration of Core State Powers. *Journal of European Public Policy, 23*(1), 42–59.

Goodhart, C. (2011). *The Basel Committee on Banking Supervision: A History of the Early Years 1974–1997*. Cambridge: Cambridge University Press.

Gloeckler, G., Lindner, J., & Salines, M. (2017). Explaining the Sudden Creation of a Banking Supervisor for the Euro Area. *Journal of European Public Policy, 24*(8), 1135–1153.

Gros, D. (2013). Banking Union Instead of Fiscal Union? In F. Allen, E. Carletti, & J. Grey (Eds.), *Political, Fiscal and Banking Union*. Philadelphia: European University Institute and Wharton and Wharton Financial Institutions Centre, University of Pennsylvania.

Hadjiemmanuil, C. (2015). *Bank Resolution Financing in the Banking Union* (LSE Law, Society and Economy Working Papers, 6/2015).

Howarth, D., & Quaglia, L. (2014). The Steep Road to European Banking Union: Constructing the Single Resolution Mechanism. *Journal of Common Market Studies, 52*, Annual Review 2013, 125–140.

Kelemen, R. D. (2002). The Politics of 'Eurocratic' Structure and the New European Agencies. *West European Politics, 25*(4), 93–118.

Kern, A. (2015). European Banking Union: A Legal and Institutional Analysis of the Single Supervisory Mechanism and the Single Resolution Mechanism. *European Law Review, 40*(2), 154–187.

Kudrna, Z. (2012). Cross-Border Resolution of Failed Banks in the European Union After the Crisis: Business as Usual. *Journal of Common Market Studies, 50*(2), 283–299.

Laffan, B., & Schlosser, P. (2016). Public Finances in Europe: Fortifying EU Economic Governance in the Shadow of the Crisis. *Journal of European Integration, 38*(3), Special Issue EU Policies in Times of Crisis, 237–249.

Majone, G. (1996). *Regulating Europe*. London: Routledge.

Majone, G. (2000). The Credibility Crisis of Community Regulation. *Journal of Common Market Studies, 38*(2), 273–302.

Mersch, Y. (2013, April 24). Europe's Ills Cannot Be Healed by Monetary Innovation Alone. *Financial Times*.

Messori, M., & Barucci, E. (Eds.). (2015). Towards the European Banking Union: Achievements and Open Problems, ASTRID, Passigli Editori, Florence.

Micossi, et al. (2014, May). *Bail-In Provisions in State Aid and Resolution Procedures: Are They Consistent with Systemic Stability?* (CEPS Policy Brief No. 318). Brussels.

Münchau, W. (2014, March 16). Europe Should Say No to a Flawed Banking Union. *Financial Times*.

Pissarides, C. (2014). Cyprus Finds Not All Nations Are Equal. *Financial Times*, 27 March 2013.

Pollitt, C., Bathgate, K., Caulfield, J., Smullen, A., & Talbot, C. (2001). Agency Fever? Analysis of an International Policy Fashion. *Journal of Comparative Policy Analysis: Research and Practice, 3*(3), 271–290.

Putnam, R. D. (1988). Diplomacy and Domestic Politics: The Logic of Two-Level Games. *International Organization, 42*(3), 427–460.

Quaglia, L. (2015). *Interview.* Florence School of Banking and Finance, Published on 10 November 2015 and Available Under http://fbf.eui.eu/lucia-quaglia-hints-at-a-convoluted-decision-making-process-on-banking-resolution/

Rey, H. (2013). Fiscal Union in the Eurozone? In F. Allen, E. Carletti, & J. Gray (Eds.), *Political, Fiscal and Banking Union in the Eurozone?* Philadelphia: European University Institute and Wharton School, University of Pennsylvania.

Rittberger, B., & Wonka, A. (2012). Agency Governance in the EU. *Journal of European Public Policy Series, 18*(6), 780–789.

Schäuble, W. (2013, May 12). Banking Union Must Be Built on Firm Foundations. *Financial Times.*

Schild, J. (2015, March 5–7). *Leading Together or Opposing Each Other? Germany, France and the European Banking Union.* Paper Presented for the 14th Biennial Conference of the European Union Studies Association (EUSA), Boston.

Schlosser, P. (2017). Still Looking for the Banking Union's Fiscal Backstop. In F. Allen, E. Carletti, J. Gray, & M. Gulati (Eds.), *The Changing Geography of Finance and Regulation in Europe.* Florence: European University Institute.

Schulz, M. (2014, January 20). *Letter of EP President Martin Schulz to Commission President Barroso.*

Thatcher, M. (2002). Delegation to Independent Regulatory Agencies: Pressures, Functions and Contextual Mediation. *West European Politics, 25*(1), 125–147.

Wojcik, K.-P. (2016). Bail-In in the Banking Union. *Common Market Law Review, 53*(1), 91–138.

Zavvos, G., & Kaltsouni, S. (2015). The Single Resolution Mechanism in the European Banking Union: Legal Foundation, Governance Structure and Financing. In M. Haentjens & B. Wessels (Eds.), *Research Handbook on Crisis Management in the Banking Sector.* Cheltenham: Edward Elgar Publishing Ltd.

CHAPTER 7

Findings and Interpretation

INTRODUCTION

The sovereign debt crisis that unravelled in Europe from spring 2010 to summer 2012 has been of an unprecedented magnitude. It has hit the European continent like no other crisis did since World War II. Economically, the crisis was characterised by a prolonged economic recession which, in turn, led to a sharp and continuous rise of debt levels in most euro area countries, pushing some countries to the brink of debt unsustainability. Socially, the crisis resulted in a severe increase in the euro area's unemployment levels, especially among Southern Europe's youth, and, overall, saw millions of people demonstrating against crisis measures. Politically, the crisis ushered in a rise of populism in Europe's crisis-ridden periphery but also in its centre. This phenomenon was partly fuelled by a growing anti-European sentiment which has also affected Europe's mainstream political parties. Perhaps for the first time in its history, European Union flags were burnt on Europe's streets as a sign of outright protest against its élite, the élite that had navigated the continent through the euro crisis. However, the crisis should be first and foremost regarded as an existential crisis for Europe, both for its currency and for its institutions. Indeed, the crisis' effects on the institutional evolution of EMU, and in particular on its fiscal powers, proved to be of significant and even of constitutional relevance.

This book claims that the height of the crisis management coincided with the institutionalization of a fiscal centre, understood as an incipient

© The Author(s) 2019
P. Schlosser, *Europe's New Fiscal Union*,
https://doi.org/10.1007/978-3-319-98636-4_7

and composite fiscal authority that runs across all EMU executive institutions without being embodied by any *primus inter pares*. Such a phenomenon is a watershed in EMU's development, in particular when compared to the early Maastricht compromise that saw no correspondence between the centralization of monetary policy and the centralization of fiscal powers. The emergence of such a fiscal centre was strongly conditioned and constrained by the path-dependence of the EU's past institutional modus operandi: an over-reliance on rules on the one hand and the empowerment of technocratic agencies on the other. In the absence of an EMU crisis management mechanism, the crisis not only generated its own pressure to define an adequate EU policy response, it also acted as a catalyst for the development of common central fiscal capacities, thus departing from the previous rules-based EMU. These newly-developed mechanisms and bodies were thus mostly designed as *ad hoc*, functional and stand-alone instruments. This flexible approach to delegation can be retraced to the EU leaders' conservative approach to institutional design, a perspective which leaned towards unsettled institutional solutions rather than towards permanently committing and irreversible alternatives.

Since these newly created facilities had to be operated under the political authority of EMU executive institutions, their creation triggered in turn institutional change at a more macro level. EMU executive institutions suddenly became informally empowered as those functions began to be more operational. A centralized yet fragmented fiscal centre has hence arisen in the middle of the crisis in Europe. Against the expectation of a neo-functionalist spill-over running from a monetary union to a fiscal union, the euro crisis – despite its magnitude – did however not result in the constitution of a genuine European Fiscal Union, understood in its most minimal form as a central fiscal capacity/budget and a common debt instrument (the so-called Eurobond). In other words, 'the euro crisis did not produce a dramatic Hamiltonian moment of general debt Europeanization' (Genschel and Jachtenfuchs 2016: 44). Such a stark and overt sovereignty transfer was resisted. The centralization process which unfolded has instead been guided by the functionalist mantra of 'form follows function' (Mitrany 1943: 236) and has seen the 'proliferation of flexible task-oriented organizations' (Rosamond 2000: 35) through incremental, covert and informal changes. Decentralized competences such as financial assistance, banking supervision and banking resolution were transferred to the central level and attributed to new mechanisms. By contrast, previously centralized policies, such as fiscal surveillance and liquidity provision were further strengthened and the respective mandate of their enforcer was extended.

The process was distinctive because fiscal powers were, in most cases, delegated to a series of *ad hoc* bodies operating in the shadow of EMU executive institutions, not to a single, federal actor. This centrifugal delegation pattern goes against the classic, pre-Maastricht delegation trend (Bickerton et al. 2015) which rested almost exclusively on an ever broader mandate entrusted to the Commission (and its agencies), an actor which occupied centre stage in the Community method. Instead, the European fiscal centre remains fundamentally fragmented among three key actors (and their respective agencies or bodies): the Eurogroup, the European Central Bank and the Commission. The main puzzle uncovered by this book is therefore that while a fiscal authority has been institutionalized, no political EU actor has been able to formally embody and exclusively claim this authority. EU leaders proved unable to go against the legacies of Europe's market integration pattern: an over-reliance on rules-based coordination and a preference for delegation to technocratic agencies at the expense of overt and formal institution-building. As the crisis forced EU leaders to go 'beyond the regulatory polity' and move towards 'integration by capacity-building' (Genschel and Jachtenfuchs 2013), the full extent of the absence of a central political authority underpinning EMU came to the fore.

This chapter recalls the four key moments of the fiscal centre formation, further substantiates the book's findings and interprets them in the light of established theories in order to best account for the fiscal authority's institutionalization logic.

THE CENTRALIZED FRAGMENTATION OF FISCAL POWERS IN FOUR ACTS

The euro crisis acted as 'a litmus test in terms of bringing the institutional properties of the EU to the surface' (Fabbrini 2015: xvii), thereby bringing both the EU's institutional logic and its integration dilemmas to the foreground. The sequence of centralization functions and the fragmented integration outcome informs the observer about the predicaments that the EU faces when it comes to pooling sovereignty in a 'high politics' area such as fiscal policy. At all critical junctures of the crisis, EU leaders agreed on the most minimal common liabilities to limit their fiscal commitments.

Instead of a grand crisis management design, they preferred to muddle-through in the face of uncertainty. They were thus reluctantly dragged into more fiscal integration by market pressure. This behavioural pattern led to periodic dramatization of the euro crisis as leaders were 'acting always behind the curve with everything happening at the last moment'.[1] Precisely because they were short-sighted and paralyzed by uncertainty, EU leaders showed their dependence on previous integration paths and proved unable to revert self-fulfilling expectations of a euro break-up by inspiring trust on financial markets. The ECB was hence left to assume this role.

Driven by unprecedented and overwhelming pressure, the euro crisis management did not, paradoxically, lead to an institutional 'big bang'. Instead, its sequence consisted in an incremental, gradual and additive centralization of fiscal functions to the EU centre. As the initial pressure following the Greek data falsification mounted, the EU first responded with a reinforcement of its rules-based fiscal regime to restore its credibility and prevent a build-up of future crises: 'member states tried to contain these spill-overs by regulation only, namely by tightening and extending surveillance' (Schelkle 2013: 118). These politically somewhat costless regulatory reforms, however, did not suffice to convince markets of EU leaders' readiness to stand behind their currency. Even worse, it fuelled market pressure further as it became obvious that EMU Member States would stick to the minimalistic spirit of the 'no-bail out clause' which had increased the likelihood of a Greek default. Therefore, in a second step, EU governments broke away from this initial logic. Given the existential threat that the sovereign debt crisis embodied as it began its contagion, money was put on the table in the form of financial assistance mechanisms. This proved to be a critical juncture in the euro crisis management and marked the moment when EU leaders truly internalized the full extent of the crisis.

However, the setting-up of financial mechanisms proved insufficient to calm down markets. In a third step, EU leaders thus committed to address a salient dimension of the crisis that was kept 'under the carpet' since the start of the Greek crisis: they recognised that Europe's banking system was fragile and should be addressed head-on through a sounder regime of supervision and resolution. The decision to institute this new regime, the Banking Union, was a crucial centralization step. Its aim was to anticipate and prevent future deteriorations in the banking sector's health and at associating the private banking sector to the recapitalization of banks in the recognition that governments did not have endless bail-out resources. A new banking resolution regime was hence instituted, centred around a new agency, the Single Resolution Board, as well as a common resolution fund, financed by a levy on banks. Yet, here too, the promise of a Banking Union did not lead to a decrease of market pressure on Southern European bonds and on the euro as a currency. The fourth decisive step, the ECB's decision to take on the role of lender of last resort, fulfilled this function. ECB President Mario Draghi's 'whatever it takes' speech of July 2012 coupled with the announcement, a few weeks later, of the creation of a new liquidity facility, the Outright Monetary Transactions instrument, constituted the final stage of euro crisis management and, as a corollary, of the institutionalization of a fiscal authority.

Quite ironically, as market panic started unravelling in March 2010, the first prominent and decisive reaction of the European leaders to the euro crisis was to set up a Task Force. The so-called Task Force Van Rompuy came up with the recommendation to strengthen the fiscal rules and enhance sanctions for fiscal 'doves'. These measures were identified as responding to the priority of the moment: restoring the credibility of the central fiscal rules and preventing any further violation of the rules-based fiscal regime. These principles would later be enshrined in the so-called 6 Pack, Fiscal Compact and the 2 Pack which led to the reinforcement, expansion and vertical institutionalization of a fiscal surveillance regime in Europe. Tougher fiscal rules did not, however, solve the crisis. Indeed it possibly made the crisis even worse as negotiations occurred against the background of mounting market pressure on Greek bond markets and, more crucially, of rising contagion to other Mediterranean countries and Ireland. It was only when governments recognized that Greece risked defaulting that they also realized – in May 2010 following the downgrade of Greek bonds to junk status – that moral posturing would not be sufficient to solve the crisis and that money had to be committed to extinguish the fire. This moment proved to be a watershed in the transition from a crisis management based on integration by rules to one based on integration by capacity-building.

The agreement on the mobilization of public money (in various forms, be it through guarantees or loans) constituted the second key step in the euro crisis management sequence and, as a corollary, in the institutionalization of a fiscal authority. This phase followed an experimental, trial-and-error dynamic. In a first period, new instruments were created and operated under the auspices of the Commission. This was the case of the Greek

Loan Facility (GLF) and the European Financial Stabilization Mechanism (EFSM). In a second step, it was however acknowledged that large-scale mechanisms – the so-called big bazookas – were needed to address the crisis. The creation of these large-scale mechanisms, namely the European Financial Stability Facility (EFSF), later the European Stability Mechanism (ESM), was a critical juncture in the constitution of a European fiscal centre. After more than a year and a half of negotiations on its design, the ultimate ESM Treaty was officially signed in February 2012. The Mechanism is a 500 bn euros firewall and represents the largest fund ever set up globally since the International Monetary Fund's creation in Bretton Woods in 1944. Its creation coincided with a very marked empowerment of the Eurogroup, at the expense of the Commission. The ESM thus operates under the authority of the Eurogroup, an informal discussion body which experienced a creeping task expansion and an ultimate conversion into an executive EMU body.

However, despite the huge financial capacity of these new mechanisms, crisis pressure persisted – and more fiscal integration was needed. After a long phase of muddling-through which lasted until spring 2012 governments realized that more common functions had to be set up. This mounting realisation ran in parallel on the one hand to a growing 'recognition that fiscal resources were not sufficient to solve the crisis'[2] and, on the other hand, to a rising awareness that a diabolic bank-sovereign loop was at play. The loop resided in a self-reinforcing dynamic between (mostly) Southern sovereigns and their domestic banks. The problem was that banks had accumulated increased levels of domestic debt on their balance sheet, thereby increasing the mutual dependence between the government and themselves. As the credit worthiness of the Southern sovereigns deteriorated, banks had weakened the financial ability of the sovereign to resolve them. The most typical illustration of this fiscal snow-ball effect was the case of Spain. The latter triggered the realization that a Banking Union with a central banking supervision and a central banking resolution regime would be needed to break this link. As a result, banking supervision and resolution became centralized. However, following a past trend of regulatory state building, the Banking Union mostly relied on the delegation to technocratic agencies (the Single Supervisory Mechanism and the Single Resolution Board) and on a dense set of rules, in particular the complex regime on bail-in (as laid down in the Bank Recovery and Resolution Directive) which is meant to ensure that the lion's share of the centralized bank resolution regime will be borne by private creditors (given the dire straits of the sovereign's public finances). The advent of the Banking Union marked the third sequence of the crisis which centred around the objective of restoring market discipline in the banking sector given that mere money could not restore the stability of the banking system.

Yet again, the new regime did however not solve once and for all the existential crisis hovering over the euro. A new centralization step appeared to be necessary to achieve this. The fourth key step came with the taking-over, by the ECB, of EMU's function of lender of last resort in the summer 2012. This consisted in the famous Mario Draghi speech of July 2012 and its celebrated line ('within its mandate, the ECB will do whatever it takes to save the euro, and believe me it will be enough') and in the OMT, an instrument which, under certain conditions, can be activated to help reduce market pressure on sovereign bond markets. This task expansion process can be summarized as the slow and fairly controversial development of a role unforeseen by the Maastricht Treaty. The ECB expanded its mandate from sole price stability to also include financial stability. Driven by the inactivity of governments and a high and persisting pressure on Southern countries' bond markets, the ECB was implicitly attributed the task of 'saving the euro' by temporarily extending its function to lending of last resort.

EMU'S POST-CRISIS FISCAL TRINITY

Beyond this vertical redefinition of powers between the EU's centre and its periphery, the crisis also affected the horizontal redistribution of powers among executive institutions. EU governments mutualized new fiscal powers without reverting to a constitutional settlement. The EU's joint-decision trap (Scharpf 1988) and its traditional tendency to end up in an institutional gridlock have been circumvented. This occurred through an informal stretching of existing executive institutions' mandate (the Eurogroup, the ECB and the Commission), a reliance on *ad hoc* international treaties that allowed EMU participating countries to go beyond the balance provided by the EU Treaty, and the delegation of residual and unsettled powers of last resort to the European Central Bank. This pattern of fiscal integration was sustainable over those years because it could be legitimated by the necessity of swift crisis management, i.e. by a 'Schmittian state of exception' (Joerges 2012; Fabbrini 2015).

From a formal perspective, the nature of the powers created is however ambiguous. The pressure-led layering of those new fiscal functions has resulted in an institutional patchwork. This complex outcome has been mainly driven by the practice of assigning the newly created functions to newly created bodies or agencies, without formalizing those bodies' political and hierarchical subordination. Instead of a classic fiscal authority, a trinity of fiscal actors has emerged, with *no primus inter pares* able to exclusively claim Europe's fiscal authority. While there is some unease on the side of the ECB to formally assume that the SSM is an ECB instrument, the institutional subordinations of the SRB and of the ESM for example appear to be only informal. In other words, as in Maastricht, post-crisis EMU is still characterised by an ambiguous division of its executive. This elusive division of labour has been recognised by ECB Board Member Benoît Coeuré in a 2012 speech in which he argues that: 'the euro is a currency with a state – but it's a state whose branches of government are not yet clearly defined. The ECB is part of the construction of Economic and Monetary Union, with a very clear but very limited mandate.[3] The other parts – I am thinking in particular of the delineation between the Commission and the Council – still require clarification' (Coeuré 2012: 7). This lack of institutional settlement has led to an inter-institutional rivalry among EMU's key executive actors and in particular between the Eurogroup and the European Commission.

In Maastricht, the ECB was constituted as a 'narrow ECB – a central bank shirking basic banking functions, such as lender of last resort to financial markets and the payments system, and supervision and regulation of banking markets' (Folkerts-Landau and Garber 1992: 35). It is worth recalling that much of the initial debate on the institutional design of EMU was monopolized by the question of central bank independence, moral hazard risks and the notion that what mattered most for the sustainability of the currency was the credibility of its issuing central bank. Besides the constitutional rules protecting the ECB's independence, the euro's stability was thus to be sustained entirely by the credibility of the ECB's monetary policy. As I have demonstrated in Chap. 5, the strong ideological foundation of the ECB can to a large extent be explained by the activist central bankers which had been tasked with determining the institutional features of the ECB, essentially disregarding the political dimension of embedding the ECB in a wider polity. As a result, the ECB became 'disembedded' (Majone 2014) from the overall EMU polity.

Accordingly, the first years of existence of the ECB were marked by a radical self-interpretation of its independence mandate that caused the Frankfurt institution to adopt a tough stance against other EU institutions – as illustrated in the OLAF case (as I have shown in Chap. 5) – from which the ECB wanted to distinguish itself. A similar dismissive approach to institutional embeddedness was also pursued in what regards the ECB's relationship with the Eurogroup, of which the Bank has been for long distrustful. The euro crisis, however, transformed the ECB. Strengthened by a generally successful track record of crisis management (if one abstracts from a few puzzling interest rate hikes in the middle of the crisis in 2011), the ECB emerges as a clear institutional winner of the euro crisis. Mostly because it was the institution that saved the euro but also because its focus on the euro area allowed it to be more decisive than the Commission or the European Council. As an interviewee recalls: 'they say that in the 1960s the ECJ stepped up to fill a vacuum, well during the euro crisis the ECB filled the vacuum of 'decision-makability''.[4] Indeed, the European Central Bank has extended its mandate to banking supervision and temporarily fulfilled a role of lender of last resort that it fiercely resisted to accept before the crisis. Its activities are now supported by an independent banking supervision/micro-prudential authority, the Single Supervisory Mechanism and by a consultative macro-prudential body, the European Systemic Risk Board (ESRB). In contrast to the narrow ECB envisaged and implemented in Maastricht, Europe's post-crisis central bank has turned into a 'thick ECB'.

The Eurogroup, as this book recalled, was created in 1997 as an informal body operating outside of the Maastricht Treaty of which it was absent. This came to the dismay of the French delegation which was supporting the creation of a *gouvernement économique* as a counter-weight to the ECB. The body became formally recognised with the Lisbon Treaty but was confined to a Protocol that insists on its deliberative and informal features. In line with its quasi-constitutionalization function, the crisis has genuinely institutionalized the Eurogroup. From an *ad hoc*, informal and deliberative body, the Eurogroup has become an EMU executive and decision-making institution, overseeing the world's largest financial firewall, the ESM. A key reason for the Eurogroup's institutionalization has been its membership basis which was restricted from the start to EMU countries. This made the Eurogroup a convenient, effective and agile institutional structure to coordinate and decide on crisis management measures. It even seems like the Eurogroup – despite being still *de jure* an informal, non-decision body – has substituted the ECOFIN in the central operation of EMU, in only two decades of existence. Its contemporary relevance is *a fortiori* illustrated by the eagerness of Poland and the UK to attend the Eurogroup meetings despite being non-euro area countries.

While the Eurogroup operates under the leadership of the European Council, it has acquired decision-making powers as well as an operational autonomy. This can be to a large extent explained by the institutional arsenal that the Eurogroup is now able to mobilize. A corollary of its development was indeed the institutionalization of its subgroup and preparatory group, the Euro Working Group. But the crucial contribution to its conversion was the creation of the € 500 bn strong ESM, which falls under its authority. Both developments have indeed marked the latest step of a long institutionalization process whose ultimate outcome has been to convert the Eurogroup from a deliberative informal body into the executive arm of EMU. The Eurogroup's empowerment remains however constrained by unanimity[5] and to a lesser extent, by its informal character. One could speculate that without these inhibiting features, the Eurogroup may have taken even more functions upon itself and could have become EMU's fiscal *primus inter pares*.

In sharp denial of the intergovernmental twist that Maastricht Treaty designers gave to EMU, the Commission has always cherished the objective of becoming EMU's uncontested executive actor. Yet, the crisis revealed that the Commission had both 'limited financial and legitimacy resources available' (Majone 2002: 375). It is undeniable that with the euro crisis, the institution has been further empowered in both means and mandate to monitor and enforce fiscal surveillance in the European Union and in particular in the euro area. Yet, in line with its narrow mandate on EMU, the Commission has been empowered along the lines of its previous delegations: fiscal surveillance and single market enforcement. A corollary effect of the strengthening of central rules was that the Commission has been further endowed with ensuring on the one hand the monitoring and compliance of the SGP and on the other, at least in theory, in enforcing sanctions on governments. The Brussels institution has thus undoubtedly layered new competences but obtained only path-dependent tasks that were in line with the role attributed to the institution in Maastricht and thereafter, namely: the role of a monitoring and compliance watchdog. However, given the density, complexity and ambiguity of the new fiscal framework, it has also increased, intentionally or unintentionally, its discretion. Yet, while the Commission has indeed extended its monitoring and controlling power over national budgets (Schlosser 2015), becoming as some have put it, the 'unexpected winner of the crisis' (Bauer and

Becker 2014), it still does not retain the final word on the enforcement of the SGP as the Treaty does not allow for automatic sanctions on EMU governments.

Moreover, when money was involved, the Commission was dismissed as an institutional alternative. Despite its operation of the small EFSM, it has been kept at 'arms' length' (Hodson 2013) of the operation of any large-scale crisis management mechanisms, the EFSF and the ESM being cases in point. Interviewed policy-makers suggested that, besides the legal reasons lying in the way of the Commission performing such tasks, its lack of empowerment on those new EMU capacities has to do with legitimacy and trust. As interviewees put it: the Commission 'can't do that'[6]; 'it is not legitimated in the eyes of Member States[7] to manage 'Other People's Money (OPM)[8]; 'we didn't trust the Commission".[9] As a result, when it comes to the provision of money, the Commission has acquired Secretariat-like functions which depart from its strong role as guardian of the single market. Such dividing line between a regulatory function and a capacity management function can also be found when assessing the Commission's role in the Single Resolution Mechanism (SRM). Through its role in clearing state aid decisions, the Commission keeps a foot in the door of banking resolution decisions. However, it has been kept at arms' length of the Single Resolution Fund.

COMPETING AND COMPLEMENTARY THEORETICAL INTERPRETATIONS

The institutionalization of a centralized yet fragmented fiscal authority in Europe lends itself to several theoretical interpretations. Yet, in line with the wider recognition that 'the processes of European integration are just too complex to be captured by a single theoretical prospectus' (Rosamond 2000: 7), I argue that no European integration theory helps to account fully and on its own for the phenomenon observed. I find that a blend of functionalism and of a more recent contribution on the dynamics of the European integration of core state powers by Genschel and Jachtenfuchs (2013, 2016) provide the closest account of the convoluted institutionalization trajectory taken by the fiscal authority over the crisis years. Distinctively, the study of the euro crisis period has revealed that the two most classic interpretation models of European integration showed their limits in accounting for the centre formation of a fiscal authority. This is largely due to the pluralist features of both neo-functionalism and liberal intergovernmentalist approaches which prove to be less helpful when applied to the integration of core state powers.

The two classic theories of European integration, i.e. neo-functionalism and intergovernmentalism, exhibit some complementarity in framing the crisis management context and thus have a value in guiding process-tracing. Several mechanisms identified by neo-functionalism have played a role during the euro crisis. The latter has indeed acted, as was reported, as a catalyst for incremental change and for the generation of new techno-cratic solutions. This goes in line with the vision of European integration incarnated by Jean Monnet and theorised by the early neo-functionalist Ernst Haas (1958). Central in the neo-functionalist model is the notion of spill-over which has been defined by Lindberg (1963: 10) as 'a situation in which a given action, related to a specific goal, creates a situation in which the original goal can be assured only by taking further actions, which in turn create a further condition and a need for more action and so forth'.

The euro proved indeed to be a policy instrument that would drive integration forward because of the functional linkages that it would imply: the crisis revealed the real degree of interdependence that countries sharing a common currency were exposed to. A neo-functionalist frame of the euro crisis generally articulates how a pressure to act leads to an expansive and incremental drive to fill gaps because of 'functional dissonances' (Niemann and Ioannou 2015: 212) in governance. This narrative is in particular appealing because it provided 'the dominant political discourse' (Niemann and Ioannou 2015: 204) throughout the crisis period. Based on this definition, one could for example claim that the move from a mon-etary union to a banking union was an instance of a functional spill-over at play. Moreover the new neo-functionalist frame provided by Ferguson et al. (2001) provides a useful insight in the dynamics of (dense) rule cre-ation and interpretation that has occurred in fiscal surveillance and which has resulted in an enhanced discretion of the Commission in this domain. However the most obvious limitation of a neo-functionalist account of the analysed case is 'that decision-makers have not yet agreed on a fully fledged fiscal union' (Niemann and Ioannou 2015: 213), against the expectation of the theory.

Furthermore, there are several dimensions on which neo-functionalism proves to be problematic in its explanatory foundations. The first aspect relates to 'political agency' (Rosamond 2000: 51). In the original neo-functionalist model, the impetus for integration is indeed provided by a plurality of actors, 'the economic technician, the planner, the innovating industrialist and trade unionist advanced the movement not the politician [...]' (Haas 1958: xix; Rosamond 2000: 51). The scope of the initial theory is thus constrained to economic or even industrial actors. This exhibits a crucial feature of neo-functionalism, namely that its logic is confined to the realm of 'low politics'. The dynamics it describes exploit the 'inherent linkages of tasks' (Nye 1971: 200) between industrial sectors as part of *economic* integration. In the examined instance, the fiscal area – an instance of *political* integration – the prime actors are however not private, they are public and consist mainly of statesmen, cabinet ministers and bureaucrats. It is recognised that the new EMU's impact on business is difficult to foresee as 'the effects are complex, indirect and hard to predict' (Genschel and Jachtenfuchs 2013: 51). As a result of this, business lobbying tends to be 'muted' (Genschel and Jachtenfuchs 2013: 51; Moravcsik and Schimmelfennig 2009: 76).

A related, crucial feature of neo-functionalism is the reliance on transnational actors to drive integration. The theory expects that as integration proceeds, sectors will 'transfer their loyalties' to the EU level as they 'seek the most effective route for the fulfilment of their material interests' (Rosamond 2000: 52). However, this analysis showed that transnational interest groups did not play a major role in advocating and shaping the design of the new fiscal centre. Some illustrative evidence of industry actions to safeguard the euro has been gathered by Niemann and Ioannou (2015: 205), mainly in the form of general communication initiatives such as joint-declarations or policy statements. Yet, if anything, this evidence points more at portraying the industry's role as a reactive agent attempting to avoid a 'spill-back' (Schmitter 2003; Vilpišauskas 2013) of integration rather than a proactive agent driving the trajectory of integration as envisaged by neo-functionalism. To be sure, financial markets played a crucial role during the crisis in exerting pressure, but as Niemann and Ioannou recognise themselves, they haven't been 'organized as a unitary actor' (2015: 206) which casts doubts on the exact agency at play. No clear evidence could be found on the assumed aggregation and intermediation function of markets' preferences through transnational actors so cherished by neo-functionalists.

The second problematic dimension in the neo-functionalist model is the central role it attributes to a 'high authority without the distracting baggage of national interests to oversee the integration' and which is given 'the ability to act as a sponsor of further integration' (Rosamond 2000:

51). While neo-functionalism may be of some help in understanding the centralization which occurred during the euro crisis, it does not explain the fragmentation logic and the centrifugal trajectory of fiscal integration. In fact it assumes that new central powers will be attributed to and concentrated in the European Commission. Yet, in practice, those powers were attributed to the Commission, the Eurogroup and the ECB both directly and through a myriad of intergovernmental bodies and supranational agencies, thereby contradicting the expectation of a concentration of powers in the hands of a single, supranational actor. At a minimum, the neo-functionalist model should be updated to accommodate for the coronation of the ECB as the new supranational actor dragging EMU integration compared to the Commission's more limited empowerment that was also constrained in scope to regulatory prerogatives. Lastly, being actor-bound, neo-functionalism has a hard time to provide a rationale for the system-wide development of EMU's fiscal pillar during the euro crisis. It does not help to explain the pattern of fiscal centre formation observed as well as the largely inefficient institutional patchwork that has emerged from the euro crisis. It can thus be admitted that functional pressures played a key role in the advent of a fiscal authority at the EU level. But this does not imply that the neo-functionalist narrative has a high explanatory value of the instance analyzed.

The second classic of European integration, intergovernmentalism (Hoffmann 1966; Moravcsik 1998), assumes instead that national governments will always have the last word on the EU integration trajectory, in line with the 'obstinate' behaviour of Charles De Gaulle in the 1960s which ushered in the Luxemburg compromise, i.e. a veto right on matters of high state interest. In the intergovernmental model, 'national governments define and control the terms and the conditions of the EU's functioning, through their periodical Inter-Governmental Conferences (IGCs) and through the regular action of formal (the Council), and for a long time informal (the European Council) intergovernmental institutions which, since the beginning of the integration process, have supervised and steered the latter' (Fabbrini 2015: 127). This type of agency is in particular expected to be at play in domains of 'high politics' (Hoffmann 1966: 865), conceptualized as an 'autonomous sphere of political activity'. In other words, intergovernmentalism assumes a 'continued centrality of nation-states' as well as the 'enduring qualities of statehood' (Rosamond 2000: 75–77). *Prima facie* the euro crisis management pattern which consisted in a high frequency of long European Council meetings seems to lend support to this set of assumptions. The crisis has been portrayed as the heydays of the European Council, which insured its institutional domination on the crucial crisis management measures (Puetter 2012). Moreover, because of its realist focus on Member States interests, the intergovernmental approach logically implies that in an area of 'high politics' which is governed by unanimity, a stalemate and joint-decision traps are likely to emerge. Rooted in realism and in the expectation that in the end, any integration decision will be in line with the interest of key European Member States, i.e. Germany, France and the UK in the case of liberal intergovernmentalism (Moravcsik 1998; Moravcsik and Schimmelfennig 2009), intergovernmentalism helps indeed explain the political practice of slow, perpetual and late-night bargaining during the crisis.

However, if one ignores for a moment the symbolism of those meetings and of the dramatic declarations announced thereafter, one can recognize that in the end the euro crisis was solved by the construction of a fiscal centre which is further eroding the fiscal autonomy of Member States. On several instances, ways out of the joint-decision trap have been found (Kudrna 2016; Laffan and Schlosser 2016). Member States, imprisoned in a 'high politics' area, had to accept policy choices that limited their sovereignty further. Pressed by the crisis, EU leaders had at times to commit both intentionally and unintentionally to delegate and centralize instruments which ran against their own interests, such as on fiscal surveillance where the Commission has been empowered and where its newly acquired discretion escapes the control of Member States. Similarly, the advent of a centralized supervision and resolution regime played against the interests of Germany's, France's and the UK's banking sectors (considerably reducing their lobbying power), and yet, liberal intergovernmentalism postulates that European integration is shaped by aligned domestic business interests in those three countries.

More generally, 'the construction of a centralized policy-making regime, regulated by automatic rules, does not fit easily with the intergovernmental assumption that the EU is based on member state governments' will and legitimacy' (Fabbrini 2015: 151). During the crisis, Member States also showed their inability to solve the crisis on their own; they had instead to rely on the supranational European Central Bank to solve it. In other words, the European Council did not control the process of integration at all stages during the euro crisis. Intergovernmentalism, lastly, does hence not explain the behavioural pattern of the ECB during the crisis. The ECB has indeed acquired substantial powers which *de facto* have been taken away from governments. The ECB thus did not act like the agent of governments, i.e. under their control and watch, one could argue that it acted like a principal, supporting the claim that portrays the EU as a multi-principal polity (Dehousse 2013). The sequence of events that led to the centralization of a fiscal authority hence appears to be based on a more complex set of factors.

Departing from the rather static and punctuated logic of intergovernmentalism, *new intergovernmentalism* assumes that states' 'interactions have gone far beyond the narrow confines of intergovernmental conferences (IGCs)' (Bickerton et al. 2015: 705). This literature thus attempts to address European integration's most contemporary paradox of a 'seemingly unrelenting expansion in the scope of European Union activity' yet 'without supranationalism' (Bickerton et al. 2015: 703). A key pillar of their approach is hence the declining role of supranational actors, 'whose relative importance in determining the character and direction of the integration process has been in question ever since Maastricht' (Bickerton et al. 2015: 706). As a result of this, a post-Maastricht delegation trend occurred towards what they term 'de novo bodies', i.e. 'newly created institutions that often enjoy considerable autonomy by way of executive or legislative power and have a degree of control over their own resources. However they fulfil functions that could have been delegated to the Commission and tend to contain mechanisms for Member State representation as part of their governance structure' (Bickerton et al. 2015: 705). In their view, the 'ECB, the ESM, the EEAS and numerous regulatory and executive agencies' constitute 'de novo bodies'. Their constitution comes at the expense of the 'empowerment of traditional supranational actors' (Bickerton et al. 2015: 713). This disempowerment, in particular of the Commission, can *a contrario,* also be observed in the 'marked proliferation of EU agencies since 1992', which has 'increased from three in 1993 to 32 by 2012' (Bickerton et al. 2015: 713). Those new institutional dynamics are attributed to a change in political economy and in preference formation with the role of élites and the fact that Western democracies are facing 'a growing disenchantment with representative politics' (Bickerton et al. 2015: 710) playing a crucial variable. In the new intergovernmentalist account, this explains the emergence of a new dynamic of constant deliberation and consensus-seeking, namely 'deliberative intergovernmentalism' (Bickerton et al. 2015: 711; Puetter 2012).

New intergovernmentalism's analytical undertaking resonates quite strongly with the centralized fragmentation of powers that this book has been getting to grips with. Similarly, its functionalist assumption that the EU 'is in a state of disequilibrium' (Bickerton et al. 2015: 716) which makes it a central 'property of the post-Maastricht phase and opens up fundamental questions about the durability of European intergovernmentalism as things stand' (Bickerton et al. 2015: 717) is in line with the findings of this book. It is also helpful when it states that 'policy-making has developed informally' (Bickerton et al. 2015: 717). New intergovernmentalism seems however incomplete both in its descriptive and explanatory account of contemporary European integration pattern. What is for example inconsistent in this model is that the delegation of powers to the ECB is not accounted for as a supranational delegation. This severely undermines their intergovernmentalist claim that post-Maastricht 'integration has taken place in the absence of supranationalism' (Bickerton et al. 2015: 717).

Yet, supranational actors have been empowered by the Banking Union whose general advent is not explained by *new intergovernmentalism*. Moreover, the claim made by this new literature that 'supranational actors are not hard-wired to seek ever-closer union' (Bickerton et al. 2015: 712), did not find supportive evidence in this analysis. On the contrary, the Commission attempted on several instances (EFSF, SRB) to acquire the operation of new mechanisms and still advocates the integration of ad hoc instruments created outside of EU law (ESM and Fiscal Compact) into the EU legal framework which has always been more favourable to the Commission's institutional interests. Lastly, what is unclear in the *new intergovernmentalism* model is why Member States decided to empower existing supranational actors with some tasks and new bodies with other tasks. The model seems indeed to assume that all policy tasks are of similar typology and does not distinguish between agenda-setting, enforcement or discretionary tasks for example.

Neo-functionalism, intergovernmentalism and new intergovernmentalism shed a useful light on the institutionalization of a fiscal authority during the crisis. However, I found their predictions to be too contained to the emergence of formal and clearly delineated powers. This goes against the untidy pattern of centre formation observed during the euro crisis. Quite unexpectedly, the early functionalism of Mitrany (1943) identified – around 70 years ago – crucial integration patterns and features that have been observed when the euro crisis unfolded.

The basic premise of functionalism is that the institutional forms taken by international cooperation should derive from utilitarian social and economic needs, not from constitutional settlements. In this model, international integration unfolds in a dynamic process where 'every function (is) left to generate others gradually, like the functional subdivision of organic cells; and in every case the appropriate authority (is) left to grow and develop out of actual performance' (Mitrany 1943: 21). A first key feature of functionalism is its depoliticized dimension: 'it is a central view of the functional approach that such an authority is not essential for our greatest and real immediate needs' (Mitrany 1943: 37). Instead, functionalism can strive in the absence of a political authority as it is the function itself that determines the body: 'the function, one might say, determines the executive instrument suitable for its proper activity, and by the same process, provides a need for the reform of that instrument at every stage' (Mitrany 1943: 35).

Another central element of functionalism according to Mitrany is the fact that the scope of the institutional arrangement rests on living functional needs: 'functional arrangements have the virtue of technical self-determination, one of the main reasons which makes them more readily acceptable. The nature of each function tells of itself the scope and power needed for its effective performance' (Mitrany 1948: 358). In other words, functionalism should be seen as 'a complete reconstruction of governmental techniques' (Mitrany 1975: 99). In line with the 'whole trend of modern government' (Mitrany 1948: 358) of which 'administration and administrative law' would be its 'characteristic tools' (Mitrany 1948: 358). As a result of this, a whole new and flexible system of *ad hoc* agencies would thus emerge. Functionalism would hence foresee 'a proliferation of flexible task-oriented organizations as the means to address the priorities dictated by human need' (Rosamond 2000: 35). Taken together, this would constitute a complex system made up of 'a cobweb of diverse and overlapping institutions of governance, differing in form as functions varied' (Rosamond 2000: 35).

A third characteristic of functionalism is that constitutional rules do not resist to developments responding to functional needs. Retracing the advent of a post-war modern government, Mitrany was strongly influenced by the *New Deal*, which he referred to as 'a great constitutional transformation' which took place 'without any changes in the Constitution' (Mitrany 1943: 27). Even in existing federations, this force is not hampered by constitutional rules: 'in times of crisis, these collective doings were expanded not by changing federal arrangements but rather by circumventing them. In no case was there any deliberate change in the formal gradation of power; the federal governments took upon themselves many new tasks with tacit national consent, and thus acquired new power by functional accretion, not by constitutional revision' (Mitrany 1948: 355). A last prominent feature of functionalism is its flexibility as to the participating countries, allowing a way around the 'obstinate problem of equal sovereignty' (Mitrany 1948: 358). Indeed, 'in this approach it is not a matter of surrendering sovereignty, but merely of pooling so much of it as may be needed for the joint-performance of the particular task' (Mitrany 1948: 358). Therefore, 'a scheme started by a few countries […] could later be broadened to include belated members, or reduced to let reluctant ones drop out. Moreover, they can vary in their membership, countries could take part in some schemes and perhaps not in others, whereas in any political arrangement such divided choice would obviously not be tolerable' (Mitrany 1948: 357–358).

These conceptual characterisations fit very closely to the fiscal integration pattern that occurred during the euro crisis. The overall functionalist dynamics canvassed by Mitrany are in line with this book's overall narrative of a centralized fragmentation of fiscal powers. The pragmatic or even 'spiritless' (Mitrany 1943: 57) approach that underpinned institution-building strove to break away from the rigidities provided by constitutional rules. The logical consequence of this approach was the creation of ad hoc, flexible and functionally-segmented bodies and agencies. Together they constituted an institutional patchwork. In the absence of an EMU political authority, the institutional redesign of EMU was indeed and at the heart a spiritless process where 'form follow(ed) function' (Rosamond 2000: 33) and where the 'design of institutional solutions' was an 'open minded and flexible process' (Rosamond 2000: 34).

This book has found that the active institutional engineering of a fiscal centre did not derive from a grand design but from the imperatives of the immediate moment: most of the new elements were 'agreed by exhausted leaders in the darkness of the night'.[10] The crisis' intensity and the resulting functional need to act, on an *ad hoc* and experimental basis, to safeguard the euro led to a series of incremental reforms. Since every manifestation of the crisis was dealt with separately and without any anticipation of the next step, functionalism prevailed over other guiding models. Like is rather typical of crisis times, leaders had an inability to anticipate the next manifestation of the crisis: 'we were not able to predict the sequence of events of the crisis; that has been the case all the time[11]'. As it anecdotally recalled in a quote from a fictional character featuring in an HBO TV Series,[12] decision-makers lack certainty when they decide on crisis management. What is specific to the euro crisis management case is that they also showed an inability to learn from their recurring shot-termist approach as the crisis persisted and the pattern of endless and frequent Council meetings repeated itself.

Overall, the institutional vacuum of EMU was thus filled with the progressive layering of new central functions which were uploaded to the central EU level but also were concomitantly fragmented among several executive actors. Informal governance prospered too during the crisis. Tuori (2012) has highlighted that 'institutional and legislative fragmentation belong to the major unintended, constitutionally relevant consequences of incrementalist European reactions to the fiscal crisis. New official, semi-official and unofficial bodies have abounded; some of them with formal decision-making powers, others without any formal competence but still exercising considerable influence.' (Tuori 2012: 46). Indeed, all those newly centralized fiscal competences were not attributed to a single fiscal and political authority: 'there has been a division of labour'[13] along functional lines, a division which remains however politically and constitutionally unsettled among the Commission, the Eurogroup, the ECB and their satellite agencies or bodies (e.g. SRB, SSM, ESM).

Moreover, although it is seldom accounted for in those terms, the euro crisis should be interpreted as a constitutional moment – in line with Mitrany's *New Deal* characterisation. The euro crisis should indeed be regarded as the largest post-Maastricht European integration history-making moment, yet one that did not involve an Inter-Governmental Conference. Numerous new rules have been adopted that constrain further the sovereignty of EMU member states, new instruments, mechanisms and bodies have been designed – some of them through international treaties – while existing institutions have been empowered, redirected to new purposes or created from scratch. As crisis management progressed, the extent of the vertical redistribution of powers between the EU centre and Member States on the one hand and of the horizontal redistribution of powers among EMU executive actors became substantial. Yet, the degree of this centralization outranks the most ambitious proposals discussed or agreed during past Treaty-making moments. As an interviewee pointed out: 'in 5–6 years we have had more integration than in the last 25 years, we have done things which in the old days would have required

Treaty change and years of negotiations'.[14] Overall, the Treaty rules did however not prevent this *de facto* constitutional changes to occur. Liberties have been taken with the Treaty where EU leaders deemed it necessary to act as the cases of the no-bail out clause circumvention or of both the Fiscal Compact and the ESM – enshrined outside of the EU order – testify. This malleability of EU law has been a cause for concern, leading notably Tuori (2012: 1) to frame the euro crisis also as a 'constitutional crisis'. In some way, the euro crisis thus functionally complemented the Maastricht Treaty's imbalanced constitutional settlement but also contradicted its inherent compromise.

Lastly, the fragmentation of fiscal powers was partly fuelled by the specific necessity of euro participating Member States – as opposed to 'outs' – to devise their own arrangements and to empower their own institutions, in particular the Eurogroup and the Euro Working Group, which as this book has documented, have become key actors in the new fiscal centre. This echoes a convenient feature of functionalism mentioned above, namely the fact that cooperation arrangements 'can vary in their membership' (Mitrany 1948: 357). Often pressured by non-euro participating countries to exclude common EU solutions, EMU participating member states had to revert during the crisis to more flexible arrangements where additional sovereignty could be shared, either through an existing provision that allowed for this (the Lisbon Treaty's article 136) or through the use of outside Treaty frameworks.

There is something remarkable about applying a functionalist frame to the instance at hand. While functionalism is quite illuminating in providing an account of the logic and of the dynamics of the fiscal centre formation process, it does so almost in complete contradiction with its fundamental (explicit or implicit) assumptions. Indeed, functionalism rests on the utilitarian assumption that functional cooperation, because it is shaped by needs, will constitute individually rational and efficient solutions which will also lead to a welfare-enhancing outcome. Functionalism was originally a model that was typically applied to the realm of 'low politics'. In Mitrany's mind for example, functional solutions would be good technical solutions if applied to the cross-border management of communication networks (e.g. railways, rivers, etc). However, in the case of the euro crisis individually efficient solutions have accumulated into a collective conundrum. The new fragmented patchwork made up of ad hoc bodies, dense and complex rules and informal executive empowerment appears uncertain in its functioning and enforcement capabilities. It can thus be argued that the institutional outcome reached is functionally inefficient. Instead, the new system was the result, one could argue, of political efficiency: it was as much as governments agreed to pool. Yet, the political agency dimension is precisely another aspect that is unspecified in the functionalist model. While law is present, politics is somehow absent from it. And yet, political actors have been the agents implementing – consciously or unconsciously – this functionalist agenda. Complementing Mitrany's analysis, Genschel and Jachtenfuchs (2013, 2016) provide a helpful frame to decipher the politics at play in this instance.

INTEGRATING CORE STATE POWERS AND MOVING FROM REGULATION TO CAPACITY-BUILDING

The dynamics that pertain to the post-Maastricht delegation of powers in 'high politics' has been identified by a more recent literature on the integration of core state powers. The literature's key claim is that contemporary EU is characterised by 'more integration, less federalization' (Genschel and Jachtenfuchs 2016: 1). This echoes the *new intergovernmentalist* argument that the EU shows a 'resistance to further supranationalization' (Bickerton et al. 2015: 7). Observing an 'increasing involvement of EU institutions in key functions of sovereign government including money and fiscal affairs', Genschel and Jachtenfuchs (2016: 42–43) find that 'in contrast to historical examples of federal state-building, where the nationalization of core state powers precipitated the institutional, territorial and political consolidation of the emerging state, the European integration of core state powers is associated with the institutional, territorial and political fragmentation of the European Union'. They suggest that state élites and mass politicization play a key role in conditioning this integration trajectory.

Genschel and Jachtenfuchs (2013, 2016) portray the EU polity as being at a crossroads. For long, they claim, the EU has been operating as a 'regulatory polity', one in which 'EU authority [was] limited to Pareto-improving issues of market creation and regulation' (Genschel and Jachtenfuchs 2013: 3). Yet, increasingly, the EU shows an inability to depart from this rules-based model which suggests that Europe's 'very strong reliance on regulatory means of integration is unusual' (Genschel and Jachtenfuchs 2016: 46). This dependence on rules, which Majone (1996) suggested has led to the advent of a 'regulatory state' in Europe, has been confirmed during the euro crisis. The EU has not only extended its regulatory scope in markets surveillance (the Banking Union being a case in point) but has also stretched its powers from markets surveillance to governments' surveillance (the 6 Pack, 2 Pack and Fiscal Compact). Through a 'creeping institutionalization', the EU's institutional evolution is therefore flirting with the 'boundaries of the regulatory polity model' (Genschel and Jachtenfuchs 2013: V; 2) and is now affecting core state powers. In particular with the 'appropriation of fiscal power' (Genschel and Jachtenfuchs 2013: 5) during the euro crisis, the EU, they contend, has now engaged into 'capacity-building', an integration path 'that pushes the EU towards state building' (Genschel and Jachtenfuchs 2013: 11). For instance, the euro crisis could not be solved by additional regulation, it required the 'creation of EU resources for exercising core state powers' (Genschel and Jachtenfuchs 2013: 6).

A key characteristic of Genschel and Jachtenfuchs's framework is that when European integration reaches the frontier of core state powers, its pattern will tend to switch from a reliance on rule creation to capacity-building production. They 'conjecture that a politicization of the cleavage between Eurosceptics and Europhiles is particularly likely if the issue involves European capacity-building because capacity-building involves a visible reallocation of ownership rights over core state powers to the European level' (Genschel and Jachtenfuchs 2016: 49). Instead, 'regulatory integration is less prone to politicization because it only strengthens European control rights over power resources that remain notionally national. The façade of national statehood remains intact' (Genschel and Jachtenfuchs 2016: 49). This makes integration by regulation convenient and less politically costly. Integration by capacity-building, i.e. 'the creation of joint-capacities immediately raises the question of who pays and who benefits' (Genschel and Jachtenfuchs 2016: 49) while regulatory integration 'tends to conceal the distributive implications of integration by imposing the same formal constraints on all member states. Compliance with these regulatory constraints is construed as a national problem to be solved by each member individually. This deflects media attention and political conflict from the European rules to the national strategies of implementing them' (Genschel and Jachtenfuchs 2016: 50). This 'political segmentation' explains the higher propensity of member states to opt-out from capacity building arrangements than from regulatory agreements.

Another feature of their model is that integration in core state power areas is associated with a change in 'dramatis personae of integration' as 'state élites and mass publics – rather than sectoral business interests' (Genschel and Jachtenfuchs 2016: 55) determine the trajectory of integration through their impact on 'government preference formation' (Genschel and Jachtenfuchs 2016: 50). They define state élites as 'all non-elected professionals who are formally responsible for the handling of national core state powers and derive status and income from it (Skocpol 1985: 9–14) – e.g., diplomats, high-ranking civil servants, military officers, central bankers, policy experts and advisers' (Genschel and Jachtenfuchs 2016: 51). Those bureaucrats are particularly fearsome about the marginalization that the centralization of core state powers would imply for them. They thus typically prefer regulatory integration over integration by capacity-building. However, in the event that there is no way around an integration mode by capacity-building, state élites would tend to prefer 'arrangements with low or no centralized capacities' (Genschel and Jachtenfuchs 2016: 52). Also, they would advocate the creation of 'intergovernmental arrangements that secure a role for national officials in managing the new created capacities' and 'will be sceptical of supranational architectures that exclusively empower Eurocrats' (Genschel and Jachtenfuchs 2016: 51). Lastly, 'state élites will prefer sector-specific capacities and regulation to more general, cross-sectoral arrangements' (Genschel and Jachtenfuchs 2016: 51–52) to maximize their power. This is why, they argue, 'the integration of core state powers is associated with a proliferation of EU institutions and a dispersion of control' (Genschel and Jachtenfuchs 2016: 46) which comes in sharp contrast to the 'historical processes of state-building [where] the nationalization of core state powers was associated with the eventual consolidation of core institutions of national government and a centralization of control (Skowronek 1982)'.

Genschel and Jachtenfuchs's framework adds an interesting explanatory layer to the understanding of the proliferation of *ad hoc* and functional solutions conceptualized and described by functionalism. Their theory has a strong focus on the EU's fragmentation dynamics which goes in line with the fact that 'the Commission's status as the EU's central bureaucracy is eroding' (Genschel and Jachtenfuchs 2016: 46). Echoing Bickerton et al. (2015), they contend that 'to the extent the creation of core state powers involves the creation of new supranational capacity, the member state often prefer vesting it into task-specific 'de novo' EU bodies and not the Commission'. Examples 'include banking supervision (ECB), diplomatic representation (EEAS), emergency lending (ESM), and a host of implementation and surveillance tasks assigned to more than 30 EU regulatory and executive agencies' (Genschel and Jachtenfuchs 2016: 47). They conclude that 'the integration of core state powers has led to the rise of new EU institutions alongside and partly in competition with, the central institutions of the traditional Community method (the Commission and the Council of Ministers)' (Genschel and Jachtenfuchs 2016: 47) and note that 'the majority of EU staff now works outside the Commission' (Genschel and Jachtenfuchs 2016: 47). A last crucial feature of their model relates to the role played by supranational actors. Compared to the 'heroic' role that they play in neo-functionalism, Genschel and Jachtenfuchs find supranational players to be more of an instrument for Member States. As they put it provocatively (Genschel and Jachtenfuchs 2016: 54), they are 'garbage trucks of integration that keep integration afloat by disposing of the unresolved problems the member states dump on them. Thus the governments of the Member States repeatedly used and abused the ECB as a 'policy-maker of last resort' in instances in which they could not, or would not, agree among themselves how to handle the crisis' (Eichengreen 2012: 131).

The frame provided by Genschel and Jachtenfuchs (2013, 2016) proves to be helpful in interpreting the institutionalization of a fiscal authority during the crisis, in particular because of its emphasis on the reliance on rules, on the conundrum that embarking on state formation implies and on the centrifugal institutional forces that this move entails. As I will show, it does not however explain to a full extent the instance under examination and is therefore complemented in the following to emphasize the role played by the original institutional design chosen in Maastricht portrayed as a critical juncture.

The Persistence and Over-Reliance on Rules

The Maastricht Treaty and the Stability and Growth Pact constituted together a form of EMU 'regulatory polity'. In Maastricht, defenders of a classic, sovereign conception of money such as Tommaso Padoa-Schioppa (2000) had alluded to a quintessential connection between fiat money and a sovereign, which would have charted a different, capacity-building path for EMU. However, these advocates – at times referred to as Cartalists (Otero-Iglesias 2015) – lost the battle against ordo-liberals and monetarists, who argued that a rules-based regime would be sufficient to support the currency. A key feature retained in Maastricht was thus a pronounced reliance on rules, assuming a capacity of rules to bind the behaviour of EMU governments. Abolishing national state capacities while relying on rules instead of transferring state capacities to the EU level was indeed a convenient solution, one that is often used in European integration. Anticipating the 'more integration without federalization' of Genschel and Jachtenfuchs (2016), Goodhart (1998: 424) emphasized that: 'what, of course, is remarkable and unique about the move to EMU and the Euro is the absence of an accompanying federalisation of governmental and fiscal functions'. Maastricht Treaty makers failed to recognize the full extent of the interdependence that sharing a currency would imply by burying any attempts to root the monetary union within a deeper banking, fiscal and political union. This would have required a different integration trajectory, i.e. by capacity-building. The question of who would bear the political authority over the euro was left institutionally unsettled and muddling-through was preferred by EU leaders.

This distinctive polity creation resulted from the alignment of three dimensions. The first is that European integration has been characterized since its beginnings by an integration through law. The single market and its 1992 programme consisting of 282 directives and regulations has been portrayed as the most telling illustration of this integration pattern. Integration through law has been perceived as being so successful that it also made its way into the institutional logic of EMU in which rules are expected to play a significant role in constraining and coordinating actors within a single monetary union. The second dimension is the fact that a central rules-based regime was in line with the interests of large Member States who did not want to share any sovereignty further than their monetary sovereignty.

As explained by Verdun (2015: 221), in Maastricht, 'member states' governments were unwilling to transfer sovereignty over fiscal policies to the EU level without there being a felt need (e.g. owing to a major shock). Yet it was assumed there would be some kind of crossroads, some kind of upset, that would force the matter back onto the agenda so that member state governments would have to commit there and then, under major pressure, to consider deeper integration' (Verdun 2007: 209). The third dimension that explains the reliance on rules has to do with the role played by the evolution of economic ideas. Ideas and contemporary economic theory played indeed a crucial role during the Maastricht negotiations and in structuring the EMU architecture (McNamara 1999). For instance, one of the crucial contributions of economic theory at the time was linked to 'credible commitments' which emphasized the necessity for rules-based coordination to avoid moral hazard or policy discretion (Kydland and Prescott 1977). While economic spill-overs stemming from fiscal policies were recognised, it was thus felt in Maastricht that rules would be an appropriate device to avoid that Member States adopt harmful behaviours to their neighbours.

Absent such central state functions, the build-up of externalities within EMU would thus have to be prevented by the creation of rules-based credible commitments embodied by the no bail out clause, the clause on the prohibition of monetary financing and by the absence of central banking supervision and resolution. In particular, the no-bail out rule, prohibited any form of fiscal liabilities acquisition among EMU governments. Such rule was partly based on the objective to avoid incentivizing moral hazard. Yet, applied to a more macro level, i.e. a multinational currency area, the effectiveness of rules to deter moral hazard behaviour was largely overestimated. To use a metaphor, it seems at times that Maastricht Treaty designers believed that if one has a rule stating that there is no fire department, then one will not have any fire. And yet the fire came.

THE CRISIS SEQUENCE SEEN AS THE SUM OF REGULATORY AND CAPACITY-BUILDING MOMENTS

The crisis made EMU's rules-based logic tumble and triggered capacity-building. However, going back to the sequence of the four centralized functions (fiscal surveillance, financial assistance, banking supervision and resolution, and lending of last resort) one can see that the institutional change pattern alternated between integration by regulation and integration by capacity-building.

The first centralized function, fiscal surveillance, was clearly a regulatory response: the rule paradigm persisted during the hey-days of the Task Force Van Rompuy. But as contagion loomed, the need for the 'creation of EU resources' (Genschel and Jachtenfuchs 2013: 6) became evident. The agreements on formal financial assistance mechanisms, instead, were an instance of capacity-building: new central resources were overtly created. Yet their political steering and decision-making was left to informal bodies: the Eurogroup and the EWG. The no-bail out rule has thus been replaced by a set of mostly intergovernmental financial assistance mechanisms managed by a newly converted institution, the Eurogroup, supported by another informally empowered institution, the EWG. Of all fiscal powers centralized to the EU level during the euro crisis, financial assistance proved to be the most contentious one, also because it implied the sharing of a tremendous amount of money and thus embodies a significant pool of sovereignty. There, euro area leaders could not rely on the creation and enforcement of common rules as banking and sovereign crises do not get solved by a rulebook. There was a need for decisive and discretionary action.

With the advent of the Banking Union, the third sequence, the integration mode switched back to the single market integration pattern, i.e. made up of rules creation and independent monitoring, compliance and enforcement by technical agencies. Banking supervision and resolution powers strove in a breeding ground characterised by the absence of central rules. Their market integration focus explains why its institutional arrangements are more in line with the typical integration patterns of the 'regulatory polity': independent agencies and a rules based system (the so-called Single Rulebook). Yet, the Banking Union also entailed the creation of a common resource, a 55 bn euros fund, which is a clear instance of capacity building integration. The last sequence, the actions of the ECB to safeguard the euro, instead, was an instance of capacity building again. The monetary financing rule has been restricted in its application scope and the ECB exploited its blurred substance to extend its capacities. It is now able to act with significant discretion on the secondary debt markets and to perform the task of lender of last resort. However, the temporary acquisition by the ECB of the lender of last resort role occurred informally and covertly.

One can thus ultimately conclude that the fiscal centre formation was the sum of convoluted regulatory and capacity-building integration steps. One of the most significant unintended consequences of the euro crisis seems to be that instead of preventing the advent of common fiscal institutions, the Maastricht reliance on rules-based governance has precipitated their institutionalization. The capacity-building dynamics that characterised the euro crisis management were however non-linear: they were overt (Héritier 2013) and predominantly formal in the case of financial assistance mechanisms whilst they proved to follow a covert and informal path in the case of the Lender of Last Resort attribution. Assuming that the creation of a European fiscal back-up would run against 'public opposition' (Genschel and Jachtenfuchs 2016: 54), Genschel and Jachtenfuchs convincingly submit that 'breaking the sovereign-banking nexus by strengthening the regulatory surveillance of deficient banks seemed like an easier political sell to sceptic publics than breaking it by the creation of a fiscal union among the member states' (Genschel and Jachtenfuchs 2016: 54). On a more general level, within the framework provided by Genschel and Jachtenfuchs, one 'would expect governments to 'undersell' integration under conditions of a constraining consensus by, for instance, emphasizing European regulation, by keeping European capacity building to a sheer minimum, by organizing capacity-building along intergovernmental lines, where it cannot be avoided [...] or by shifting politically controversial decisions to supranational institutions' (Genschel and Jachtenfuchs 2016: 54). While I find this politicization-based explanation helpful in accounting for the complex trajectory of the fiscal authority centralization, their frame does not explain the variation of capacity-building solutions during the crisis. Why did governments agree to create financial mechanisms in Spring 2010 and refrained from doing so in 2012 when it was clear that even the creation of the Banking Union did not lead to a decrease in market pressure, leaving the 'dirty job' to the ECB?

CENTRIFUGAL FORCES AT PLAY

In line with Genschel and Jachtenfuchs (2016: 47), this book has found that the centralization of a fiscal authority was concomitant to the 'proliferation of EU institutions' and to the fragmentation of the EU's executive. This occurred around the Council of Ministers. To use their terminology, it happened 'above' (e.g. the European Council), 'beside' (the Eurogroup, the Single Supervisory Mechanism) and 'below' (e.g. the European Stability Mechanism, the Single Resolution Board) the Council of Ministers. While it is yet unclear how intergovernmental and/or supranational those bodies will prove to be, it is already obvious that taken together they contribute to the erosion of the Commission's bureaucratic centrality. Following the reference of Genschel and Jachtenfuchs (2016) to EU staff figures, a quick calculation reveals that the cumulated staff numbers of the new EMU agencies (ESM, SSM, SRB) amount to around 1500 staff which considerably outweighs the staff number of EMU's institutional incumbent, the Commission (i.e. both DG ECFIN and DG FISMA).

Can the Commission's disempowerment be totally explained by the fact that national bureaucrats 'will be sceptical of supranational architectures that exclusively empower Eurocrats' (Genschel and Jachtenfuchs 2016: 51)? In line with their expectations, the new intergovernmental arrangement indeed gathers the 'state élites' in its decision-making bodies while a classic supranational agent, the Commission, has been left out of it. Yet, Genschel and Jachtenfuchs (2016: 47) also point at possible countervailing forces in that 'new supranational agents' have appeared on the EU scene too. This book's findings seem to confirm that the president of the European Council, the President of the Eurogroup and to a lesser extent, the President of the Euro Working Group contribute to a form of 'executive centre formation' (Trondal 2014). All this, 'leaves the EU institutionally fragmented to an extent that, when it wins the Nobel Prize, it has to send three presidents to collect it because no single one can claim to represent the EU as a whole' (Genschel and Jachtenfuchs 2016: 47). More recently the latter representation conundrum has been publicly illustrated by the now famous Four Presidents (2014) or Five Presidents (2015) reports. Beyond the institutional interests of national state élites, this therefore suggests that the fragmentation of EMU's fiscal authority could be ultimately linked to a matter of representation and legitimacy.

Lastly, the fragmentation is undeniably fuelled by the persistence of 'special rules' (Genschel and Jachtenfuchs 2016: 46) for core state power areas. The possibility of opting out goes against the advent of EU's territorial consolidation. While the euro was initially supposed to be a driver of unity since every EU Member States was expected to join the euro sooner or later, with time, it contributed to the territorial fragmentation of Europe which, in turn, has resulted in an increased institutional fragmentation. This trend has been accentuated as the EMU institutional evolution has been proceeding forward, in part thanks to the Lisbon Treaty's new article 136, which, has argued by Tuori (2012: 8) 'reflects resignation in front of a lingering bifurcation of the Union into the euro area and non-euro area Member States'. The irreversibility of the euro which, since Maastricht, fundamentally structured the EU polity has been further questioned by the euro crisis. Such a development has been reinforced by the proliferation of isomorphic institutions, functional for EMU countries only: the Eurogroup, but now also the ESM, the SSM and the SRB. This all derives from a peculiar feature of the integration of core state powers, namely that 'the EU's formal authority over core state powers is limited to subsets of member states' (Genschel and Jachtenfuchs 2016: 48). One can indeed see that instead of an institutional consolidation, the fiscal authority in EMU is characterised by a 'dispersion of control' (Genschel and Jachtenfuchs 2016: 46).

The theoretical framework provided by Genschel and Jachtenfuchs (2013, 2016), despite its merits in accounting for most of EMU's institutional evolution during the crisis, entails however a few blind spots when applied to this instance.

The first implicit yet major assumption made is that actors operate in an environment where constitutional rules do not act as a strong constraint. One can see there a connection with the functionalism of Mitrany. Yet, in particular domestic constitutional systems played a key role in shaping and structuring the institutional design of fiscal arrangements during the crisis (e.g. the Inter-Governmental Agreement on the SRF or the ESM Treaty) and it is somehow surprising that Genschel and Jachtenfuchs (2013) does not consider the constraining power of national constitutional frameworks as European integration gets closer to core state powers. Constitutional rules at both EU level and national level however severely constrained the design of new institutions, and to some extent, also contributed to the EU polity's further fragmentation. I submit that those barriers act as key constraints that explain why one observes 'more integration without federalization' and why the integration of fiscal powers during the euro crisis has not led to solid and overt formalization and consolidation of powers within one institution. The institutional evolution of the ESM, an intergovernmental, unanimity-based body controlled by state élites will provide an interesting litmus test for their theory (will the ESM be consolidating fiscal powers going forward?). Secondly, Genschel and Jachtenfuchs (2013) seems to assume that state élites are in a position to design the institutions the way they see fit, as if the politicians to whom they report would not have any autonomous preference formation to decide on institutional design. For the model to function, the powers of bureaucrats should hence trump the power of politicians. Connected to this, is the fact that the model under-specifies how state élites satisfy their institutional interests by ultimately determining the shape of institutional arrangements. Considering these two elements would probably lead to tame down the implicit rationalist assumption of their theory.

In line with the above limits lined out, I contend that the theory could be enriched by a starker emphasis put on legal and institutional constraints when explaining EU/EMU institutional design. Path-dependency and the stickiness that is in the EU system played a strong role during the euro crisis suggesting that the EU polity is first and foremost a very conservative polity. This institutionalization process uncovered by this book has been heavily constrained by path dependent processes, be they legal constraints as formulated in the Treaty, existing regulatory practices (rules-based fiscal surveillance) or also institutional practices and actor-empowerment (growing powers of the Eurogroup, EWG and ECB; maintenance of the Commission in a Secretariat-like function). Previous features of EMU's fiscal regime have been confirmed and reinforced by the euro crisis. This observation accounts for a fundamental rigidity in EMU's economic governance. While Genschel and Jachtenfuchs (2013) brilliantly accounts for the fact that the regulatory system has been reproduced and expanded beyond its previous strict focus on market integration providing apparent support for the claim of an emerging regulatory state in fiscal surveillance (Schelkle 2009: 829; Majone 1994, 1996), they disregard the path-dependence constraining the actor's institutional evolution. For instance, their reliance on state élites's institutional interest as an explanatory variable does not account for the empowerment of the ECB as the latter has restricted the sphere of powers of national state élites. Lastly, the absence of a legitimate, European central actor able to aggregate core state powers is not considered by Genschel and Jachtenfuchs as an explicit explanatory variable. Yet this analysis has illustrated that the perceived illegitimacy of the Commission partly fuelled the fragmentation of EMU's institutional order. In fact, a classic way out of Europe's democratic deficit has been to 'satisfy the self-interest of all EU institutions to keep its polity legitimate' Möllers (2015: 3).

How Much Can EMU's Stateless Nature Be Embraced?

This book has argued that EMU's inherent institutional flaws go a long way in explaining the distinctive pattern through which the European fiscal centre has been constituted: the Maastricht's unsettled institutional features and its rules-based regime are an explaining factor of the European fiscal union's trajectory. Future research could go a step further and ask the more far-reaching question whether EMU's unfinished structure, and in particular the theories used to justify the 'stateless' nature of EMU, *caused* the euro crisis.[15] Approaching the phenomenon more in-depth, one realizes indeed that the crisis acted as a revelation trigger of the underlying forces that underpin a currency.

The atypical, 'stateless' (Otero-Iglesias 2015) design of EMU was not only recognised and acknowledged in Maastricht, it was also praised as a post-modern achievement. Wim Duisenberg, the inaugurating ECB

President stressed that the euro 'is the first currency that has not only severed its link to gold, but also its link to the nation state. It is not backed by the durability of the metal or by the authority of the state' (Duisenberg 2002: 1, cited in Otero-Iglesias 2015: 355). The euro was embraced at the time as a monetary and political innovation: 'we have given rise to an entirely new type of monetary order' (Padoa-Schioppa 1999: 1), one that is disconnected from the traditional anchors of currency, 'a commodity, usually gold; and the sovereign, i.e. the political power' (Padoa-Schioppa 1999: 1). The euro was thus conceived as a 'currency without a state' (Padoa-Schioppa 1999). This fact is embodied in the very design of euro banknotes which feature architectural monuments but no state or cultural personalities, thereby breaking away from past traditions in Europe and the world. Ottmar Issing, first chief economist of the ECB (Issing 2008: 234) went even further when he claimed that 'the euro represents depoliticized and hence stable money'.

The whole intellectual rationale of EMU was based on its disconnection from state power. Instead of being anchored to a sovereign, EMU was based on the so-called 'metalist theory of money' where 'money emanates spontaneously in the market' with a view to minimizing transaction costs (Otero-Iglesias 2015: 351). The original rationale underpinning the euro creation was summarized by the Commission slogan 'one market, one money' (European Commission 1990). By necessity, it was argued, the development of trade within the single market would automatically lead to the creation of a single currency. As documented by Goodhart (1998), this approach implicitly rooted the existence of currencies within the multiplication of exchanges and the need to minimize transaction costs through the use of a common currency. This microeconomic logic is also at the core of the Optimum Currency Areas (OCA) theory, which theoretically underpinned the creation of the euro (Eichengreen 2012).

However, to the extent that the crisis has led to a reinforcement of the ties between the currency and sovereign functions, as also shown by Genschel and Jachtenfuchs (2016), it could be argued that the crisis has lent support to the rival of the metalist theory: the Cartalist theory of money that sees the sovereign as the ultimate driver and anchor of a currency. The ultimate responsible authority of the euro, the European Central Bank, seems itself to have followed the pendulum from one theory to the other, moving away from the claim that the euro needed to be a depoliticized currency towards making the public request that it actually needs a political union underlying it (Otero-Iglesias 2015). If one pushes the hypothesis provided by the Cartalist theory of money to its extreme, it can indeed be argued that a currency without a credible taxpayer backing it up will always be subject to suspicion in periods of crises. The market dynamics and the speculation that occurred against the euro lend some support to this thesis. And yet, the question of the extent of the euro's sovereign-less nature in producing the euro crisis has never been used as an autonomous explanatory factor. This is an approach that future researchers might thus consider exploring.

NOTES

1. Interviewee 40 – EU Council official.
2. Interviewee 38 – European Central Bank official.
3. Obviously, one can however disagree about his claim that the ECB has a 'very clear but very limited mandate'.
4. Interviewee 30 – Finnish Ministry of Finance official.
5. With the exception of the new emergency procedure in the ESM.
6. Interviewee 40 – EU Council official.
7. Interviewee 46 – European Parliament official.
8. Interviewee 47 – EU Council official.
9. Interviewee 30 – Finnish Ministry of Finance official.
10. Interviewee 30 – Finnish Ministry of Finance official.
11. Interviewee 32 – European Central Bank official.
12. 'Actually I have another thing I want to mention. Just something I want to throw out there. If we'd known in 2001 we were staying in Afghanistan this long, we would have made some very different choices. Right? Instead our planning cycles rarely look more than 12 months ahead, so this hasn't been a 14 year war we've been waging, but a one-year war, waged 14 times'. *Extract from HBO TV Series Homeland, Season 4, Episode 1 S. Berenson, former CIA Director in the fiction.*
13. Interviewee 40 – EU Council official.
14. Interviewee 30 – Finnish Ministry of Finance official.
15. See also Honohan (2016).

REFERENCES

Bauer, M., & Becker, S. (2014). The Unexpected Winner of the Crisis: The European Commission's Strengthened Role in Economic Governance. *Journal of European Integration, 36*(3), 213–229.

Bickerton, C. J., Hodson, D., & Puetter, U. (2015). *The New Intergovernmentalism: States, Supranational Actors, and European Politics in the Post-Maastricht Era.* Oxford: Oxford University Press.

Coeuré, B. (2012, December 1). *Speech,* Forum Eco Libération ESCP, Reprendre confiance en (l')Europe. Paris. https://www.ecb.europa.eu/press/key/date/2012/html/sp121201.en.html

Dehousse, R. (2013). *The Politics of Delegation in the European Union.* Paris: Centre d'Etudes Européennes de Sciences Po, Cahiers européens de Sciences Po.

Duisenberg, W. (2002, May 9). *Acceptance Speech by Dr. Willem F. Duisenberg, President of the European Central Bank.* International Charlemagne Prize of Aachen for 2002, Aachen. https://www.ecb.europa.eu/press/key/date/2002/html/sp020509.en.html

Eichengreen, B. (2012). European Monetary Integration with Benefit of Hindsight. *Journal of Common Market Studies, 50*(s1), 123–136.

European Commission. (1990, October). *One Market, One Money: An Evaluation of the Potential Benefits and Costs of Forming an Economic and Monetary Union.* European Economy, Commission of the European Communities, Directorate-General for Economic and Financial Affairs.

Fabbrini, S. (2015). *Which European Union? Europe After the Euro Crisis.* Cambridge: Cambridge University Press.

Ferguson, N., Sandholtz, W., & Stone-Sweet, A. (2001). *The Institutionalization of Europe.* Oxford: Oxford University Press.

Folkerts-Landau, D., & Garber, P. M. (1992, March). *The European Central Bank: A Bank or a Monetary Policy Rule* (NBER Working Paper No. 4016).

Genschel, P., & Jachtenfuchs, M. (Eds.). (2013). *Beyond the Regulatory Polity? The European Integration of Core State Powers.* Oxford: Oxford University Press.

Genschel, P., & Jachtenfuchs, M. (2016). More Integration, Less Federation: The European Integration of Core State Powers. *Journal of European Public Policy, 23*(1), 42–59.

Goodhart, C. (1998). The Two Concepts of Money: Implications for the Analysis of Optimal Currency Areas. *European Journal of Political Economy, 14*(3), 407–432.

Haas, E. (1958). *The Uniting of Europe: Political, Social, and Economic Forces (1950–1957).* Stanford: Stanford University Press.

Héritier, A. (2013). Covert Integration of Core State Powers: Renegotiating Incomplete Contracts. In P. Genschel & M. Jachtenfuchs (Eds.), *Beyond the Regulatory Polity? The European Integration of Core State Powers.* Oxford: Oxford University Press.

Hodson, D. (2013). The Little Engine That Wouldn't: Supranational Entrepreneurship and the Barroso Commission. *Journal of European Integration, 35*(3), 301–314.

Hoffmann, S. (1966). Obstinate or Obsolete: The Fate of the Nation-State and the Case of Western Europe. *Daedalus, 95*(3), 862–915.

Honohan, P. (2016, April 28). *Dinner Speech.* EUI Conference on 'Filling the Gaps in Governance: The Case of Europe', San Domenico di Fiesole.

Issing, O. (2008). *The Birth of the Euro.* Cambridge: Cambridge University Press.

Joerges, C. (2012). The European Economic Constitution in Crisis: Between "State of Exception" and "Constitutional Moment". In M. Poiares Maduro, B. De Witte, & M. Kumm (Eds.), *The Democratic Governance of the Euro,* RSCAS Global Governance Programme, Rscas Policy Paper 2012/8, pp. 39–44, Florence, San Domenico di Fiesole: European University Institute.

Kudrna, Z. (2016). Financial Market Regulation: Crisis-Induced Supranationalization. *Journal of European Integration, 38*(3), 251–264.

Kydland, F., & Prescott, E. (1977). Rules Rather than Discretion: The Inconsistency of Optimal Plans. *Journal of Political Economy, 85*(3), 473–492.

Laffan, B., & Schlosser, P. (2016). Public Finances in Europe: Fortifying EU Economic Governance in the Shadow of the Crisis. *Journal of European Integration, 38*(3), 237–249.

Lindberg, L. N. (1963). *The Political Dynamics of European Economic Integration.* Stanford: Stanford University Press.

Majone, G. (1994). The Rise of the Regulatory State in Europe. *West European Politics, 17*(3), 77–101.

Majone, G. (1996). *Regulating Europe.* London: Routledge.

Majone, G. (2002). The European Commission: The Limits of Centralization and the Perils of Parliamentarization. *Governance, 15*(3), 375–392.

Majone, G. (2014). *Rethinking the European Union: Has Integration Gone Too Far?* Cambridge: Cambridge University Press.

Mcnamara, K. R. (1999). *The Currency of Ideas: Monetary Politics in European Union.* Ithaca: Cornell University Press.

Mitrany, D. (1943). *A Working Peace System : An Argument for the Functional Development of International Organization.* London: The Royal Institute of International Affairs, Oxford University Press.

Mitrany, D. (1948). The Functional Approach to World Organization. *International Affairs* (Royal Institute of International Affairs), *24*(3), 350–363.

Mitrany, D. (1975). *The Functional Theory of Politics.* London: London School of Economics and Political Science, Martin Robertson.

Möllers, C. (2015, May 22). *Presentation given at the European University Institute as Part of the Conference on 'European Banking Union – Democracy, Technocracy and the State of Integration'.* For a Link to the Conference's Write Up: http://cadmus.eui.eu/bitstream/handle/1814/36481/FBF_EB_2015_02.pdf?sequence=1

Moravcsik, A. (1998). *The Choice for Europe: Social Purpose and State Power from Messina to Maastricht.* Ithaca: Cornell University Press.

Moravcsik, A., & Schimmelfennig, F. (2009). Liberal Intergovernmentalism. In A. Wiener & T. Diez (Eds.), *European Integration Theory.* Oxford: Oxford University Press.

Niemann, A., & Ioannou, D. (2015). European Economic Integration in Times of Crisis: A Case of Neofunctionalism? *Journal of European Public Policy, 22*(2), 196–218.

Nye, J. (1971). Comparing Common Markets: A Revised Neo-Functional Model. In L. N. Lindberg & S. Scheingold (Eds.), *Regional Integration*. Cambridge: Harvard University Press.

Otero-Iglesias, M. (2015). Stateless Euro: The Euro Crisis and the Revenge of Chartalist Theory of Money. *Journal of Common Market Studies, 53*(2), 349–364.

Padoa-Schioppa, T. (1999, February 24). EMU and Banking Supervision. *Lecture by Tommaso Padoa-Schioppa*, Member of the ECB Executive Board, London School of Economics, Financial Markets Group, London.

Padoa-Schioppa, T. (2000). *The Road to Monetary Union in Europe: The Emperor, the Kings and the Genies*. Oxford: Oxford University Press.

Puetter, U. (2012). Europe's Deliberative Intergovernmentalism: The Role of the Council and European Council in EU Economic Governance. *Journal of European Public Policy, 19*(2), 161–178.

Rosamond, B. (2000). *Theories of European Integration*. Basingstoke: Macmillan Press.

Scharpf, F. (1988). The Joint-Decision Trap. Lessons from German Federalism and European Integration. *Public Administration, 66*(2), 239–278.

Schelkle, W. (2009). The Contentious Creation of the Regulatory State in Fiscal Surveillance. *West European Politics, 32*(4), 829–846.

Schelkle, W. (2013). Fiscal Integration by Default. In P. Genschel & M. Jachtenfuchs (Eds.), *Beyond the Regulatory Polity? The European Integration of Core State Powers*. Oxford: Oxford University Press.

Schlosser, P. (2015). '*Tightening the Knot: Strengthening Fiscal Surveillance in EMU during the Euro Crisis*', LUISS Guido Carli School of European Political Economy (Working Paper 12/2015).

Schmitter, P. (2003). Neo-Neo-Functionalism. In A. Wiener & T. Diez (Eds.), *European Integration Theory*. Oxford: Oxford University Press.

Skocpol, T. (1985). Bringing the State Back In: Strategies of Analysis in Current Research. In P. B. Evans, D. Rueschemeyer, & T. Skocpol (Eds.), *Bringing the State Back In* (pp. 3–43). Cambridge: Cambridge University Press.

Skowronek, S. (1982). *Building a New American State: The Expansion of National Administrative Capacities, 1877–1920*. Cambridge: Cambridge University Press.

Trondal, J. (2014). The Rise of a European Public Administration: European Capacity Building by Stealth. In P. Genschel & M. Jachtenfuchs (Eds.), *Beyond the Regulatory Polity?* Oxford: Oxford University Press.

Tuori, K. (2012). *The European Financial Crisis – Constitutional Aspects and Implications* (EUI Working Papers). Department of Law, 2012/28.

Verdun, A. (2007). A Historical Institutionalist Analysis of the Road to Economic and Monetary Union: A Journey with Many Crossroads. In S. Meunier & K. McNamara (Eds.), *Making History: European Integration and Institutional Change at Fifty*. New York: Oxford University Press.

Verdun, A. (2015). A Historical Institutionalist Explanation of the EU's Responses to the Euro Area Financial Crisis. *Journal of European Public Policy, 22*(2), 219–237.

Vilpišauskas, R. (2013). Eurozone Crisis and European Integration: Functional Spill-Over, Political Spill-Back?'. *Journal of European Integration, 35*(3), 361–373.

CHAPTER 8

How to Reform EMU?

INTRODUCTION

EMU's original set up was functionally flawed (De Grauwe 2013; Giavazzi and Wyplosz 2015). Maastricht-designed EMU proved to be highly geared towards its monetary pillar, under-developed in its banking and fiscal dimensions, over-specified in its battery of rules and under-equipped in its arsenal of crisis management capabilities. The 'crisis revealed that the Union lacked sufficiently solid instruments to act swiftly and decisively in response to challenges to its financial stability' (EC 2017a: 17). As a result, no EU instruments were in place to deal with the risks or vulnerabilities that originated in, or were largely amplified by, the financial sector. Sapir and Schoenmaker (2017: 1) neatly captured the essence of the problem: 'there was no common instrument in case a sovereign faced a liquidity or solvency crunch. For banks, there was not even a common instrument for the surveillance of risk, and there was no common instrument in case of a liquidity or solvency crisis. Everything was left in the hands of individual member countries'.

In this context, I have articulated why and how the euro crisis acted as a catalyst for the institutionalization of a centralized yet fragmented fiscal authority in Europe. I argued that acting under severe market pressure, EU leaders were primarily motivated by stability concerns to safeguard the integrity of the euro rather than by institutional considerations over the grand design of a European fiscal union. During the crisis, the permanent state of emergency ensured that functionalist considerations trumped

© The Author(s) 2019
P. Schlosser, *Europe's New Fiscal Union*,
https://doi.org/10.1007/978-3-319-98636-4_8

institutionalist contemplations. However, as crisis pressure ebbs away, institutional questions will ineluctably come back to the fore. All the more so because it became ever clearer with time, as an interviewee argued, that 'there is a collective decision-making problem'[1] in the EU. The years and decades to come will therefore fully expose the implications of crisis management measures on EMU's institutional evolution.

I have shown that the euro crisis management pattern relied on the incremental creation of complex rules, on the dense production of *ad hoc* and functional mechanisms and bodies and on the mostly informal empowerment of existing EMU institutions. The history of European integration reminds us however that path-dependence and institutional lock-in forces are often at play to transform context-dependent solutions into a permanent system. Past trends suggest that the institutional piecemeal that resulted from the euro crisis could become 'sticky' and, because of the 'economies of scale' that reinforce existing institutions (Pierson 2000), can be expected to solidify over the years to come. As an interviewee suggested, 'the crisis did not break the path-dependency'.[2] To break the path-dependency, EU leaders will need to find a way out of the collective action problem in which they are currently trapped. Yet, initiating institutional consolidation would necessitate that the European Council moves away from its past tendency towards stalemate, reaches an agreement on the institutional direction it wants to give to the European Union and agrees on the necessity of Treaty change. This will require a significant departure from heads of states and governments' previous navigation by sight. In other words, the only exit from muddling-through implies some form of constitutional settlement of the EU polity.

Against this background, this closing chapter assesses the reform prospects of EMU's polity going forward. It canvasses the crucial features of muddling-through in the current institutional framework, an outlook which I consider as the most likely for the years to come. Evaluating three key policy ideas put on the table by the Commission in December 2017, it then discusses the costly implications of the perpetuation of this status quo. Departing from muddling-through, the chapter then sets out three competing medium term scenarios for the development of EMU's polity. After having clearly spelled out the possible institutional directions that EU leaders could embark on, the chapter suggests three policy reform steps to make EMU sustainable, describes the 'technology' behind institutional settlement and provides the closing remarks of this book.

The Outlook: 'Muddling-Through' and Its Limitations

Since it can be assumed that a constitutional settlement will be discounted in the short term by EU leaders as too electorally costly, the most likely development for the years to come is thus that the EU embraces post-crisis EMU as its new working arrangement. Quite expectedly, the large share of actors interviewed imagined Europe's future along those lines. Muddling-through within an incomplete EMU entails however certain costs, mainly in terms of democratic practice, legitimacy and effectiveness of the new framework. Whether the post-crisis regime sails forward will thus depend on how it deals with these deficiencies.

Given that the newly created EMU arrangements display a pronounced technocratic character, muddling-through will first imply the ability of European institutions to withstand calls for democratic reforms. As has been shown by the number of demonstrations that the euro crisis response triggered in the streets of European capitals, by the renewed interest of national parliaments in European affairs and by the increased invasiveness of national constitutional courts on the design choices of European crisis management mechanisms, the intrusiveness of the European fiscal centre poses serious democratic problems. It is hard to deny that the euro crisis management fared poorly in terms of democratic participation and deliberation: big decisions were mostly made under closed doors and in the 'darkness of the night'.[3] With the crisis, European citizens suddenly realized that they had no direct leverage over those big decisions made over their own faith within the European Council. This decision pattern comes for instance in sharp contrast with the transparency and accountability standards of Europe's parliamentary democracies.

Moreover, crisis management was characterised by a mushrooming of new bodies, facilities and mechanisms. The proliferation of the 'loci of the EU decision-making machinery' (Bartolini 2006: 31) – of which many appear to be un-formalized decision-making institutions – have blurred the lines of political responsibility. As a result, two eminently political questions are now becoming increasingly difficult to answer when it comes to Europe's fiscal governance: who decides, and who is responsible for what? In a classic political system, functional bodies would not be as much in the limelight as European instruments and bodies are. However, in the absence of central political and institutional mechanisms that simplify and clarify where political responsibility lies exactly, European citizens quite rightly perceive that all those instruments and bodies dispose of some political authority. And indeed, can a 'normal citizen' reasonably understand the difference between what the ECB (the European Central Bank), the EBA (European Banking Authority), the ESM (European Stability Mechanism), the SRB (Single Resolution Board), the Single Supervisory Mechanism (SSM), the European Systemic Risk Board (ESRB), the ECOFIN, the Eurogroup, the Euro Working Group, the Commission's DG ECFIN, DG COMP or DG FISMA do? Can we expect them to disentangle the power of those technocratic actors from the powers of political actors? Furthermore, it appears misleading to expect citizens to be able to decipher Europe's convoluted fiscal governance when even European policy-makers involved in the files recognise – as several interviewees did – that they do not understand how the rules work exactly and admit a lack of comprehension of its processes. Muddling-through with a high number of actors is therefore costly for the legitimacy of the European Union as a whole.

In my view, a key reason of Europe's unpopularity lies in its inherent incapacity to design formal political solutions that go beyond the creation of rules. During the euro crisis, Europe has indeed pushed regulatory integration to its limits, to the extent, as an interviewee conjectured, that 'the EU is world-champion in making rules'.[4] As another interviewee explained: 'on rules we can go no further, we have used all we got'.[5] Yet another interviewed policy-maker explained that this rule proliferation could in reality be the result of a negative choice: 'in a system without a strong centre and not enough trust among countries, maybe rules and algorithms acting as benchmarks are better, even if it is sad to say this'.[6] Integration through law has been rather successful when it came to developing a single European market. Yet, as I have shown, the European arsenal of rules, fines and sanctions fares poorly when it comes to controlling core state powers such as fiscal policy. Enforcing rules on economic agents and on state governments are two different endeavours. Because the EU does not dispose of the autonomous legitimacy to ensure rule enforcement on state actors, the problem with the reliance on rules in the area of core state powers seems to be that they are only enforceable to those Member States who deem them legitimate (Laffan and Schlosser 2016).

Europe is thus stuck with a complex rules-based regime that is difficult to decipher and ultimately almost useless: 'we have created a disaster'.[7] To allow for action, discretion in the interpretation of the rules has therefore been performed during the crisis with varying levels of success. While the rule-making process is thus underpinned by Europe's Treaty-makers and co-legislators and therefore meets basic democratic legitimacy standards, the discretion taken by EMU's executive actors from the rules is all the more problematic because the ECB, the Eurogroup and the Commission all fared quite poorly in terms of democratic legitimacy and accountability already pre-crisis.

The crisis made things worse. A consequence of the crisis was indeed that all EMU executive actors significantly drifted away from their initial mandate. The ECB stretched its Treaty-based mandate to be able to perform lending of last resort and has been informally vested with the performance of tasks which would normally be exercised by a political authority. Yet, it is for instance unclear how the ECB will be held accountable to its decisions in case of supervisory or liquidity provision mistakes. The Eurogroup, for its part, has acted flexibly on the enforcement of the rules-based bail-out and bail-in regimes, displaying a discretionary power. Despite its lack of formal decision-making powers and accountability obligations, it made wide-ranging decisions – together with its subgroup, the EWG – when agreeing on and setting the conditionality of assistance programmes. Those decisions affected the lives of millions of European citizens but could not be directly contested, either democratically or judicially. The Commission, lastly, has been lenient on the interpretation of fiscal surveillance rules. Yet, in the absence of an activist European Court of Justice which could hold the Commission in check and without the existence of a sound accountability channel to Commission action, the Commission's discretion is exercised without sufficient checks and balances.

For different reasons, the current EMU polity therefore displays a lack of legitimate actors. In a context marked by legitimacy scarcity, a horizontal redistribution of powers has occurred on the European continent. Because of the 'lack of democratic legitimacy of the Commission', one observes a 'drift from the Commission towards Member States',[8] who are even more pushed at the centre of EMU institutional-building. In other words, because of the Union's 'depleted legitimacy resources […] the Union has had to turn to its Member States for salvation. Solutions will still have to be Europe-wide, but they will not be ideated, designed and crafted using the classical 'community method' but will be negotiated among and validated by the Member States' (Weiler 2012: 827). Hence the post-Maastricht 'desire to define a viable intergovernmental alternative to the transfer of powers to the Commission' (Dehousse 2013: 3). As an interviewee explained: 'in the early 2000s, the Commission was the driving force; with the crisis, the intergovernmental method came to the fore'.[9] An additional reason that might explain why the Commission has been pushed away from EMU's core is that European integration was for long legitimated through a 'political messianism' (Weiler 2012) which was incarnated by the Commission, acting as a champion of the 'ever closer union'. And indeed, the 'whole ethos of the organization is to promote further integration'.[10] In the current Eurosceptic context, this is likely to contribute to tilt the institutional balance in favour of the Commission's rival, the Eurogroup, despite the latter's legitimacy pitfalls. I contend that the only way out of this rules and discretion conundrum is therefore to design common and legitimate institutions as this appears to be the only way that is susceptible to lead to a steady-state EMU. The drive towards common institutions has been a recurring recommendation of interviewees: as one of them explained, 'my conclusion is that rules don't work and that there is no alternative than going to common institutions'.[11] It is also the line advocated by ECB President Mario Draghi (Draghi 2014, 2015).

Besides its poor performance in democratic and legitimacy terms, muddling-through within the post-crisis framework entails several shortcomings in terms of efficiency. As I have highlighted, the new fiscal regime involves countless actors in its daily operation. This preference for a high division of labour among institutions and bodies is harmful because it leads to unnecessary costs. The set-up of the SRB – which features an annual operational budget of 57 million euros for the year 2016 – is a case in point. A higher concentration of instruments could instead have brought benefits in terms of economies of scale and of learning/experience effects. The preparation of Eurogroup meetings offers another, more anecdotal, example of this damaging fragmentation. Since its creation, the Eurogroup relies on two secretariats, one which is located in the Council and another one sitting in the Commission's DG ECFIN (but reporting directly to the chairman of the Economic and Financial Committee). Yet, instead of being complementary, a deeper foray into the secretariats' daily operations revealed that in the almost twenty years of the Eurogroup's existence, both secretariats have been independently preparing separate briefings for Eurogroup members before every monthly meeting, clearly duplicating work. Asked about this inefficiency, an interviewee explained that while 'in practice they know each other', 'institutionally it is a big mess and there is a competition between the two secretariats'.[12]

On top of the new fiscal regime's inefficiency, its effectiveness can also be contested since the enforceability of some newly created powers is doubtful. This is the case in particular when it comes to the fiscal surveillance and banking resolution regimes. Despite their far-reaching powers, the newly adopted regimes have already proven to be tumbling as the enforceability of those powers largely depends on the existence of a pro-enforcement coalition in the Council. Besides, Court challenges could also threaten the success of the new regimes. One can for instance expect that some newly created instruments which push fiscal intrusiveness to a high level (e.g. the *ex ante* check of draft budgetary plans or the enhanced surveillance foreseen by the Two-Pack) could be legally contested (De Witte and Kilpatrick 2014) as they may violate fundamental rights such as pension rights for instance. Similarly, improper implementations of EU bail-in provisions could impinge on the property rights of EU citizens.

Lastly, in terms of the strongest powers centralized during the crisis – the newly created liquidity instruments of the ECB – their effectiveness is weakened by the fact that their advent followed an informal trajectory and has not been settled by any Treaty revision. The sustainability of the ECB's lending of last resort can therefore be questioned. Will the ECB keep on acting as an effective backstop in the future? This is far from certain as such an expectation is largely conditional on the ECB's current presidency, or at a minimum, on the existing composition of the ECB's executive board. Regardless of the persistence of the OMT regime and by extension, of the Quantitative Easing regime, the appointment of a German ECB President (FT 2018), for instance, could lead to a spill-back in terms of the credibility of these newly acquired functions. Lastly, should Member State governments procrastinate too much on the reforms that the ECB has repeatedly encouraged them to conduct, the ECB could deem it necessary to backtrack on its liquidity arsenal to muscle up the credibility of its requests.

Three Policy Ideas to Muddle Through a Little Longer

Despite the obvious risks of muddling through, the consensus view among policy-makers is to look for all possible ways to complete EMU without a big bang. Three policy ideas have emerged as good illustrations of this approach: the creation of a fiscal backstop (see Schoenmaker 2017: Micossi

2017), the transformation of the European Stability Mechanism into a European Monetary Fund (see Sapir and Schoenmaker 2017) as well as the creation of a new position of EU Minister of Finance (Enderlein and Haas 2015). Not surprisingly, the fiscal backstop, the European Monetary Fund and the European Finance Minister have been at the core of a package of new measures released by the Commission in December 2017, to 'strengthen unity, improve efficiency and enhance democratic accountability' (EC 2017a: 2). Having been ideated within the limits of the current Treaty, the package sharply captures what EMU could look like in a few decades if muddling-through and the crisis-like, permanent and quasi-constitutional reform spirit would proceed. Assessing the package thus helps identify where the reform tensions are located and why muddling through is so costly. I will therefore examine these three ideas in turn. They all constitute imperfect solutions to the problem of institutional and instrumental fragmentation that the crisis produced. Moreover, all three ideas are likely to stay at the centre of the debate on EMU's institutional architecture over the next decades.

Much has been done during and after the euro crisis to make Europe's banking system more resilient. On the prudential side, stricter and more demanding capital rules and procedures have been adopted with the Capital Requirements Directive IV and the Capital Requirements Regulation package while a new, two-level micro-prudential supervisory regime has been established with the creation of the Single Supervisory Mechanism (SSM). In parallel, a whole new banking resolution regime has been set up. The Commission is thus correct to recall that compared to the pre-crisis situation, 'new EU rules on banking supervision and resolution developed in the aftermath of the crisis have significantly reduced the likelihood and potential impact of bank failures' (EC 2017c: 6). Moreover, those rules are about to be strengthened with the adoption of yet another Banking Package (EC 2016). However, despite those advances, EMU's crisis management capacity remains weak as the Banking Union's elephant in the room has not been addressed: who is backstopping the Banking Union and with which instrument? The absence of a fiscal backstop is indeed disturbing because the idea of creating EU-level mechanisms to support ailing banks in fiscally vulnerable countries was always considered to be a qualitative jump towards breaking the doom-loop. The Single Resolution Fund and the ESM instruments, designed to that effect, are however too weak and too difficult to mobilize to backstop the Banking Union (Schlosser 2017).

Put differently, Europe's financial stability will not be guaranteed until the EU as a whole can endure the failure of its largest systemic units, and all the more of several of its largest systemic units (e.g. BNP Paribas, Crédit Agricole, Deutsche Bank, Santander) at the same time. This means that the 'too big to fail principle', still characterises Europe's banking system, despite the advent of a new European banking resolution regime. This is why a fiscal backstop is needed to complete the Banking Union. Such a fiscal backstop instrument is a very salient element of the Commission's December 2017 Package which the Commission expects 'to decisively weaken the link between Member States finances and their banking systems' (EC 2017c: 10). In the Commission's view, the fiscal backstop would be 'a last resort to be activated if the Single Resolution Fund's immediately available resources proved to be insufficient for capital or liquidity purposes' (EC 2017c: 6). Such a backstop would be able to be mobilized only after a significant bail-in: 'it may be used to finance resolution costs, provided that all conditions of the regulatory framework are met, including the bail-in of 8% of total liabilities of the bank concerned' (EC 2017a: 6).

A crucial design feature is indeed that the fiscal backstop is 'fiscally neutral so that industry repays any potential disbursements from the fund and the use of public resources is limited' (EC 2017d). More concretely, the Commission proposal foresees that 'the combined amount of outstanding commitments for backstopping the SRF is subject to a ceiling of EUR 60 000 million' (EC 2017c: 15) but provides also that 'the Board of Governors should have the power to increase the ceiling accordingly' (EC 2017c: 25). In its proposal, the Commission also seeks to ensure that a 'reinforced qualified majority, in which 85% of the votes are required' is applied to the 'deployment of the backstop' (EC 2017a:6). Overall, the fiscal backstop would mean yet another fiscal authority transfer to the central level.

The creation of a European Monetary Fund (EMF), transforming the existing European Stability Mechanism (ESM), is the second salient element of the Commission's December 2017 Package. Because the ESM remains paralysed by an internal decision-making ruled by unanimity which means that *de facto*, it is 'not a real lender of last resort' (Enderlein and Haas 2015: 9). Hence the idea that the EMF 'should take over the existing responsibilities from the ESM, but expand them and adopt a different governance model' (Sapir and Schoenmaker 2017: 4). Compared to the fiscal backstop idea which can be narrowed down to the creation of a new instrument in the broader toolbox, the EMF idea has more to do with institution-building (Sandbu 2017). This makes it by essence problematic. The Commission's overarching goal with this proposal is to 'further strengthen its institutional anchoring' (EC 2017c: 4) and to ensure that 'the EMF will establish itself as a robust crisis management body within the Union framework, working in full synergy with other EU institutions' (EC 2017c: 4). The Commission's EMF proposal puts a strong emphasis on the need to have a more accountable financial stability actor. To that effect, the Commission foresees to turn the EMF into a "unique legal entity' called a 'Union body' (EC 2017c: 4); it proposes to generalize the use of qualified majority voting for decisions on the disbursement of funds; it foresees a more direct involvement of the EMF, alongside the European Commission' when it comes to managing financial assistance programmes (EC 2017a: 6); it relocates the EMF's discretionary powers within the ECOFIN and provides for an 'endorsement by the Council of discretionary decisions taken by the European Monetary Fund' (EC 2017c: 6).

However, aside from the ESM's suboptimal governance, there is a deeper and more convincing reason behind the idea of creating a full-fledged European Monetary Fund. The euro is a currency without a state and as such is missing a sovereign that can support its value when its credibility or the credibility of its single constituents is attacked. This is why the ESM's existence contributes not only to the reactive management of sovereign debt crises, it also – proactively – 'prevents self-fulfilling crisis in sovereign debt markets' (Wolff 2017: 5). In theory, this can be extended to dynamics of the banking system, since 'ultimately the standing of a banking system depends on the strength of the fiscal authority behind it and on its ability to provide a fiscal backstop' (Schoenmaker 2017). Sapir and Schoenmaker (2017) spelled out the larger implications of an ideal European Monetary Fund, in contrast to the narrower EMF imagined by the European Commission. In their assessment, 'EMU 2.0 still suffers from three main weaknesses' (Sapir and Schoenmaker 2017: 2–3): 'it still lacks an instrument to deal in an orderly way with insolvency crises [...], this makes the no-bailout clause of the Maastricht Treaty toothless' (Sapir and Schoenmaker 2017: 1); the Banking Union is incomplete as the EDIS[13] is not yet up and running and the SRM fails to have a credible backstop: 'use of the ESM's direct recapitalisation instrument is subject to such strict conditions that it falls short of a credible ex-ante fiscal backstop to the SRF' (Sapir and Schoenmaker 2017: 3). Thirdly, 'ESM decisions require unanimity and the prior approval of some national parliaments. The unanimity rule also applies for lending under the direct recapitalisation instrument' (Sapir and Schoenmaker 2017: 3).

This is why Sapir and Schoenmaker (2017: 1) advocate to 'design the EMF as part of a broader risk-sharing and market-discipline agenda' and make several suggestions on the new capacities that such a Fund should have. A key reason why they support such a new mechanism is also to give relief to the ECB: 'in the euro area, the ECB can or should be able to prevent or to manage a sovereign or a banking crisis as long as it is a matter of providing liquidity on a temporary basis. Beyond that, it should be the responsibility of the EMF, as the fiscal agent of euro-area governments, to protect the stability of governments and banks' (Sapir and Schoenmaker 2017: 4). They stress that 'the EMF should be fully capable of acting as the fiscal counterpart of the ECB to guarantee the financial stability of the euro area in the event of a sovereign or banking crisis, or a threat of a crisis' (Sapir and Schoenmaker 2017: 4). In other words, Sapir and Schoenmaker aim for the following: 'the EMF should not deal only with sovereign crises or only with banking crises. It should deal with both in order to effectively prevent the occurrence of sovereign-bank 'doom loops' (Sapir and Schoenmaker 2017: 6). In their expectation, 'the EMF's involvement will contribute to breaking the negative feedback loops between sovereigns, banks and the real economy, which is crucial for a smooth functioning of the EMU' (Sapir and Schoenmaker 2017: 2). Ultimately, the Commission's proposal thus appears to fall short of any significant breakthrough in terms of stabilisation of the euro area. This is largely due to the fact that it is framed in a muddling-through logic.

A third crucial element of the Commission's EMU Package is the proposed 'creation of the post of European Minister of Economy and Finance' (EC 2017b: 1) which follows on the earlier idea of creating a 'super-Commissioner' to veto national budgets (Karagiannis and Guidi 2014: 1). Here is how the Commission justifies the creation of such a position: 'compared to monetary policy, which is unified for euro area Member States and easily identified by citizens, economic policy is essentially managed by individual Member States and coordination efforts at EU and euro area level are conducted by many actors' (EC 2017b: 1). The Commission goes on in stressing that such institutional patchwork 'has led to complex decision-making processes, which have often been criticized for not being sufficiently understandable and efficient' (EC 2017b: 1). Overall, 'coordination efforts at EU and euro area level are conducted by many actors' (EC 2017b: 1). This echoes the argument made earlier by Enderlein and Haas (2015: 8) that 'there are too many actors involved in crisis management negotiations' (Enderlein and Haas 2015: 8) while 'no one seems to be fully in charge' (Enderlein and Haas 2015: 8).

Looking at the solutions that this reform can bring about, the Commission considers that the 'minister will be instrumental in strengthening the coherence, efficiency, transparency and democratic accountability of EU economic governance' (EC 2017b: 10). The Commission expects that 'the minister would help to create synergies and thus improve the overall coherence and effectiveness of EU economic policy-making' (EC 2017b: 1). The Commission stresses that 'certain functions could be combined under a European Minister in order to pursue the general interest of the EU and euro area economy, to strengthen policy coordination and to deliver an improved policy mix at all levels' (EC 2017b: 10). Lastly, it is anticipated that 'the minister would also contribute to strengthening the transparency of EU policy-making, accountability towards the European Parliament and the interaction with national authorities' (EC 2017b: 1), thereby leading to a more 'effective governance and further strengthening democratic accountability' (EC 2017b: 1). The final goal would be that the reform ushers in the 'ultimate merger of the function of Commission Vice-President in charge of the Economic and Monetary Union with that of President of the Eurogroup' (EC 2017b: 2), a move which the Commission insists 'is already possible under the current EU Treaties' (EC 2017b: 10). In reality, the Finance Minister would altogether cumulate three different 'hats' as he would also be the Chair of the ESM's (or indeed the EMF's) Board of Governors.

Two years before the Commission came out with their proposal, Enderlein and Haas (2015) laid out a first vision for the possible role and accountability of a European Finance Minister. They distinguished two models, 'a EMU supervisor', a German-inspired declination that would focus on 'risk-sharing' through 'negative integration' (Enderlein and Haas 2015: 5) and 'an EMU manager', a French-inspired declination, characterised by 'sovereignty-sharing' through 'positive integration' (Enderlein and Haas 2015: 5), recognising that 'there seems to be little to no overlap between the two concepts' (Enderlein and Haas 2015: 4). It is unclear whether the Commission's model intends to turn the Finance Minister into a manager or a supervisor. What is however certain is that the covert institutionalization strategy, followed by the Commission, comes in stark contrast with the recommendation provided by Enderlein and Haas

(2015) that 'any solution coming close to our proposal would require a change of the European treaties' (Enderlein and Haas 2015: 14).

In this light, Patrin (2018: 4) uncovers that the model which inspired the new Finance Minister post, the position of High Representative of the Union for Foreign Affairs and Security Policy, 'was agreed by Treaty revision, its role and functions are spelled out in the Treaties and the administrative reform underpinning it was the result of an inter-institutional political bargain that led to the creation of the External Service as a special administrative apparatus shared between the Council and the Commission'. Patrin (2018: 7) stresses that 'the position admittedly would ensure better representation of the interest of the euro-area as a whole, however at the expenses of the separation of powers and functions between the institutions'. Lastly, 'the creation of a Finance Minister would necessarily lead to the institutionalisation of the Eurogroup. This in turn, would however raise the question of the relation between the newly formalised Eurogroup and the ECOFIN Council, and, more importantly of the relation between the latter and the Finance Minister' (Patrin 2018: 10). It is fair to ask 'how would an official Minister preside over an informal institution?' (Patrin 2018: 11). These critiques point here again at a half-baked proposal by the Commission. I argue that the proposal is undermined and weakened by the fact that it is framed in a muddling-through and technocratic logic.

The Institutional Limits of Those Ideas

Whereas the creation of a small fiscal backstop is rather convincing on functional grounds and institutionally less problematic, the EMF and the Finance minister ideas have something disturbing in common. Rather than being justified by the instrumental returns than their functions will bring to the EMU system, they strive more on the promise that their institutional creation offers to the Commission's state-building fantasies. In other words, their establishment seems to be more motivated by their symbolic but also grandiloquent contribution to EMU state-building rather than by the solutions that they will bring to bear to EMU in the long term. How else could the disregard of easier and simpler institutional alternatives – the revision of the Treaty of the European Stability Mechanism and the establishment of a full-time Eurogroup Chairman – be explained? As Sandbu (2017) argues, 'mistaking institution-building for policymaking is an ingrained bad habit of European policymakers. In the context of euro reform, one needs to ask the question why a changed institutional set-up would make for better policy when leaders have made avoidable mistakes in the current set-up. Seen from another perspective, why not use the existing institutional set-up better? Many of the improvements the eurozone is claimed to need can be achieved with current tools' (Sandbu 2017: 1). This reasoning however assumes the ability 'to distinguish form from function, or put differently, institutions from mechanisms'. Indeed, 'policy or mechanism choice can be made separately from institutional choices' (Sandbu 2017; Guttenberg 2017).

Justifying the rationale for EMU reforms, European Commission President Juncker benignly declared in his September 2017 State of the Union address: 'we must complete the European House now that the sun is shining' (Juncker 2017). By throwing concrete ideas on the table for EMU reform and putting the ball on the side of Member States who have in the past committed to mutualizing more, in particular France and Germany, the Commission is doing its job of enforcing Member States' commitments. In reality, the current institutional set up gives a rather ungrateful role to the Commission. When the Commission puts forwards bold reform proposals it is criticised for its idealism. When it is too wary of Member States' interests and does not table new proposals, it is criticised for being in the hands of large Member States and for not taking its independent role seriously enough. This means in some way that regardless of the course of action that the Commission decides to follow, it will always be wrong. This is why, despite the critique on the design of their proposals, one can praise the Commission for its determination to fuel the much needed debate on EMU reforms.

However, the nature of the Commission proposals also indicates the institution's dissatisfaction with its current role in EMU. It is fairly obvious that the Commission's December 2017 Package was not only driven by the pressing need to consolidate EMU in good times. It was also an attempt by the Commission to reclaim an institutional territory that it lost to the Eurogroup during the crisis, an intention that the Commission had openly stressed in its Reflections Paper when it underlined the necessity to find 'a 'new balance' between the Commission and the Eurogroup' (EC 2017a: 27). Indeed, the first 'victim' of a communitarized EMF and of a Finance Minister creation would indeed be the ever more central Eurogroup. The Package should thus be seen as an attempt for the Commission to put itself at the centre of EMU after having been strongly marginalised during the crisis. This effort can be for example observed in a blatant reframing of the ESM genesis where the Commission attributes the creation of the

ESM outside of the EU legal order only to the intensity of the crisis: 'the pressure of events at the time led to an intergovernmental solution being found' (EC 2017a: 4). It omits to stress that large Member States refrained from granting any additional budgetary powers to the Commission because they didn't want to entrust them durably and irreversibly to the European Commission. Meanwhile, the Commission appears to cherish the dream of applying the Community method to EMU. Yet, as the first chapter of this book explained, the functions granted to the Commission by the Maastricht Treaty can overall be assimilated to Secretariat-like functions.

Despite the Commission's claim that form should follow function, the Commission's way forward seems to be more inspired by the opposite mantra of 'function follows form'. First one sets up an EMF and a Finance Minister in a way that is reinforcing the Commission's role in EMU and then it will be seen what those new actors do exactly to increase EMU's overall welfare. In this the Commission's package is in denial of the political reality: it 'favours a model that puts the Commission at the centre of fiscal policy decision-making' (Wolff 2017: 1) and which 'ignores the reality of the strong intergovernmental nature of European fiscal policy coordination' (Wolff 2017: 2). It also disregards a related dimension: the growing lack of trust or even 'mistrust' (Wolff 2017: 2) that Member States express towards the Commission. This book's empirical analysis found confirmation for the claim that Member States generally want to keep the Commission at 'arm's length' (Hodson 2013). Despite its strengthened role in fiscal surveillance – uncovered in Chap. 3 – the new ideas put in the negotiation by the Commission should thus be interpreted as an admission of its weakness and of its soul-searching in the interinstitutional game. This attitude is reinforced by the fact that the Commission seems to be paralysed by the prospects of an increasingly differentiated integration. And indeed it is uncertain whether such an integration channel would still rely on the Commission as a central executive actor or whether it would empower *ad hoc*, sector agencies instead.

What the Commission seems to be trying to do is to go down the road of functionalism (i.e. by creating new functions and instruments at the EU level) instead of acknowledging that the priority for the future development of the EMU polity is to recognise its new actors and to discuss and determine which one among the two main EMU executive actors should be EMU's fiscal *inter pares*. Of course this is a Pandora box because Treaty change would involve parliamentary ratifications and, at times, ratifications via referenda. However, this argument is brushed aside by the Commission. Yet, if a brighter future for Europe's stability goes through the completion of the Economic and Monetary Union as the Commission seems to indicate in its Communication, then a different method must be considered. A more democratic one. A more inclusive one. A more far-sighted one. Such an approach would entail to revisit the roles and responsibilities of all EMU actors including first and foremost the ECB and the Eurogroup but also the role of the Commission in EMU. The half-backed Commission Package thus leaves the observer with a series of unanswered questions: Doesn't a reform of the ECB's mandate stand in the way of a sustainable EMU? Twenty years after its creation, shouldn't the Eurogroup become a formal EU institution? What is the real action perimeter of new bodies created during the crisis such as the European Stability Mechanism (ESM) and the Single Resolution Board (SRB)? Last but not least, what are the merits of institutional consolidation if the EU Treaty should be left untouched?

SOME CONCERNS OVER TREATY OPTIMISATION

The genuine contradiction at the core of the package is the intention by the Commission to normalize and streamline EMU's architecture, to enhance democratic accountability while at the same time stretching the existing provisions of the Treaty to its most extreme limits. Under the functional excuse of completing EMU, the Commission is proposing to create a European Monetary Fund, to establish the function of a European Finance Minister and, beyond that, to create new financial instruments at the disposal of these new central actors. In other words, it is advocating further functional layering in a logic of executive federalism and state-building. While many will agree that European integration is facing a 'constraining dissensus' (Hooghe and Marks 2008) recently illustrated by the massive surge in populism throughout Europe, the European Commission – obviously in denial of new these political dynamics – looks eager to kick the can further down the road.

The Commission seems to look at the Lisbon Treaty and perceive it only as a set of constraints preventing its development into EMU's executive. In this vision the Treaty's constitutional and democratic nature is denied while the Commission focusses on how to exploit existing loopholes and how to optimize under constraint. While this pragmatism could derive from the French and Dutch referenda and from Brexit, this approach reveals however an imbalance between the type of grand institution that the Commission would like to create and the legal act that will bring it to life. For example, the International Monetary Fund was established by the United Nations Monetary and Financial Conference – also known as the Bretton Woods conference – which gathered more than 700 delegates from 44 nations and was later ratified by every signatory member state's parliaments. By contrast, setting up a European Monetary Fund by a mere Council Regulation clearly looks like institutional design by stealth. A key question in that regard is: what is the merit of formalising the European Stability Mechanism into something else if after the formalisation the EMF will become a 'unique legal entity' which does not mean anything tangible legally speaking. Why can't the European Stability Mechanism be converted into an EU agency?

More provocatively, if it is agreed that in the future the EMF will per-form the tasks of an EMU treasury, shouldn't this treasury become an EU institution? The Commission explicitly declares that the EMF would also be in all likelihood in charge of the stabilisation function, this means that in a dynamic perspective, the EMF will really be a future EMU treasury: 'the proposal refers to the possibility for the European Monetary Fund to develop new financial instruments. Over time, such instruments could supplement or support other EU financial instruments and programmes. Such synergies could prove particularly useful if the European Monetary Fund were to play a role in support to a possible stabilisation function in the future' (EC 2017c: 7). Such a dynamic view of the EMF is further substantiated when the Commission argues – in rather cynical terms – that 'article 352 could also be used to confer additional tasks on the ESM when it is integrated into the Union' (EC 2017c: 11). This seems to con-firm that the only reason why the EMF under EU law is set up is that it can be tasked with new prerogatives. The current *raison d'etre* of the EMF is hence to be an embryo of a more long term solution. Given those broad-based implications, one can wonder whether a simple modification of the European Stability Mechanism Treaty wouldn't be a better way forward. Surely the fiscal backstop could be established in this way.

What is therefore striking to the observer is that the Commission's EMF proposal is half-cooked. It focuses only on the tip of the iceberg (the mechanism) whereas what ought to be discussed is EMU's institutional structure and the role, competences and democratic accountability of an EMU fiscal institution formalised as part of a Treaty change. As Guttenberg stresses: 'the ESM debate is used in these cases as a vehicle to discuss much larger issues relating to the institutional structure of EMU' (Guttenberg 2017: 4). This is also underlined by Sapir and Schoenmaker (2017: 7): 'the transformation of the ESM into an EMF should not be viewed as a stand-alone initiative. It should be considered as part of a wider institutional reform of the fiscal organisation of the euro area'. Such a reform will also impact on the role of the European Central Bank. Although the Commission tries hard to hide it, a key driver for the constitution of a fiscal institution is the ECB's 'institutional loneliness' (Padoa-Schioppa 1999) and the fact that the ECB needs a fiscal counterpart to be relieved from its too central role in EMU crisis management. Over time, EMU would ideally have only two crisis management institutions: one monetary (the ECB) and one fiscal (the EU Treasury). In this regard, the ECB's semantic objection to calling this new fiscal institution a 'monetary fund' has some valid ground. Ironically, 'the institution most actively calling for such a voice has been the ECB, arguing that if needed a political counterpart in charge of overseeing member states' fiscal policy and economic policy coordination at the euro-area level' (Enderlein and Haas 2015: 4, referring to a speech by ECB Board Member Benoît Coeuré). To ensure that EMU's monetary institution is flanked with a counterpart of equal weight, a fiscal institution should thus be created and enshrined in the Treaty.

The imbalance between the institution-building ambitions of the Commission and the legal vehicles used to that effect is also striking in the case of the Finance Minister. The function and competences of Ministers in domestic constituencies are typically foreseen by constitutions whereas in this instance, the Commission seems to believe that a mere non-binding Communication can outline its role. The Commission strangely indicates that 'by combining existing functions and available expertise at EU level, the Minister would help create synergies and thus contribute to a more efficient governance framework' (EC 2017b: 5). Moreover, 'the minister would not create a new supranational bureaucratic layer, nor would the Minister impinge on national competences' (EC 2017b: 5). But then how much of a Minister would this new position be? Usually, 'a finance minister should be in charge of a substantial budget, with, ideally, taxation and spending powers and the capacity to borrow' (Wolff 2017: 6). There is indeed something puzzling about the asymmetry that the new function would entail: the minister would have no administration and no treasury, the minister would be part of no government, the minister would have no prime minister. Which authority would the minister have? Why would it be a minister at all then and who would take the job? By carefully avoiding to settle on who should become such a fiscal actor, among the Eurogroup, the ECOFIN and the Commission, and most importantly – settling on who should no longer exercise those functions – the Commission's proposal merely offers the continuation of the status quo. A transformation of the role of the existing Chair of the Eurogroup who could become permanent, as EU Member States have discussed (European Council 2011), would be a simpler and more operational solution.

Moreover, the merging of roles bears inter-institutional and inner-institutional consequences. 'Juncker's plan to merge the role of the chair of the Eurogroup with that of the Economic and Financial affairs Commissioner is institutionally problematic. In fact, the proposal would amount to asking the prosecutor to preside as the chief judge over fiscal decision-making' (Wolff 2017: 2). Inter-institutional balance issues but also 'conflicts of interests' (Wolff 2017: 3) arise. A connected doubt is how such a new position would co-exist with the Commission's internal principle of collegiality (Patrin 2018). Another dimension which is worth debating is the fact that such a new function misleadingly gives the impression of autonomy. In reality however, the Minister would be strictly subject to the authority of the President of the European Commission. Yet, by proposing the creation of a Finance Minister it is jumping fast to a too specific and imperfect solution that, for now, appears to mostly suit its institutional interest. Where the Commission is more convincing is that the EU needs a fiscal counterpart to its monetary institution, the ECB.

A Look at Three Competing Medium-Term Scenarios

I see three possible scenarios for the medium term evolution of EMU. Reflecting a diversity of political systems, these scenarios logically differ in the varying degree of centralized powers and in the type of decision-making that they imply. Crucially, they also entail varying assumptions on what the European Union is: an administrative or a constitutional undertaking (Lindseth 2010). I contend that going forward, the crucial question that EU political leaders will have to face is how to engineer an EMU fiscal state-formation in a way that internalizes the currently poor legitimacy resources of the European Union. I also argue that a new constitutional settlement will be needed over the medium term to formalize the institutional changes made during the euro crisis. On several instances, institutional practices have indeed drifted too far away from the letter and spirit of the Lisbon Treaty. Such a settlement would clarify the separation of powers and checks and balances of the EU polity. In this context, Treaty makers will also have to make a crucial choice as to the type of European polity that they envisage for European citizens: will it be an executive technocracy, an intergovernmental confederation, or a federal democracy?

The model of an *executive technocracy* constitutes a path-breaking scenario from muddling-through because the scenario revolves around a more effective and efficient EU polity. It is based on limited institutional simplification and consolidation and on the creation of a small fiscal centre. The scenario also implies Treaty change. Institutionally, it rests on the empowerment of both supranational and intergovernmental technocratic actors. More specifically, the *executive technocracy* model would rely on a dominant ECB (formalized in its status as EMU's lender of last resort), on an ultra-central Commission and on a full-time Eurogroup president who would also supervise a European Treasury. The European Parliament would remain marginal in this set-up. The integration trajectory towards *executive technocracy* would follow the neo-functionalist logic encapsulated in the famous line of Jean Monnet that 'Europe will be forged in crises and will be the sum of the solutions adapted for those crises' (Monnet 1988). Compared to a pure functionalist logic, this scenario assumes however that EU leaders show the capacity to periodically punctuate the process of an 'ever closer union' by episodes of institutional rationalization.

In terms of its functional shape, *executive technocracy's* new mutualisation steps would include on the one hand the completion of the remaining pillars that are envisaged to reach a full Banking Union. According to the Five Presidents Report (2015) this means a common deposit guarantee scheme, a fiscal capacity and eventually, probably in a limited form, an EU/EMU unemployment benefit scheme likely to provide some degree of stabilization through shock absorption in the euro area. On the other hand, it can be expected that the functional pressures provided by the sovereign-bank loop which already led the way to the Banking Union will be exploited further to reach a deeper Fiscal Union too. This would be in line with the current trend of creating a fiscal union 'through the back door' (Schelkle 2012), i.e. pushing forward the integration of fiscal instruments on the basis of their expected insurance benefits for the stability of the Banking Union. Illustrative measures of this crossbreed area of the banking and fiscal unions is the creation of a European Safe Bond (Brunnermeier et al. 2011) and the introduction of risk-weights for the treatment of sovereign debt (ESRB 2015; ESM 2016) to limit the doom-loop between banks and sovereigns.

In terms of genuine fiscal integration, an interviewee underlined that the key aim of this small fiscal centre should be to have 'a legitimizable centre that sets key parameters for fiscal policy', but looks only at 'financial stability' not 'redistribution'.[14] In this regard, the same interviewee conjectured that 'it would be probably sufficient to set the fiscal stance'.[15] A key feature of this small fiscal centre is that it would be underpinned by the creation of a euro area Treasury, for which a consensus is slowly gathering pace: 'among experts, there is a growing consensus for a euro area treasury'.[16] While different functions – e.g. a fiscal capacity, an investment fund (Enderlein and Haas 2015) – could be attributed to this state-like structure, the added-value of this new construct would reside in the consolidation and concentration of fiscal powers within one administration. Moreover, 'gradually, it would get a much larger role'.[17] The consolidation however will imply Treaty change, and would require an ESM Treaty revision too. A variation of *executive technocracy* would see the appointment of a European finance minister at the helm of this new Treasury.

In line with its focus on the construction of a more powerful and lean executive arm within EMU, the *executive technocracy* scenario clearly privileges efficiency over democratic legitimacy concerns. The model builds on a stronger degree of power concentration to credibly warrant the stability of the euro. It does so however through a marked empowerment of technocratic experts and a disregard of democratic and accountability processes as the current framework does. A key weakness of this scenario is hence its short-termist nature: it does not provide any sustainable solution to EMU's legitimacy conundrum as it simply assumes that a more effective set-up will ensure this. The proposal of a euro area finance minister is particularly illustrative of this limitation. Being deprived of a government as the constitution of the latter would require another type and degree of political integration, this stand-alone minister would be more likely to be a technocrat. Its function would be closer to the function of a judge than to a politician as its central likely responsibility would be the enforcement of rules. This led an interviewee to characterise the idea of a Euro Area Finance Minister as 'a joke'.[18]

The scenario further assumes that constitutional reform and institutional consolidation will allow for the advent of a fiscal centre. However, fragmentation forces are likely to prevail while domestic constitutional constraints could block the emergence of a single fiscal authority at the

EU level. A further limitation of this model is that it does not entail a definitive answer on the nature of the EU polity as either an administrative or a constitutional polity. The functionalist mantra that foresees that 'form follows function' (Mitrany 1943: 236) fuels indeed institutional ambiguity. Key constitutional principles would thus be sacrificed for the achievement of a wider functional good, a stronger fiscal centre that would instead guarantee the stability of the euro area. To the extent that the scenario extrapolates the current muddling-through, the political feasibility of the *executive technocracy* scenario seems to be moderate.

The model of *intergovernmental confederation* departs from the institutional engineering that characterised Europe during the crisis. Whilst also requiring Treaty change, it revolves around a vertical redistribution of powers in the European Union between the central level and the national level. It also breaks away from path-dependency and rests on a constitutional settlement that clearly favours intergovernmental actors at the expense of supranational actors. This scenario relies indeed on the assumption of the 'cultural persistence of national democratic and constitutional legitimacy in the European system of governance' (Lindseth 2010: xii). Member States are thus considered to be the 'primary locus of democratic and constitutional legitimacy in the European system' (Lindseth 2010: xiv). Assuming that the European 'integration has gone too far' (Majone 2014) in expanding its powers, the scenario hence implies the repatriation of some powers to the Member State level to ensure that the EU polity stays in line with its purely administrative nature. The outcome of this scenario would be 'a significantly lower level of institutionalization' (Majone 2014: 5). As such, *intergovernmental confederation* would provide that EU Member States would never be outvoted by their peers in case a legislation or a decision is affecting a Member State's core interest.

Institutionally, powers would have to be taken away from the EU centre. An *intergovernmental confederation* would attribute a dominant role to the European Council which would rule by unanimity in all areas of core state powers, including evidently fiscal policy. In line with this intergovernmentalist bias, a deliberative Eurogroup would occupy centre stage, yet its focus would lay on the exchange of best economic policy practices with almost no constraints falling on the sovereignty of EU leaders. In other words, the Eurogroup's operation would be closest to its current Treaty-based, purely discussion-oriented and informal rationale. To ensure that risks of agency drift are avoided, the Commission would be functionally limited in its action scope. For example, it would be deprived of any fiscal power other than the management of the EU budget. While remaining the central actor that it is on the single market, it would also no longer be granted a right of initiative. The European Parliament, for its part, would be denied its existing co-legislator function in the sensitive policy-areas in which the spill-back would occur. The ECB's mandate, instead, would be very close to the letter and spirit of the Maastricht Treaty which largely focussed on price stability. The Bank would therefore stick to its narrow and conservative mandate— in particular when it comes to liquidity provision.

Concretely, this scenario would see no need for a fiscal centre. By contrast, it would involve a higher *de jure* autonomy of fiscal and economic policies at national level, meaning a complete abandonment of the Stability and Growth Pact in exchange for a twin reliance on decentralized hard constitutional budget constraints and on market discipline, i.e. credit markets exerting pressure on deficit prone countries to limit excessive deficits. The other side of the same coin is also the fact that to be credible, these hard constraints would need to be accompanied by a debt restructuring regime. Tougher participation rules in the EMU would therefore ensure that discipline is exerted through the threat of a euro exit. In its most extreme declination, this scenario would imply the dismantling of the European Stability Mechanism as its existence assumes the persistence of common liabilities among EMU Member States. A less radical version of the scenario would rest on strict conditionality and on a new rule that would ensure that the ESM can only be mobilized once a debt restructuring has occurred, in order to internalize moral hazard considerations.

The added value of this scenario is that it would address current democratic and legitimacy concerns that the EU 'is doing too much' and would hold in check what is at times perceived as an ineluctable drive towards an 'ever closer union', a drive forward also portrayed as 'integration for its own sake' (Majone 2014: 8). The model appears to be the closest to contemporary political dynamics at domestic level. It is more in line with what the current European median voter would expect from its national political leaders: a re-appropriation of political sovereignty. Such a propensity for 'taking back control' has been evidenced for example during the Brexit debate but is also more generally the mantra of rising populist parties also in founding members of the European Union such as Italy, France and last but not least, Germany. One can argue that such a power repatriation would be performed at the benefit of a higher democratic legitimacy in the short term, which over time, could also profit in turn to the sake of

European integration as it would lead to a safer management of EU Member States legitimacy resources.

The key weakness of an *intergovernmental confederation* is that it entails however so limited centralization that it is doubtful whether its minimalist agenda internalizes at all the existence of the euro, and overall, the inter-dependence that EU membership implies. As this model is likely to foster divergences of economic performance within EMU (it does not foresee the existence of any central mechanism to counter-act this), it therefore implicitly includes a disintegrationist dimension. In the absence of strong imbalances correcting institutions, members of the EMU club who are unable to sustain market pressure over the long term would indeed have to face the consequences of this reality and exit the euro. The future of the euro as a currency is thus threatened by this scenario. Another key diffi-culty is the fact that the scenario rests on a dual architecture within the EU, the single market on the one hand and the core state powers on the other. Such a distinction is indeed central to delineate the role of the European Council and of the Commission on the one hand, and the type of decision-rule (unanimity vs. qualified majority) on the other. Yet, in practice, it is utterly challenging to draw a clear line between internal mar-ket and core state powers. Is banking supervision a core state power? What about banking resolution? These considerations cast high doubts on the political feasibility of this scenario.

The model of *democratic federalism* would consist in a significant EU institutional rearrangement that would result in a grand, federal political scheme, elaborated by a European Convention and implemented through Treaty change. Among the three medium-term models offered, *demo-cratic federalism* is the most radical in terms of its departure from the existing institutional change path and in terms of the magnitude of its leap forward. Accordingly, it is also the least politically feasible given the cur-rent domestic constraints on European integration.

The scenario's starting point is that European citizens strive to have a clear and understandable EU political system with few actors and clearly delineated powers, an outcome that can only be provided by a federal system. The model is thus centred on the provision of a more democratic and legitimate European Union based on an institutional reform that aims, like in classic federations, to attribute key powers to central level actors but also to clarify where the political responsibility lies. *Democratic federalism* builds on the assumption that the EU has a constitutional nature and that democracy can go beyond the borders of the nation-state. In this regard, it rests on the notion that European integration should follow an entirely different trajectory than the one it is pursuing since the Rome Treaty. Instead of accepting the principle that economic integration will naturally lead to political integration which this perspective contests, *democratic federalism* follows a logic *à la Spinelli*. It hence assumes that the EU should overtly become a genuine federation through the overt constitution of a parliamentary Convention. The model furthermore contends that the creation of state capacities at the EU level requires the constitution of such a federalist system to ensure that the capacities are exercised by legitimate and democratic transnational actors. In terms of vertical and horizontal power distribution, *democratic federalism* would be the 'cleanest' way out of the capacity building conundrum in which the EU is currently trapped. Further, because of its democratic embeddedness and of the existence of a thick fiscal centre, it is the only scenario that could lead to the advent of a legitimate single fiscal actor, *a primus inter pares*, at the European level.

Institutionally, the scenario mostly relies on the empowerment of supranational actors which would however be rooted within and be legitimated by democratic processes. The new EMU fiscal actor would thus become the undisputed EU executive which would be accountable to a more central European Parliament while the European Council would be turned into the upper legislative chamber of the EU and be strapped of its current *de facto* executive powers. To be more specific, the new EMU fiscal actor would therefore manage a larger EU budget, would manage the ESM as its instrument to safeguard financial stability and would be able to issue debt. The ECB's would be made more accountable to the European Parliament. The EP, in turn, would be the main forum for the debate over the economic policy in EMU. In this light, it could request a spontaneous audition by both the ECB president and by the President of the new EMU fiscal actor, should controversial measures taken by those institutions go against the stability and growth of the euro area. Who would the new EMU fiscal actor be? Given the distrust of Member States towards the Commission, the latter is unlikely to come EMU's *primus inter pares*. In my view, a Switzerland-inspired federal council made up of a hand-full of EMU finance ministers and directed by a full-time Brussels-based President would be a more promising solution.

Concretely, the *democratic federalism* model would allow for the constitution of a strong and potentially growing fiscal centre. Fiscal stabilization and limited fiscal redistribution functions would be attributed to the EU level. Accordingly, I contend that this is the only scenario that would for instance allow the creation of Eurobonds, i.e. a mutual debt instrument that could be issued by all EMU participating member states, thereby embedding fiscal solidarity in EMU durably. Alongside Eurobonds, the fiscal union foreseen by *democratic federalism* could feature a direct source of income, a stronger budget, an unemployment benefit scheme as well as the key fiscally relevant instruments of a full Banking Union (i.e. a deposit guarantee scheme and a fiscal backstop). This scenario could hence virtually see, over the very long term, the co-existence of a full banking union and of a full fiscal union. This model would allow a stronger reliance on discretion than on law.

Democratic federalism fairs equally well in terms of democratic nature, legitimacy performance and effectiveness. Its political feasibility is however very low. The scenario's materialization faces a high hurdle as it is unclear how heads of state and governments would naturally and deliberately hand-over their powers to an EU government in a peaceful context. What is therefore unknown is how to create the context for such a jump into the unknown. The history of federations suggest that the emergence of such a new political order could only come from a security crisis, a typical situation in which effectiveness trumps all other considerations. A second caveat of this model is that it is expected to trigger territorial fragmentation. Based on the recognition that the creation of overt capacity-building institutions – which would form the backbone of the federation – tends to create domestic opposition, *democratic federalism* is unlikely to develop in a format that involves all participating EU Member States. In other words, the clarity gained by a more strict delineation of vertical powers would have to be assessed and measured against an increased horizontal patchwork as it would be likely that participation on fiscal arrangements would vary across fiscal capacities. Lastly, and this is probably the most important limitation of the scenario, the model assumes that European citizens would ratify such a huge integrationist step forward which is far from evident, given the diversity of preferences over European integration even in the medium-term.

What Should EU Leaders Do Now to Make EMU Sustainable?

Against this background, what should EU leaders do to make EMU sustainable? My view is that the scenario I termed 'democratic federalism' offers the most valuable and promising prospects for EMU's future. Why? Because I believe that EMU will only be able to function properly if its actors perform what their constitutional mandate asks them to perform. In other words, political responsibilities should be very clearly attributed in EMU's polity. This is a crucial condition for a genuine trust in the currency and its underlying institutions.

While institutional engineering could take on various forms and a myriad of instruments could be generated, I believe that three key reforms should be performed. In my view, the EU should (1) move away from a crisis management that is too reliant on the ECB, (2) it should constitute a fiscal institution that becomes the legitimate and lead actor in crisis management, (3) it should create new fiscal instruments at EU level and should simplify and revisit the fiscal rules. All those reforms require Treaty change. But, let's face it: if one wants to make the euro crisis-proof, then Europe needs a Treaty change. It is hypocritical to keep on claiming the opposite.

Step 1: Re-dimension and Clearly Delineate the Role of the European Central Bank

Over the years of the euro crisis, unconventional monetary policy instruments have mushroomed to safeguard the euro and Emergency Liquidity Assistance (ELA) has been largely mobilized by Eurosystem central banks. Yet, the use of central banking solutions should be restricted to last resort situations and be subject to the real discretion of the central bank. During the crisis, the opposite seemed to be true. As Chap. 5 documented, liquidity provision instruments appeared to be increasingly of a business as usual nature and were used at times reluctantly by the ECB, simply because there was no other actor left to save the euro.

However, the European Central Bank cannot be the mother of all crisis management forever: 'depending on the ECB alone is economically dangerous and politically unsustainable' (De Geus et al. 2017: 2). And yet, Europe's existing crisis management arsenal still assumes the implicit support of the ECB, whose actions stopped the euro crisis from escalating further. After all, it was only with the 'whatever it takes' declaration by Mario Draghi and the following launch of the Outright Monetary Transactions that the concerns of a pervasive doom loop between fragile Southern European banks and fiscally vulnerable governments ebbed away. Because of the absence of an EU or EMU treasury, the Bank suffered from a Padoa-Schioppian 'institutional loneliness' during the crisis. Compared to other OECD central banks whose long-term sustainability is implicitly provided by the Treasury of the country in which they are based, the ECB has indeed no federal EU counter-part which can absorb risks like the FED can do. In my view, the ECB has reached the limit of the tasks it can concentrate, both in terms of the spirit of the Treaty but also in terms of EMU's overall inter-institutional balance.

The ECB's paradox is that on the one hand, 'it has never been so powerful' (Honohan 2017: 1) and on the other, it still does not dispose of a sufficient portfolio of tasks to ensure a crucial central banking mission, namely: be EMU's lender of last resort. To put this in further perspective: 'central banks were put on this earth to be lenders of last resort. Dealing with complex situations in which banks are running out of liquidity and may or may not be solvent should be a core part of every central bank's tasks. The ECB, however, does not currently play this role in a coherent and comprehensive manner' (Whelan 2014: 19). I thus believe that the existing Emergency Liquidity Assistance regime that falls under the responsibility of Eurosystem Central Banks but grants a veto to the ECB, is not sustainable. ELA should be federalized. In this regard I concur with Whelan when he stresses that 'the ECB should be required to approve each and every ELA programme and have the risk shared among the Eurosystem' (Whelan 2014: 4[19]). This will require Treaty change, also with a view to enhancing the transparency and accountability of such decisions (see Transparency International 2017).

However, this additional task granted to the ECB will contribute to the concentration of powers that the ECB has gathered during the crisis and which is unsustainable from an inter-institutional point of view. The ECB cannot and should not be at the same time Europe's monetary policy authority, its lender of last resort authority, its macro-prudential authority as well as its micro-prudential authority. It will have to let go of something. Therefore, going forward, I believe that the ECB should refocus its tasks on its core central banking function and abandon both its macro-prudential and its micro-prudential roles. Why? Because it fundamentally mixes its role and risks to turn the ECB into an authority which *de facto* exerts legislative powers as recently illustrated by the Non-Performing Loans inter-institutional saga.[20]

Once the SSM's smooth operation and its market credibility is fully established, I suggest to strip the ECB from its prudential supervision tasks and to transfer them to an independent agency which will have to be merged with the European Banking Authority and the European Insurance and Occupational Pensions Authority while an independent financial markets supervisor elaborated on the current European Securities Markets Authority (ESMA) would be set-up contemporaneously. This elaborates on but also pushes further the logic of the twin-peak supervisory model proposed by Schoenmaker and Véron (2017). However, such a techno-cratic supervision model can in my view only be followed if those two authorities do not perform fiscal powers. These tasks should be taken up by a genuine and political fiscal institution.

Step 2: Constitute a Fiscal Institution as a Lead Actor of Crisis Management

In order to move away from a technocratic EMU towards a democratic EMU, re-dimensioning the role of the ECB through Treaty change will however not be enough. What is needed is to formalize and consolidate the fiscal instruments and agents which have been created during the euro crisis as part of a deeper and more ambitious state-building exercise. It is indeed time to recognise that a multinational currency such as the euro, shared among 19 countries which still display huge disparities cannot be simply governed by a set of rules and an independent monetary actor. The crisis has demonstrated that such a minimalist institutional set-up is both dangerous and insufficient.

Fiscal institution-building occurred during the crisis. It did however in a covert fashion. It is thus overdue to recognise that several of the most significant institutional creations performed during the crisis to increase EMU's crisis management capacity – in particular the European Stability Mechanism and the Single Resolution Board – are fiscal creations. They both constitute key parts of what would, in other jurisdictions, be an EMU Treasury. Similarly, both the Eurogroup and the Euro Working Group – who together direct the European Stability Mechanism – have consolidated as key fiscal actors during the crisis. Another potentially fiscal actor which is often less considered, is the European Systemic Risk Board. Lastly, the European Commission while remaining like all other actors mentioned in an ambiguous situations as to its ultimate role in EMU, also exerts fiscal powers.

EU leaders need to create a fiscal executive actor as part of a Treaty revision. Europe needs a fiscal *primus inter pares* to be sustainable. Such actor would be politically in charge of crisis management in the sense that it would be responsible for the deployment of all of EMU's safety nets, both those which currently exist and those which might be designed in the future (such as the European Deposit Insurance Scheme or such as a future European Stabilisation Function). It would address those banking and sovereign risks which fall outside of the scope of the ECB's lender of last resort function. Concretely, the fiscal actor would regroup and rationalize the current functions performed by the ESM, by the SRB, by the ESRB and also by the Commission's DG ECFIN and to some extent DG FISMA. The EMU treasury would be made up of three key divisions: the first would be in charge of the oversight of systemic sovereign and banking vulnerabilities, the second would be in charge of the crisis management of the banking sector while the third would be in charge of the crisis management of sovereigns. This would be a democratic breakthrough since a European level fiscal actor would finally be created and thereby would be the direct representative of European citizens and tax-payers in crisis management actions. It would also mark a step change in EMU's stability: going forward, a federal discretionary actor would be in a position to respond to crisis in a swift and proportionate manner. This would address precisely the current Achilles' heel of EMU.

Step 3: Restore Incentives for Sound Fiscal Policies in Good Times and Bad Times

Another paradox at the core of EMU is that while the crisis has turned EMU into a much more *fiscal* construct, the basic fiscal incentives of its regime are flawed, in three key dimensions. EMU displays a lack of credibility of its no-bail out clause, a missing enforceability of its post-crisis fiscal surveillance arsenal and an unlikely way out of the doom-loop through the sole reliance on domestic tools. What those three issues have in common is that they reveal the existence of too weak incentives to push Member States towards domestic fiscal sustainability. This indicates the need to design a fiscal regime that entails both stronger 'sticks' and better 'carrots'

- EMU's so-called 'no bail-out' clause, so central in EMU's original design has been violated in its spirit when the large-scale financial firewalls were set up in Spring 2010. In its no-bail out clause, the Lisbon Treaty's article 125 foresees indeed that 'the Union shall not be liable for or assume the commitments of central governments, regional, local or other public authorities, other bodies governed by public law, or public undertakings of any Member State' and the same article specifies the same for single Member States. Functional imperatives – i.e. the safeguard of the euro – led to the no bail-out clause logic being put in abeyance. However, in a steady-state in which financial stability risks emerging from single EMU Member States can no longer threaten the sustainability of the euro, EMU's basic fiscal incentives should be restored. Member States' governments should therefore be exposed to disciplining actions in case they behave irresponsibly. A possible way to achieve this would be by moving towards a conditional bail-out in case a Member State loses market access. Such a scheme would entail financial assistance from the ESM but would also entail a prior automatic debt restructuring, as suggested by Pisany Ferry et al. (2018). This way moral hazard concerns would be partially addressed.

- The second problematic dimension is the fact that EMU's fiscal framework has become a conundrum. Fiscal surveillance is now characterised by opacity and unpredictability. Such a system cannot lead to any clear fiscal incentives production. When combined with the reality that ever since the creation of the SGP in 1997, the sanctions foreseen by the SGP's Excessive Deficit Procedure (EDP) have never been applied, one can only face the truth that EMU's fiscal framework is close to an institutionalised hypocrisy. While an increasing number of EMU actors recognise the need to simplify the almost Kafkaian nature of the post-crisis fiscal framework, the EU did not yet come up with a large-scale proposal to address this issue in a comprehensive and sustainable way. I believe that simpler rules must be adopted and that more credible sanctions must be enforced. As things stand, a fiscally profligate country can violate the letter and spirit of the SGP for years before any credible correction is performed by the Member State. Italy and France have been living proofs of such a situation.

Using the flexibility of the newly revised fiscal surveillance rules, the Commission has showed that the new framework was full of loopholes and that the road followed since the revision of the SGP in 2005 – which gave more consideration to fiscal inputs compared to its previous look at outputs (the famous 3% and 60% of GDP) – would lead to never-ending disagreements on the calculation of economic values and formula. I am hence convinced that a radically different approach must be explored now, an approach that would combine credible and intelligent sanctions such as a reduced access to a number of existing public investment windows and mechanisms provided by the EU today but also in the future (for example a safe asset). Another possibility would be to engineer a link between SGP sanctions and the contributions of participating Member States to the ESM (Schlosser 2017).

- The third dimension is that despite the advent of a single currency, EMU's debt markets remain fragmented along national lines. As the doom loop illustrated, banks' debt holdings are on average poorly diversified as financial undertaking's portfolios tend to be biased towards domestic sovereign debt holdings. For example, sovereign debt holdings by resident banks remain high in Europe. It has been starkly decreasing in France and Germany over the past decade but the share of domestic debt owned by resident banks remains above 19% in Spain, Greece, Italy, Ireland and Portugal (Merler and Pisani-Ferry 2012). There is a need to increase the portfolio diversification of banks to safeguard their stability. As Philipp Lane argued[21] (2018): 'when they [economic shocks] hit, financial markets fragment along national lines. Shocks therefore get amplified by pre-existing local fragilities, rather than mitigated by a broad-shouldered common market in which private investors share risks'. Such a safe asset could provide the necessary carrot and the operational instrument to Southern Member States to both consolidate their public finances in good times and to break the doom loop between sovereigns and banks. Northern Member States should understand that if designed carefully and intelligently (ESRB 2018), safe assets can be a much more promising and cheaper way to make EMU sustainable compared to functional alternatives.

How to Precipitate Such an Institutional Settlement?

European integration tended from its beginning to proceed forward through the support of stake-dramatizing crises which fuelled the ever-closer union and concomitantly, empowered the European Commission. In line with this trend one can therefore expect that a new crisis will be necessary to trigger a constitutional settlement in Europe. Such a crisis could take various forms: the failure of a systemic bank or insurance undertaking in a large European country, a banking crisis in a large EMU member state or the decision by a large member state to exit the euro.

High-magnitude crises of such nature could in theory break the forces of path-dependency and provide a context in which a constitutional settlement could impose itself on the policy agenda. The euro crisis period has shown that crises are a necessary condition for institutional-building at the EU level. They can act as catalysts to produce solutions – sometimes even of constitutional nature – to the pressure which has been building up. Yet, an exogenous crisis appears to be an insufficient condition to produce the constitutional settlement that would be needed for the European Union to reach a stable equilibrium. I submit that such a settlement can only occur when there is political leadership to ensure the long-term alignment of political actors towards this objective. This alignment does not occur automatically. A political actor must drive and shape the politics in such a direction.

In the absence of a *Deus ex Machina*, the EU's current political actors should ensure that this settlement occurs. When presenting the three above medium-term scenarios, an essential question has thus been ignored: in the absence of a central political authority in the EU, which actor can provoke such path-breaking shifts? The European Parliament, while disposing of a voice to call for such a step change, has weak autonomous power resources and above all, is not in a position to rally national political classes around such reformist projects. The European Commission, despite having been in the past the driving engine of European integration, is no longer in a position to drive system development. The institution seems indeed to be much more influential when it comes to specific and technical policy issues (mostly relating to market regulation), than when it should provide a significant political breakthrough to the EU polity as a whole. Another argument that goes against any leadership role being provided by the European Parliament or by the European Commission is that, as I have stressed, they do not possess sufficient legitimacy resources to initiate such large-scale institutional change: in other words, 'the supranational engine has been exhausted' (Bartolini 2016). The most likely actor of the European scene that could trigger such an institutional recast thus remains the European Council, which is the EU's only Treaty-making institution. However, the body is composed of 28 Heads of State and Government and has displayed during the euro crisis how prone it is to collective action problems and to stalemate.

A way out of the European Council's stalemate can however be found: I claim that the French-German tandem could be relied on as a leadership solution to precipitate those institutional choices. This proposal is based on the rationale that legitimacy resources of national Member States should be tapped in to project Europe towards a new constitutional settlement. Why the French-German couple? Mainly because the euro was from the beginning a French-German project, notwithstanding the important contributions made by leaders from Luxemburg, Belgium, the Netherlands and Italy. It would thus be logical to expect that the political responsibility and authority for the euro's sustainability is provided by its original founding fathers. Moreover, I consider that the French-German couple, despite its limits and pitfalls, remains an opportune and capable political authority to forge compromises. It is hence best placed to precipitate an institutional choice in Europe and drag other Member States towards serious and committing institutional soul-searching that may end up in constitutional change. Germany and France's key commitment would be to act as honest brokers towards reaching a constitutional settlement. Instead of a dominant *directoire,* they would act as a benevolent catalyst (as a form of orchestrator) to lead Europe towards an institutional bifurcation. The acquisition of this leadership role by the French-German couple is however conditional on overcoming two implementation barriers.

The first implementation challenge relates to the decline, over the last years, in the appeal of the French-German couple among European Union Member States. For instance, European leaders and citizens alike proved dismayed by the way in which Angela Merkel and Nicolas Sarkozy ("Merkozy") monopolized the public scene at the height of the crisis, giving the impression that the show was run by them and them only. In Deauville in 2011, Merkozy reached its apex as a decision-making body, setting the main terms of the negotiations of the Six Pack (formally conducted in parallel by the EU's co-legislators) and deciding on an *ad hoc* debt restructuring plan. The Deauville deal seems to have acted as a lasting trauma: 'Deauville was so out of place'.[22] It was problematic because it abused the very essence of the French-German couple. The latter has always been an effective form of leadership when it was based on visionary decisions that only engaged, at least in its first step, France and Germany, but kept an open and inclusive approach to other Member States. The French-German tandem never worked as an operational duopoly. Perhaps it would be helpful in this regard for the French and the German governments to perform a *mea culpa* on Deauville.

The second key barrier lying on the way is that both capitals diverge over the ultimate shape and goal of a European fiscal centre: 'the main impediment is that Germany and France have different conceptions'[23] and are trapped in a 'game of chicken' (Otero-Iglesias 2015: 361). This deviation can be narrowed down to three key political differences which lead to varying expectations as to the exact role and function of a political core: republicanism vs. ordo-liberalism (Dyson and Featherstone 1999); federal vs. centralized system; parliamentary vs. executive regimes. On top of this, the two countries feature divergent guiding principles of economic policy. If the jump from a monetary to a fiscal union is a tall order, bridging those cultural differences appears as a big challenge too. The situation is reinforced by the fact that, compared to the hey-days of French-German cooperation in the 1970s and 1980s, their respective power resources have been altered ever since. As an interviewee explained: 'the reunification of Germany has tilted the balance'.[24] Meanwhile, France 'exerts less power in the game'[25]: it is striking for instance 'how weak France has been'[26] during the crisis, testified an interviewee. However, despite these limits, France and Germany remain the two principals of the euro, have always shown in the past an ability to bridge stark differences and have already explained that they would issue a common proposal in a near future for a closer integration of the Eurozone.[27] After all, no other nations can indeed credibly provide the political and principled leadership needed to stand behind the euro.

CLOSING REMARKS

Several scholars and political leaders alike have emphasized the *sui generis* character of European integration – and *a fortiori* of EMU – which would thus be justified in its structure to be functioning 'against the law of gravity' (Tsoukalis 2011). Yet, it remains questionable whether a multinational currency can be sustainable without a state to support its credibility and protect it in times of crises. A currency should also be embedded to be sustainable. In the very speech that arguably saved the euro, Mario Draghi (2012: 1) alluded to the fact that 'the euro is like a bumblebee. This is a mystery of nature because it shouldn't fly but instead it does'. To push the metaphor to its extreme, one should however be reminded that nature is full of examples of species which have renounced to some of their fundamental features (such as flying) because they had to mimetically adapt to their environment, in an urge for survival. Geese and swans have wings but they seldom use them as necessity has made them more embedded in their daily habitat, water. By analogy, the euro started as a de-politicized

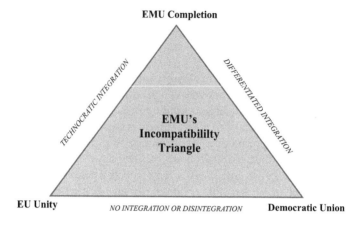

Fig. 8.1   EMU's incompatibility triangle

currency as part of a technocratic polity whose legitimacy rested mainly on national democracies. The crisis suddenly and dramatically re-politicized the currency, reminding advocates of an anchorless currency that the euro has an environmental habitat in which it naturally evolves and is socially and politically embedded in. This habitat is constituted by Europe's democracies. Now, regardless of whether the euro is a bumble-bee or a swan, not recognizing the need to root and embed the currency effectively and durably in a democratic polity and to ensure that it has solid democratic institutions underlying it, is very likely going forward to increase the likelihood of severe economic and social crises occurring in Europe.

In truth what this book has uncovered is that Europe appears to be constrained by an impossibility triangle between its new aspiration to form a democratic union, its ambition to maintain European unity and its need to complete EMU (Fig. 8.1).

Given the weak democratic equilibrium in which post-crisis EMU finds itself in, I contend that only two of those three objectives will be able to be achieved simultaneously:

- **The completion of EMU and the safeguard of European unity but without the flourishing of a democratic union**: as the Commission demonstrated in its December 2017 package, aiming to complete

EMU while concomitantly preserving EU unity comes at the cost of promoting a democratic union.

- **The flourishing of a democratic union and the safeguard of European unity but no completion of EMU**: As the intergovernmental confederation scenario illustrated, striping EMU of a few of its key mutualisation mechanisms and ensuring a better alignment between its Treaty basis and the fiscal tasks it performs would ensure a more legitimate and democratic union while also safeguarding the EU order. It would however fall short of leading to any new mutualisation measures needed to complete EMU.

- **The completion of EMU and the flourishing of a democratic union but without the safeguard of European unity**: EMU can be completed through the large scale Treaty reform which I advocated earlier and which would ensure a better alignment between EMU actors' tasks and their democratic mandate. However, given the magnitude of the institutional changes needed to complete EMU (e.g. ECB as lender of last resort, creation of a central treasury), one cannot reasonably assume that such a grand integration jump will be done among all EMU members and that European unity will be safeguarded.

If time confirms this impossibility triangle, then it means that EMU's future polity will necessarily have to come out of differentiated integration, i.e. an integrative initiative sponsored and led by only a small group of EMU Member States. Yet, lingering doubts remain as to the circumstances under which a new political order be created. As Fabbrini concludes (2015: 288), quoting Federalist No. 1, the true question is 'whether societies of men are really capable or not of establishing good government from reflection and choice, or whether they are forever destined to depend for their political constitutions on accident and force' (Hamilton 1787).

My deep conviction is that the only possible remedy to EMU's instability which does not rely on accident and force is a French-German led reform agenda. After all – and despite the contribution made by other EMU founding Member States – it was France and Germany who committed Europe to creating the euro, in a move that was expected to propel Europe towards genuine solidarity after centuries of wars. Germany and France should now show the way on how to reconcile the euro with European solidarity and thereby fix their own creation.

NOTES

1. Interviewee 47 – EU Council official.
2. Interviewee 47 – EU Council official.
3. Interviewee 30 – Finnish Ministry of Finance official.
4. Interviewee 30 – Finnish Ministry of Finance official.
5. Interviewee 40 – EU Council official.
6. Interviewee 18 – Italian Ministry of Finance official.
7. Interviewee 47 – EU Council official.
8. Interviewee 39 – European Central Bank official.
9. Interviewee 44 – European Commission official.
10. Interviewee 30 – Finnish Ministry of Finance official.
11. Interviewee 40 – EU Council official.
12. Interviewee 10 – EU Council official.
13. EDIS: European Deposit Insurance Scheme.
14. Interviewee 40 – EU Council official.
15. Interviewee 40 – EU Council official.
16. Interviewee 32 – European Central Bank official.
17. Interviewee 32 – European Central Bank official.
18. Interviewee 41 – Independent analyst.
19. http://www.ucd.ie/t4cms/WP16_09.pdf.
20. http://www.huffingtonpost.it/2017/11/09/la-bce-replica-stizzita-a-tajani-ma-apre-uno-spiraglio-a-modifiche-alle-regole-sui-crediti-deteriorati_a_23271667/.
21. http://www.ilsole24ore.com/art/commenti-e-idee/2018-01-27/a-safe-asset-for-europe-133629.shtml?uuid=AExHPAqD.
22. Interviewee 42 – European Commission official.
23. Interviewee 32 – European Central Bank official.
24. Interviewee 33 – European Central Bank official.
25. Interviewee 33 – European Central Bank official.
26. Interviewee 42 – European Commission official.
27. http://www.euractiv.com/section/euro-finance/news/france-and-germany-dither-over-the-eurozones-future/.

REFERENCES

Bartolini, S. (2006, March). Politics: The Right or the Wrong Sort of Medicine for the EU? *Notre Europe Policy Paper N°19.*

Bartolini, S. (2016, July 6). *Private Conversation with the Author.* Florence.

Brunnermeier, M. K., Garicano, L., Lane, P.R., Pagano, M., Reis, R., Santos, T., van Nieuwerburgh, S., & Vayanos, D. (2011). European Safe Bonds: ESBies. *Euro-nomics.com.*

De Geus, A., Enderlein, H., & Letta, E. (2017, May). *Seizing the Moment for Euro Area Reform* (Policy Paper). Gütersloh/ Paris: Bertelsmann Stiftung/Jacques Delors Institute.

De Grauwe, P. (2013, February). *Design Failures in the Eurozone: Can they Be Fixed?* LSE 'Europe in Question' Discussion Paper Series, LEQS Paper No. 57/2013. London

De Witte, B., & Kilpatrick, C. (2014). *Social Rights in Times of Crisis in the Eurozone: The Role of Fundamental Rights' Challenges.* EUI Working Papers, Law 2014/2015.

Dehousse, R. (2013). *The Politics of Delegation in the European Union.* Paris: Centre d'Etudes Européennes de Sciences Po, Cahiers européens de Sciences Po.

Draghi, M. (2012, July 26). *Speech by Mario Draghi, President of the European Central Bank.* In Global Investment Conference, London.

Draghi, M. (2014, November 27). Stability and Prosperity in Monetary Union. *Speech* by Mario Draghi, President of the European Central Bank, at the University of Helsinki, Helsinki.

Draghi, M. (2015, March 16). Speech by the President at SZ Finance Day 2015. *Speech* by Mario Draghi, President of the ECB, Frankfurt am Main.

Dyson, K., & Featherstone, K. (1999). *The Road to Maastricht: Negotiating Economic and Monetary Union.* New York: Oxford University Press.

Enderlein, H., & Haas, J. (2015, October). *What Would a European Finance Minister Do? A Proposal.* Jacques Delors Institut Berlin, *Policy Paper N°145.*

ESM. (2016, March). *Tackling Sovereign Risk in European Banks* (Lenarčič, A., Mevis, D., & Siklós, D., Ed.). Discussion Paper Series/1.

ESRB. (2015, March). Report on the Regulatory Treatment of Sovereign Exposures. *European Systemic Risk Board.*

ESRB. (2018, January). *Sovereign Bond-Backed Securities: A Feasibility Study.* European Systemic Risk Board.

European Commission. (2016, November 23). *EU Banking Reform: Strong Banks to Support Growth and Restore Confidence.* European Commission Press Release.

European Commission. (2017a, December 6). *Communication from the Commission to the European Parliament, The European Council, The Council and The European Central Bank Further Steps Towards Completing Europe's Economic and Monetary Union: A Roadmap.* Brussels.

European Commission. (2017b, December 6). *Communication from the Commission to The European Parliament, The European Council, The Council and The European Central Bank a European Minister of Economy and Finance.* Brussels.

European Commission. (2017c, December 6). *Proposal for a Council Regulation on the Establishment of the European Monetary Fund.* Brussels.

European Commission. (2017d, May 31). *Reflection Paper on the Deepening of the Economic and Monetary Union.* Brussels.

European Council. (2011, December 9). *Statement by the Euro Area Heads State or Government.*

Fabbrini, S. (2015). *Which European Union? Europe after the Euro Crisis.* Cambridge: Cambridge University Press.

Five Presidents Report (2015, June 22). *The Five Presidents' Report: Completing Europe's Economic and Monetary Union.* Report by Jean-Claude Juncker (President of the European Commission), in Close Collaboration with Donald Tusk, Jeroen Dijsselbloem, Mario Draghi and Martin Schulz, Brussels.

FT. (2018, March 7). *Germany Hesitates at Weidmann's Nomination for ECB Presidency.*

Giavazzi, F., & Wyplosz, C. (2015). EMU: Old Flaws Revisited. *Journal of European Integration, 37*(7), 723–737.

Guttenberg, L. (2017, December 4). *Looking for the Silver Bullet – A Guide to the ESM Debate.* Policy Paper, Jacques Delors Institute Berlin.

Hamilton, A. (1787, October 27). *Federalist Number Paper.*

Hodson, D. (2013). The Little Engine that Wouldn't: Supranational Entrepreneurship and the Barroso Commission. *Journal of European Integration, 35*(3), 301–314.

Honohan, P. (2017, November 26). Central Banking in Europe Today: Over-Mighty or Under-Powered? *Lecture.* Florence: European University Institute.

Hooghe, L., & Marks, G. (2008). A Postfunctionalist Theory of European Integration: From Permissive Consensus to Constraining Dissensus. *British Journal of Political Science, 39*(1), 1–23.

Juncker, J.-C. (2017, September 13). Speech, *State of the Union Address.* Brussels.

Karagiannis, Y., & Guidi, M. (2014). Institutional Change and Continuity in the European Union: The Super-Commissioner Saga. *Acta Politica, 49*(2), 174–195.

Laffan, B., & Schlosser, P. (2016). Public Finances in Europe: Fortifying EU Economic Governance in the Shadow of the Crisis. *Journal of European Integration, 38*(3, Special Issue EU Policies in Times of Crisis), 237–249.

Lane, P. (2018, January 29). A Safe Asset for Europe. *Il Sole 24 Ore.*

Lindseth, P. (2010). *Power and Legitimacy: Reconciling Europe and the Nation-State.* Oxford: Oxford University Press.

Majone, G. (2014). *Rethinking the European Union: Has Integration Gone Too Far?* Cambridge: Cambridge University Press.

Merler, S., & Pisani-Ferry, J. (2012, February). *Who's Afraid of Sovereign Bonds.* Bruegel Policy Contribution.

Micossi, S. (2017, November 27). *A Blueprint for Completing the Banking Union.* CEPS Policy Insights.

Mitrany, D. (1943). *A Working Peace System: An Argument for the Functional Development of International Organization.* London: The Royal Institute of International Affairs, Oxford University Press.

Monnet, J. (1988). *Mémoires.* Paris: Fayard.

Otero-Iglesias, M. (2015). Stateless Euro: The Euro Crisis and the Revenge of the Chartalist Theory of Money. *JCMS: Journal of Common Market Studies, 53*(2), 349–364.

Padoa-Schioppa, T. (1999, February 24). *EMU and Banking Supervision. Lecture by Tommaso Padoa-Schioppa,* Member of the ECB Executive Board, London School of Economics, Financial Markets Group, London.

Patrin, M. (2018, April). *A European Finance Minister: Form Follows Function But Is It Legal?* ADEMU Working Paper, European University Institute.

Pierson, P. (2000). Increasing Returns, Path Dependence, and the Study of Politics. *American Political Science Review, 94*(2), 251–267.

Pisany Ferry, J. et al. (2018, January). *Reconciling Risk-Sharing with Market Discipline: A Constructive Approach to Euro Area Reform.* CEPR.

Sandbu, M. (2017, December 6). Eurogroup Reform: Poor Craftsmen Blame their Tools. *Free Lunch.*

Sapir, A., & Schoenmaker, D. (2017, October 30). *The Time Is Right for a European Monetary Fund.* Bruegel Policy Brief.

Schelkle, W. (2012). European Fiscal Union: From Monetary Back Door to Parliamentary Main Entrance. *CESifo Forum 1/2012, 13*(1), 28–34.

Schlosser, P. (2017). Still Looking for the Banking Union's Fiscal Backstop. In F. Allen, E. Carletti, J. Gray, & M. Gulati (Eds.), *The Changing Geography of Finance and Regulation in Europe.* Florence: European University Institute.

Schoenmaker, D. (2017). Resolution of International Banks: Can Smaller Countries Cope? *International Finance, 2018,* 39–54.

Schoenmaker, D., & Véron, N. (2017, November). *A 'Twin Peaks' Vision for Europe.* Policy Contribution N°30, Bruegel.

Transparency International. (2017). *Two Sides of the Same Coin? Independence and Accountability of the European Central Bank.* Transparency International EU.

Tsoukalis, L. (2011). The JCMS Annual Review Lecture – The Shattering of Illusions – And What Next?. *Journal of Common Market Studies, 49,* (Annual Review), 19–44.

Weiler, J. H. (2012). In the Face of Crisis: Input Legitimacy, Output Legitimacy and the Political Messianism of European Integration. *Journal of European Integration, 34*(7), 825–841.

Whelan, K. (2014, November). *The ECB's Collateral Policy and Its Future as Lender of Last Resort.* Document Requested by the European Parliament's Committee on Economic and Monetary Affairs, European Parliament.

Wolff, G. (2017, May 17). What Could a Euro-Area Finance Minister Mean? *Bruegel Blog Post.*

Index

© The Author(s) 2019
P. Schlosser, *Europe's New Fiscal Union*,
https://doi.org/10.1007/978-3-319-98636-4